Disrupted Economic Relationships

CESifo Seminar Series
Edited by Clemens Fuest

Disrupted Economic Relationships

Disasters, Sanctions, and Dissolutions

Edited by Tibor Besedeš and Volker Nitsch

CESifo Seminar Series

The MIT Press
Cambridge, Massachusetts
London, England

This book was set in Palatino by Westchester Publishing Services. Printed and bound in the United States of America.

Library of Congress Cataloging-in-Publication Data

Names: Besedeš, Tibor, editor. | Nitsch, Volker, editor.
Title: Disrupted economic relationships : disasters, sanctions, dissolutions / edited by Tibor Besedeš and Volker Nitsch.
Description: Cambridge, MA : MIT Press, [2019] | Series: CESifo seminar series | Includes bibliographical references and index.
Identifiers: LCCN 2018039317 | ISBN 9780262039895 (hardcover : alk. paper)
Subjects: LCSH: War—Economic aspects. | Disasters—Economic aspects. | Economic sanctions. | International economic relations.
Classification: LCC HB195 .D57 2019 | DDC 330—dc23 LC record available at https://lccn.loc.gov/2018039317

10   9   8   7   6   5   4   3   2   1

Contents

Series Foreword

This book is part of the CESifo Seminar Series. The series aims to cover topical policy issues in economics from a largely European perspective. The books in this series are the products of the papers and intensive debates that took place during the seminars hosted by CESifo, an international research network of renowned economists organized jointly by the Center for Economic Studies at Ludwig-Maximilians-Universität, Munich, and the Ifo Institute for Economic Research. All publications in this series have been carefully selected and refereed by members of the CESifo research network.

Acknowledgments

This book collects a selection of papers presented at a CESifo Summer Institute workshop that took place on the island of San Servolo in Venice in July 2016. We thank Pramila Crivelli, Stefan Goldbach, Melise Jaud, Sebastian Krautheim, Daniel Mirza, and Vincent Vicard, who acted as discussants at the workshop, for their comments and suggestions for improvement, and CESifo for the provision of financial, logistical, and human resources support.

Tibor Besedeš and Volker Nitsch

Introduction

Tibor Besedeš and Volker Nitsch

For a long time, cross-border interactions have been characterized by a strengthening of economic relationships. After the end of World War II, barriers to trade were gradually removed, and there were also massive improvements in the communication and transportation infrastructure. As a result, for most of the postwar period, international trade and investment have grown faster than output, a process that has frequently been labeled "globalization."

In recent years, however, economic relationships have become more fragile. Established relationships appear to be increasingly threatened by various types of shocks. In view of the increased interdependencies between economic actors (as exemplified by the establishment of global value chains), these disruptions seem to be particularly costly and may require appropriate policy responses.

The first type of major shock with the potential to lastingly disrupt cross-border interactions comprises disasters, both natural and man-made. Natural disasters that have recently affected international economic relationships include the 2004 Indian Ocean tsunami; the 2010 eruption of the Eyjafjallajökull volcano, which grounded the flights of 10 million passengers; and the 2011 Great Tōhoku earthquake, which led to the catastrophe in Fukushima. Man-made disasters include conflicts such as the Russia-Ukraine crisis, war, and terrorism.

Another reason for the sudden disruption of economic relationships is the imposition of sanctions, which may include trade sanctions, financial sanctions, and/or asset freezes. Sanctions may be targeted against countries or against individuals or entities. According to the European Commission, sanctions are an essential tool of European Union foreign policy; most prominently, they have recently been imposed on Russia, with ongoing controversy about their impacts on both the target and the senders.

Finally, economic relationships may seriously suffer from the dissolution of existing institutional arrangements. Examples of disintegration include tendencies toward secession in several European countries (such as the United Kingdom, Spain, and Belgium) or the exit of countries from international arrangements (such as the United Kingdom's decision to leave the European Union). Among other campaign promises, US president Donald Trump was voted into office on a promise to walk away from both negotiated and implemented trade agreements such as the Transatlantic Trade and Investment Partnership (TTIP) and the North American Free Trade Agreement (NAFTA).

In such an environment, this is a particularly timely volume. It offers a number of studies examining causes and consequences of disruptions in economic relationships. Given the breadth of issues and dimensions involved, and in view of an active body of literature on some issues, various selected aspects are addressed. Chapters 1 and 2 focus on conflicts and examine their causes theoretically. Then, chapters 3–5 empirically analyze the various effects of economic sanctions, largely motivated by the reemergence of discussions on the role of economic sanctions as a diplomatic instrument coinciding with the restrictive measures imposed on Russia in the wake of its annexation of Crimea. Next, chapter 6 examines the related issue of the consequences of a (consumer) boycott on international trade, while chapter 7 discusses the effects of natural disasters on trade. Finally, chapters 8–10 deal with disruptions, examining causes of the collapse of the Soviet Union and the duration of trade relationships. Overall, we believe that this book provides a thought-provoking (if necessarily incomplete) overview of methods and research questions on disrupted economic relationships.

On Conflict

A major impediment to cross-border economic interaction is political conflict. Consequently, a sizable amount of literature, not only in economics, examines a wide range of issues related to conflicts, from identifying their determinants to quantifying their effects.

Enrico Spolaore and Romain Wacziarg contribute to this literature by providing an interesting new perspective on the association between cultural heterogeneity and conflict. In particular, they argue that the impact of ethnic and cultural dissimilarity on conflict varies according to the types of goods over which groups are fighting. For public goods, which are characterized by nonrivalry in consumption and are commonly shared by all within a jurisdiction, heterogeneous populations are likely to experience more conflict. For private (rival) goods, in contrast, it is populations that are more similar, sharing closer preferences, that are more likely to fight with each other. Building on their earlier work, Spolaore and Wacziarg provide convincing theoretical and empirical evidence in support of their argument.

Arthur Silve and Thierry Verdier examine another interesting feature of conflicts. Based on the observation that civil wars (and, more generally, weak state institutions) often tend to cluster in time and space, they provide a theoretical framework to analyze the diffusion of conflicts. In their model, the possibility of conflict spillovers from abroad induces a regional complementarity between governments choosing their own national political regimes. In view of the resulting possibility of multiple regional political regime equilibria, an important policy lesson of their analysis, therefore, is the importance of regional institutions in coordinating national policies in order to avoid regional clusters of civil conflicts.

Sanctions, Boycotts, and Disasters

Conflicts come in different forms and intensities. Therefore, when analyzing their effects, it is essential that this heterogeneity be taken into account. In this respect, the implementation of sanctions is a particularly interesting form of cross-border dispute. While sanctions are less intense than military conflict, they imply an action and therefore go (far) beyond other diplomatic measures in order to achieve foreign policy goals.

Julian Hinz adds to the growing literature that aims to empirically assess the effects of sanctions on international trade. Applying a structural gravity framework, three recent episodes of sanctions are examined: those against Iran, Russia, and Myanmar (Burma). Overall, Hinz estimates that during these sanction regimes, trade was reduced by more than US$50 billion in 2014, or about 0.4 percent of world trade, with the bulk of this lost trade carried by a few countries.

Tristan Kohl and Chiel Klein Reesink are concerned with a related issue. While they are also interested in the effects of sanctions on trade, they differentiate between the threat of sanctions and their actual imposition. Analyzing a large sample of almost 1,500 sanction cases, they find that, in contrast to impositions, threats do not have a significant (negative) impact on international trade, despite their often extensive media coverage, which causes considerable uncertainty among economic agents.

Daniel Ahn and Rodney Ludema apply a more direct approach to assess the economic impact of sanctions. The business performance of companies targeted by sanctions is examined by analyzing sanctions against Russia. According to Ahn and Ludema's estimates, a sanctioned company loses, on average, about one-third of its operating revenue, over one-half of its asset value, and about one-third of its employees after being targeted compared to nonsanctioned companies. Consequently, targeted sanctions seem to have a powerful impact on the targets themselves. For the overall economy, however, the effects are found to be small.

Kilian Heilmann examines another form of trade disruption, consumer boycotts. Using a natural experiment, the boycott of Danish brands in Muslim countries after the publication of the so-called Muhammad cartoons in a Danish newspaper in 2005, he examines the effects of this measure on trade in services. Heilmann shows that service trade was significantly disrupted after the boycott was announced, although the effect turned out to be short lived and was mainly concentrated in the recreational and travel service sectors.

Chenmei Li and Peter van Bergeijk offer a new, perhaps provocative, perspective on the effects of natural disasters on trade. Contrary to findings that disasters may reduce trade, it is argued that natural disasters are associated with a positive shift in the real annual growth rates of imports and exports. Plausible explanations for these findings include the need for reconstruction and the replacement of domestic production destroyed by the disaster as well as greater export orientation because of a reduction in domestic demand.

Disruptions and Duration

Sudden disruptions of existing cross-border interactions have to be analyzed in context. Recent empirical findings suggest that international trade relationships are often extremely short lived. If trade is highly flexible, however, the economic costs of disruptions may generally be limited.

Maria Persson and Wolfgang Hess examine the literature on trade duration in detail. Their survey not only illustrates that short trade durations are a very robust empirical finding, but they also explore a large set of explanatory variables that have been found to affect the duration of trade. Interestingly, Persson and Hess also show that explanatory factors that have previously been identified as relevant are not enough to explain the variation in trade survival over time.

Melise Jaud, Madina Kukenova, and Martin Strieborny focus on a specific determinant of trade duration, a country's level of financial development. Analyzing product-level exports from ten developing countries in the Middle East and North Africa (MENA) region and sub-Saharan Africa, they argue that a significant portion of financial costs related to exports of agricultural goods emerges as a result of required compliance with sanitary and phytosanitary standards. They find that the long-term export survival of products with high export-related financial needs indeed benefits from financial development, as a well-developed financial system helps export firms establish a long-term presence in foreign markets.

Marvin Suesse examines a particularly strong form of disintegration, the dissolution of a country, using the end of the Soviet Union as a case study. After critically reviewing the hypothesis that oil played a decisive role in the collapse of the Soviet economy, alternative explanations are offered. In particular, it is argued that policy measures and territorial disintegration carry substantially greater explanatory power than oil for understanding the Soviet collapse.

Overall, the studies in this book cover a broad range of (selected) issues. By applying a variety of methods and approaches, both theoretically and empirically, it is hoped that they will provide suggestions and ideas for further research.

1 The Political Economy of Heterogeneity and Conflict

Enrico Spolaore and Romain Wacziarg

1.1 Introduction

Conflicts within and between nations are paramount sources of economic and social disruption. International wars—such as the two world wars in the twentieth century—account for some of the largest losses of lives and physical capital in human history. Conflicts that are more localized can also produce large economic and human costs, especially when they persist over time. As noted by Blattman and Miguel (2010), since 1960, over 50 percent of nations in the world have experienced internal armed conflict, and in 20 percent of them, conflict has lasted for at least 10 years, often causing extensive fatalities and displacement of entire communities. For example, the current conflict in Syria, which started in 2011, has already resulted in over 290,000 victims (International Institute for Strategic Studies 2017) and millions of refugees, with global political, social, and economic repercussions. Other areas directly affected by conflict between armed groups in recent years include Afghanistan, Burma (Myanmar), Iraq, Israel/Palestine, South Sudan, Ukraine, and many others. At the same time, terrorism and other forms of political violence have played a disruptive role in the economic and political lives of numerous societies all over the world and have affected the political debate in Europe, the United States, and elsewhere.

As the world continues to experience warfare and tensions, observers have wondered to what extent these conflicts may be linked to the heterogeneity of cultural, linguistic, and religious traits. Does diversity of cultural and ethnic origins go hand in hand with more conflict between different groups?

Social scientists have often held polarized views on this question. At one extreme is the optimistic view that historically heterogeneous populations, by interacting and cooperating with each other, can converge on common norms and values and achieve peaceful and sustainable integration. For instance, versions of this view inspired the functionalist approach to European integration (Haas 1958, 1964) as well as broader theories about communication and political cooperation across communities (Deutsch 1964). Indeed, after World War II, Europeans managed to create common institutions through peaceful integration of a growing and more dissimilar set of populations. However, the recent wave of crises and disruptions in Europe—including Britain's vote in June 2016 to exit the European Union ("Brexit") and the surge of anti-EU political movements in several countries—has challenged such optimistic assumptions, raising questions about costs and instability associated with political and cultural heterogeneity.[1]

At the other extreme is the pessimistic view that ethnic and cultural dissimilarities prevent cooperation and bring about conflicts and wars. This "primordialist" view has a long intellectual pedigree (see, for instance, Sumner 1906) but has received renewed attention in recent decades, especially since the collapse of the Soviet Union. A well-known example of this position is Huntington's (1993, 1996) "Clash of Civilizations" hypothesis, stressing religious and cultural cleavages as major sources of violent conflict since the Cold War.

While wars and conflicts are traditionally studied by historians and political scientists, there exists a growing body of literature that attempts to understand these important phenomena using the theoretical and empirical tools of contemporary political economy (for overviews, see Garfinkel and Skaperdas 2007; Blattman and Miguel 2010). In particular, recent empirical studies have focused on the relation between measures of ethnic and cultural diversity and civil conflict (e.g., Montalvo and Reynal-Querol 2005; Esteban, Mayoral, and Ray 2012; Desmet, Ortuño-Ortín, and Wacziarg 2012; Arbatli, Ashraf, and Galor 2015), while in our own work we have explored the relation between historical relatedness and international conflict (Spolaore and Wacziarg 2016a).

Motivated by findings from this empirical literature, in this chapter we present a conceptual framework that provides insights on the relation between conflict and cultural heterogeneity. Our central point is that the impact of heterogeneity should depend on whether groups are fighting over control of public goods or rival goods. Heterogeneous preferences and traits negatively affect the provision of public goods, which are nonrival in consumption and must be shared by all within a jurisdiction, whether one likes them or not. In contrast, diversity across individuals and groups comes with benefits when considering interactions about rival goods, because a diversity of preferences and cultures should be associated with lower levels of antagonism over a specific private good. In such cases, it is similarity of preferences that should bring about more conflict.

This chapter's main idea can be illustrated with a simple example. Consider two people in a room with two sandwiches: a chicken sandwich and a ham sandwich (rival goods). People who share preferences that are more similar are more likely to want the same kind of sandwich, and possibly to fight over it, while people with preferences that are more diverse are more likely to be happy with different sandwiches. In contrast, suppose that there is a television set in the room, which both individuals must share (public good). Each can watch television without reducing the other person's utility from watching, but they may disagree over which channel to watch and fight over the remote control. In this case, people with preferences that are more similar are less likely to fight, because they can agree on the same show.

If this distinction is relevant for understanding actual conflict, we should observe more conflict over public goods among groups that are more dissimilar but more conflict over rival goods among groups that are closer to each other in preferences, values, and cultures. In order to bring these hypotheses to the data, we must be able to measure the heterogeneity and distance between different groups and populations. Such measurements are complex and conceptually tricky, but, as already mentioned, there is now a large and growing volume of empirical literature that has made substantial progress on these issues. In our own work on this topic, we have taken a genealogical approach to heterogeneity across different populations (for a recent discussion, see, for example, Spolaore and Wacziarg 2016b). This approach is based on the idea that all human populations are related to each other but that some share common ancestors who are more recent than others, with direct implications for the extent to which they are more similar in several relevant characteristics and preferences. As different populations have split from each other over a long time, they have gradually diverged regarding sets of traits that are transmitted from one generation to another, including language, values, and norms. As a result, on average, populations with a more recent common history have had less time to diverge regarding such intergenerationally transmitted traits and tend to be more similar. Hence, we can use measures of long-term relatedness between populations to test whether heterogeneity across different groups is associated with more or less conflict among them.

Our empirical findings on heterogeneity and conflict, focused on international wars (Spolaore and Wacziarg 2016a), are consistent with the central hypothesis of this chapter. In particular, we found that, over the past two centuries, sovereign states inhabited by populations that are more closely related have been more likely to engage in violent conflict over rival goods, such as territories and natural resources (fertile soil in the nineteenth century, oil in the twentieth). On the other hand, evidence on civil conflict, such as the already mentioned contributions by Esteban, Mayoral, and Ray (2012), Desmet, Ortuño-Ortín, and Wacziarg (2012), and Arbatli, Ashraf, and Galor (2015), is broadly consistent with the hypothesis that ethnic and cultural diversity is associated with greater levels of internal violence when different groups fight over the control of public goods and policies.

The rest of this chapter is organized as follows. In section 1.2, we provide an analytical framework, capturing our main ideas about the links between intergenerational transmission of preferences, heterogeneity, and conflict over rival goods or public goods. In section 1.3, we discuss recent empirical studies of conflict that strongly support the implications of our analytical framework. Our conclusions are presented in section 1.4.

1.2   Heterogeneity and Conflict: An Analytical Framework

In this section, we present a theoretical framework linking the intergenerational transmission of preferences, genealogical distance, and the probability of conflict between populations. As far as we know, this is the first model that explicitly connects such variables within a unified formal setting. First, we model the transmission of preferences over time with variation across populations in order to explain why differences in values, norms, and preferences are linked to the degree of genealogical relatedness between populations. We show that populations that are more closely related—that is, those at a smaller genealogical distance—tend to have preferences that are more similar. Second, we model conflict over rival goods and show that conflict is more likely to arise when different populations care about the same rival goods and resources. Third, we show how the effect of relatedness on conflict changes if the dispute is about control of nonrival goods (public goods). Finally, we present a generalization of the framework, which includes conflict over rival goods and conflict over nonrival goods as special cases.

1.2.1 Intergenerational Transmission of Preferences

Our starting point is a simple model of the intergenerational transmission of preferences over the very long run. Consider three periods: o for origin, p for prehistory, and h for history. In period o, there exists only one population: population 0. In period p, the original population splits into two populations: population 1 and population 2. In period h, each of the two populations splits again into two separate populations: population 1 into population 1.1 and population 1.2, and population 2 into population 2.1 and population 2.2, as displayed in figure 1.1. In this setting, the genealogical distance $d_g(i, j)$ between population i and population j can be simply measured by the number of periods since they were one population:

$$d_g(1.1, 1.2) = d_g(2.1, 2.2) = 1 \tag{1.1}$$

and

$$d_g(1.1, 2.1) = d_g(1.1, 2.2) = d_g(1.2, 2.1) = d_g(1.2, 2.2) = 2. \tag{1.2}$$

These numbers have an intuitive interpretation: populations 1.1 and 1.2 are sibling populations, sharing a common parent ancestor (population 1), while populations 2.1 and 2.2 are also sibling populations, sharing a different common parent ancestor (population 2). In contrast, populations 1.1 and 2.1, for example, are cousin populations sharing a common grandparent ancestor (population 0).

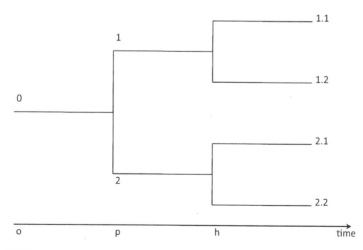

Figure 1.1
Population tree.

For simplicity, preferences are summarized by two types (A and B). At time o, the ancestral population 0 is either of type A or of type B. For analytical convenience and without loss of generality, we assume that population 0 is of type A with probability 1/2 and of type B with probability 1/2.[2] Populations inherit preferences from their ancestors with variation—a population i' descending from a population i will have preferences of the same type as their parent population i with probability μ and of the other type with probability $1-\mu$.

We capture the fact that populations inherit preferences from their ancestors by assuming $\mu > 1/2$ and capture the fact that there is variation (inheritance is not perfect) by assuming $\mu < 1$.[3] Thus, on average, populations at a smaller genealogical distance from each other will tend to be more similar in preferences. For instance, the probability that two sibling populations (say, 1.1 and 1.2) have identical types is

$$F(\mu) = \mu^2 + (1-\mu)^2, \tag{1.3}$$

while the probability that two cousin populations (say, 1.1 and 2.1) have identical types is

$$G(\mu) = \mu^4 + 6\mu^2(1-\mu)^2 + (1-\mu)^4. \tag{1.4}$$

It can be easily shown that[4]

$$F(\mu) > G(\mu) \quad \text{for } 1/2 < \mu < 1, \tag{1.5}$$

which implies the following proposition.

Proposition 1.1 The probability that two populations are of the same type is decreasing in genealogical distance.

This result plays a key role in our analysis of conflict that follows.

1.2.2 Conflict over Rival Goods

Consider two populations (i and j), each forming a sovereign state. For simplicity, we assume that each state is a unified agent, formed by one population with homogeneous preferences.[5]

Suppose that sovereign state i is in control of a valuable prize of type t, from which it obtains the following benefits b_i,

$$b_i = (1 - |t - t_i^*|)R, \tag{1.6}$$

where t_i^* denotes state i's ideal type, and $R > 0$ is the size of the prize. If the prize is of type A, $t = t_A$, and if it is of type B, $t = t_B$. Without loss of generality, we assume that the prize is of type A with probability 1/2 and of type B with probability 1/2. State i's ideal type is also equal to either t_A or t_B. We assume that the state benefits from controlling the prize even if it is not of its favored type; that is,

$$|t_A - t_B| < 1. \tag{1.7}$$

The prize can be interpreted as any valuable good that can be controlled by a sovereign state—natural resources, land, cities, trade routes, colonies, protectorates, and so on (we return to the interpretation of the model later when we discuss possible extensions). Sovereign state j also values the prize, and would gain benefits if it could control the prize. State j's benefits b_j from controlling the prize are

$$b_j = (1 - |t - t_j^*|)R. \tag{1.8}$$

State j can try to obtain control over the prize by challenging state i—that is, state j can take two actions: "challenge" state i (C) or "not challenge" (NC) it. If state j chooses action NC, state i keeps full control over the prize and obtains a net utility equal to b_i, while state j obtains net benefits equal to 0. If state j challenges state i for possession of the prize, state i can respond either with "fight" (F) or "not fight" (NF). If state i does not fight, state j obtains control of the prize and net benefits equal to b_j, while state i obtains net benefits equal to 0.

If state i decides to fight in response to the challenge, a war takes place.[6] When a war occurs—that is, when actions {C, F} are taken—the probability that state i wins, denoted by π_i, is a function of the two states' relative military capabilities (denoted respectively by M_i and M_j),

$$\pi_i = \frac{M_i}{M_i + M_j}, \tag{1.9}$$

while the probability that state j wins the war is $1 - \pi_i$. This is an instance of a contest success function of the ratio type (Hirshleifer 1989). In general, the literature on the technology of conflict assumes that the probability of success is a function of either the ratio or the difference between military capabilities (for a general discussion, see Garfinkel and Skaperdas 2007).[7] In our model, it is the ratio.

Ex ante, each state obtains an expected utility, respectively given by

$$U_i = \pi_i b_i - c_i \tag{1.10}$$

and

$$U_j = (1 - \pi_i)b_j - c_j, \tag{1.11}$$

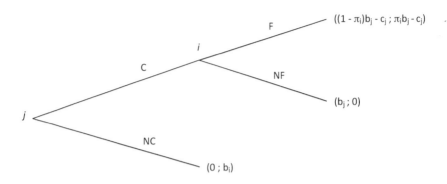

In parentheses: (state *j*'s payoff ; state *i*'s payoff)

Figure 1.2
Extensive-form game.

where $c_i > 0$ and $c_j > 0$ denote the respective costs of going to war. The extensive form of the game is illustrated in figure 1.2.

It is immediate to show the following.

Lemma 1.1   War is subgame perfect equilibrium if and only if $\min\{U_i, U_j\} \geq 0$. War is the unique subgame perfect equilibrium when $\min\{U_i, U_j\} > 0$.[8]

Proof   When $U_i > 0$ and $U_j = 0$, two subgame perfect equilibria exist: $\{C, F\}$ and $\{NC, F\}$. When $U_i = 0$ and $U_j > 0$, there are also two subgame perfect equilibria: $\{C, F\}$ and $\{C, NF\}$. When $U_i = U_j = 0$, three equilibria may occur: $\{C, F\}$, $\{C, NF\}$, and $\{NC, F\}$. When $\min\{U_i, U_j\} < 0$, the only subgame perfect equilibria are peaceful. If $U_i < 0$, the only subgame perfect equilibrium is $\{C, NF\}$. If $U_i > 0$ and $U_j < 0$, the only subgame perfect equilibrium is $\{NC, F\}$. Finally, when $U_i = 0$ and $U_j < 0$, there are two (peaceful) equilibria: $\{NC, F\}$ and $\{C, NF\}$. QED.

We are now ready to investigate how similarity in preferences between the two states affects the probability of war. To simplify the analysis, we assume equal capabilities $(M_i = M_j = M)$ and costs $(c_i = c_j = c)$. Let $P(i, j)$ denote the probability of a war between state i and state j.

A war *never* occurs (that is, $P(i, j) = 0$) if each state's expected utility from going to war is negative even when the prize is of its preferred type. This happens at a very high cost of war:

$$c > \frac{1}{2}R. \tag{1.12}$$

In contrast, a war *always* occurs (that is, $P(i, j) = 1$) if each state's expected utility from going to war is positive even when the resource is not of its favored type. This happens at a very low cost of war:

$$c < \frac{1}{2}R(1 - |t_A - t_B|). \tag{1.13}$$

Therefore, we focus on the more interesting case where war may occur with probability between 0 and 1 (that is, $0 < P(i, j) < 1$), which happens when the cost of war takes on an intermediate value:[9]

$$\frac{1}{2}R(1 - |t_A - t_B|) < c < \frac{1}{2}R. \tag{1.14}$$

Under these assumptions, a war will occur if and only if the two states have the same preferred type, and that type is equal to the type of the prize under dispute—that is, $t_i^* = t_j^* = t$. If the two states always had identical preferences, the probability of a war would be $1/2$. This would occur, for instance, if preferences were transmitted without variation across generations: $\mu = 1$. In contrast, if the preferences of each state were independently distributed, with each state having a 50 percent chance of preferring type A to type B (and vice versa), the probability of war would be $1/4$. This would occur, for instance, if preferences were transmitted purely randomly across generations: $\mu = 1/2$.

In general, for $1/2 < \mu < 1$, the expected probability of war between states i and j depends on the degree of relatedness (genealogical distance) of their populations. For two states i and j with $d_g(i, j) = 1$—that is, states formed by sibling populations—the probability that both states have the same type as the prize under dispute is half the probability that both states have the same preferences; that is,

$$P\{i, j \mid d_g(i, j) = 1\} = \frac{F(\mu)}{2} = \frac{\mu^2 + (1 - \mu)^2}{2}. \tag{1.15}$$

By the same token, for states such that $d_g(i, j) = 2$—that is, states formed by cousin populations—the probability that both states' types are equal to the type of the prize is

$$P\{i, j \mid d_g(i, j) = 2\} = \frac{G(\mu)}{2} = \frac{\mu^4 + 6\mu^2(1 - \mu)^2 + (1 - \mu)^4}{2}. \tag{1.16}$$

As already shown in subsection 1.2.1, $F(\mu) > G(\mu)$ for all $1/2 < \mu < 1$. Therefore, it immediately follows that

$$P\{i, j \mid d_g(i, j) = 1\} > P\{i, j \mid d_g(i, j) = 2\}, \tag{1.17}$$

which can be summarized as our main result in the following proposition.

Proposition 1.2   States with populations that are more closely related (smaller genealogical distance) are more likely to go to war with each other.

A simple spatial example illustrates the model. Assume that space is unidimensional. Three states divide the territory among themselves as in figure 1.3, with the border between state i and state j at point x and the border between state j and state i' at point y. Assume that state i and state j are of type A, and state i' is of type B. The parameters are such that equation (1.14) is satisfied. Now, consider the territory between x' and x. If that territory is of type B, state j will not challenge state i for its possession, but if that territory is of type A, a war will occur. In contrast, consider the territory between y and y'. If that territory is of type B, state j will not challenge state i' for its possession, while if it is of type A, state j will challenge state i', and state i' will surrender it peacefully. In either case, no conflict will occur.

This example illustrates how the probability of conflict between states in similar geographical settings varies because of preferences over the prize: states with preferences that are more similar are more likely to go to war with each other, other things being equal. In this example, the prize is a contiguous territory, but similar effects would hold for control over noncontiguous territories (colonies, protectorates, ports and harbors along trade routes) or other rival goods that states may care about with different intensities (for instance, monopoly rights

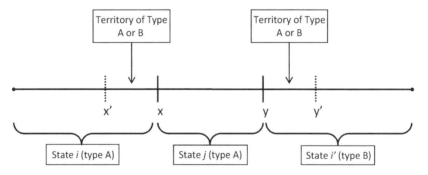

Figure 1.3
An illustration of the model.

over trade, fishing, or other valuable sources of income in specific waters or regions). History abounds with examples of populations that fought over specific rival goods (territories, cities, religious sites) because they shared a common history and common preferences, inherited with variation from their ancestors. For instance, genealogically close populations (Jews and Arabs) who share similar preferences over Jerusalem have fought and continue to fight over control of that rival good. In general, we can expect that populations may share preferences that are more similar over specific types of land and resources because they have inherited similar tastes and demand functions (as in the example about Jerusalem), because they have inherited similar technologies and methods of production, or both.[10]

1.2.3 Conflict over Public Goods

In our basic model, the prize is a rival and excludable good: either one or the other state obtains full control, and the population in the state without control receives no net benefit. How would our results change if the prize were a public good (nonrival and nonexcludable in consumption)? Then, state j would obtain some external benefits when state i is in control of the good, and vice versa. In itself, this extension would only reduce the likelihood of war, because the externalities would reduce the gap in utility between controlling and not controlling the good. However, the implications would change dramatically if we also allowed the state in control to select the characteristics or type of the public good.

In our basic model, the prize is a rival and excludable good, and the type of the rival good is given (that is, it cannot be changed by either player). We now consider the different case, where the prize is a pure public good, nonrival in consumption, and the player in control can choose whether the public good is of type A or B. In this case, we refer to "players" rather than "states," consistent with our view that conflict over types of public goods is more likely to occur among agents engaged in intrastate conflict rather than interstate conflict. Conceptually, two states could also fight over a type of public good that both must share. However, it is unlikely that this would have occurred historically in a world where most public goods are provided at the national level, not at the supranational level. In general, the nature of the conflict is not determined by whether players are sovereign states or intrastate agents. The key consideration is whether they are fighting over the control of a rival good or a nonrival good. Two states (or other agents) that fight over the control of a territory are fighting over a rival good. When that territory comes under the control of a specific state, different agents within that state might fight over what public policies to provide to the inhabitants of the territory (the territory itself, however, continues to be a rival good).

Therefore, we are now focusing on the case where conflict is *not* about controlling access to the good (both players benefit from the good no matter who "owns" it) but rather about controlling the *type* of public good (for example, as already mentioned, the characteristics of a public policy or service): the winner will select his or her favored type of public good. Utilities from the public good are given as follows:

(a) If player i and player j are of the same type, both obtain maximum benefits R from the good no matter who is in control:

$$b_i = b_j = R. \tag{1.18}$$

(b) If the two players are of different types and player i is in control of the public good, the respective benefits are

$$b_i = R, \tag{1.19}$$

$$b_j = (1 - |t_A - t_B|)R. \tag{1.20}$$

(c) Conversely, if the two players are of different types, and player j is in control of the public good, we have

$$b_i = (1 - |t_A - t_B|)R, \tag{1.21}$$

$$b_j = R. \tag{1.22}$$

Now, there is no reason for conflict between two players of the same type. If player i is of the same type as player j, player j will obtain the same utility as if he or she were in control of the good. In contrast, if player i is of a different type, player j could increase his or her utility by seizing control of the good and changing the type. Hence, a necessary condition for war is that the players be of different types. Player i's expected utility from going to war is

$$\pi_i R + (1 - \pi_i)[1 - |t_A - t_B|]R - c_i, \tag{1.23}$$

and he or she will prefer to fight when

$$\pi_i R + (1 - \pi_i)(1 - |t_A - t_B|)R - c_i > (1 - |t_A - t_B|)R, \tag{1.24}$$

which can be rewritten as

$$\pi_i\left(|t_A - t_B|\right)R - c_i > 0. \tag{1.25}$$

By the same token, player j will prefer war over not challenging the other player for control when

$$(1 - \pi_i)(|t_A - t_B|)R - c_j > 0. \tag{1.26}$$

In the symmetric case ($\pi_i = 1/2$ and $c_i = c_j = c$), the two conditions become

$$c < \left(|t_A - t_B|\right)\frac{R}{2}. \tag{1.27}$$

If condition (1.27) is satisfied—that is, the war costs are small enough—the probability that player i and player j engage in conflict is equal to the probability that they are not of the same type. For sibling populations ($d_g(i, j) = 1$), the probability that they are not of the same type is

$$P\{i, j \mid d_g(i, j) = 1\} = 1 - F(\mu) = 1 - [\mu^2 + (1 - \mu^2)], \tag{1.28}$$

while for cousin populations ($d_g(i, j) = 2$), the probability that both are of different types is

$$P\{i, j \mid d_g(i, j) = 2\} = 1 - G(\mu) = 1 - [\mu^4 + 6\mu^2(1 - \mu)^2 + (1 - \mu)^4]. \tag{1.29}$$

As we have shown, $F(\mu) > G(\mu)$ for all $1/2 < \mu < 1$, which immediately implies

$$P\{i, j \mid d_g(i, j) = 1\} < P\{i, j \mid d_g(i, j) = 2\}. \tag{1.30}$$

Consequently, we have the following proposition.

Proposition 1.3   When conflict is about the control of public-good types, the probability of violent conflict is higher between groups that are less closely related.

The intuition is straightforward. Suppose conflict is not about control of the public good per se but about determination of its type. Then, populations that are more closely related, sharing preferences that are more similar about the characteristics of the public good, are less likely to engage in conflict. In contrast, populations that are historically and culturally more distant tend to disagree more over the type of public good.

1.2.4   A General Framework

The two basic models—conflict over pure rival goods and conflict over pure public goods—can be viewed as two special cases of a more general framework where (a) there may be externalities in consumption and (b) the player in control of the prize may be able to change the good's type. Formally:

(a) When player i is in control of the prize, player j's benefits are $\delta(1-|t-t_j^*|)R$, and when player j is in control, player i's benefits are $\delta(1-|t-t_i^*|)R$, where $0 \le \delta \le 1$.

(b) When a player is in control of the prize of type A, he or she can change the type to B (and, conversely, a player in control of the prize of type B can change the type to A) with probability γ $(0 \le \gamma \le 1)$.

Our basic model of conflict over rival goods is the case $\delta = \gamma = 0$, while the model of conflict over public goods is the case $\delta = \gamma = 1$.

In general, two players with the same preferences will go to war with each other at low levels of δ (for all γ), while two players with different preferences will go to war with each other for high levels of γ, when $\delta > 0$. These results generalize the insights from the basic models: similarity in preferences leads to more conflict over goods with zero or low externalities (low δ), while dissimilarity in preferences leads to more conflict when agents in control of a nonrival good ($\delta > 0$) can change the good's type (high γ). Formally, we have the following proposition.

Proposition 1.4   For all γ, there exists a critical $\delta^* = 1 - \dfrac{2c}{R}$ such that two players of the same type will go to war for $\delta < \delta^*$ and will not go to war for $\delta > \delta^*$.[11]

Proof   Two players of the same type X (X = A, B) will not go to war over a good of type X if

$$\frac{1}{2}R + \frac{1}{2}\delta R - c < \delta R \tag{1.31}$$

and will not go to war over a good of type Y $\ne$ X if

$$\frac{1}{2}[\gamma R + (1-\gamma)(1-|t_A - t_B|)R] + \frac{1}{2}\delta[\gamma R + (1-\gamma)(1-|t_A - t_B|)R]$$
$$- c < (1-\gamma)(1-|t_A - t_B|)R, \tag{1.32}$$

which can be rewritten, respectively,[12] as

$$\delta < 1 - \frac{2c}{R} \tag{1.33}$$

and

$$\delta < 1 - \frac{2c}{R[1 - (1-\gamma)|t_A - t_B|]}. \tag{1.34}$$

For all $0 \leq \gamma \leq 1$, we have

$$1 - \frac{2c}{R} \geq 1 - \frac{2c}{R[1 - (1-\gamma)|t_A - t_B|]}. \tag{1.35}$$

Therefore, for all $\delta > \delta^* \equiv 1 - \frac{2c}{R}$, we also have $\delta > 1 - \frac{2c}{R[1 - (1-\gamma)|t_A - t_B|]}$, and no war ever takes place between two players with the same preferences. In contrast, for $\delta < \delta^*$, the two players will go to war. QED.

In contrast, conflict between players with different preferences is characterized by the following proposition.

Proposition 1.5 For all $\delta > 0$, two players with different preferences will go to war for $\gamma > \gamma^*$, where[13]

$$\gamma^* = \frac{1}{|t_A - t_B|} \min \left\{ 1 - \frac{1}{\delta}\left(1 - \frac{2c}{R}\right); \frac{2c}{R} - (1-\delta)[1 - |t_A - t_B|] \right\}. \tag{1.36}$$

Proof When two players have different preferences, the player whose preferred type is the same as the prize will go to war if

$$\frac{1}{2}R + \frac{1}{2}\delta[\gamma(1 - |t_A - t_B|)R + (1-\gamma)R] - c > \delta[\gamma(1 - |t_A - t_B|)R + (1-\gamma)R], \tag{1.37}$$

while the other player will go to war if

$$\frac{1}{2}[\gamma R + (1-\gamma)(1 - |t_A - t_B|)R] + \frac{1}{2}\delta(1 - |t_A - t_B|)R - c > \delta(1 - |t_A - t_B|)R. \tag{1.38}$$

The preceding equations can be rewritten as

$$\gamma > \frac{1 - \frac{1}{\delta}\left(1 - \frac{2c}{R}\right)}{|t_A - t_B|} \tag{1.39}$$

and

$$\gamma > \frac{\frac{2c}{R} - (1 - \delta)(1 - |t_A - t_B|)}{|t_A - t_B|}. \tag{1.40}$$

Both conditions hold if $\gamma > \gamma^*$. QED.

1.3 Empirical Evidence on Heterogeneity and Conflict

Our conceptual framework implies that conflict over rival goods is likely to be more severe among groups that are more similar in terms of culture, preferences, and ethnic origins, while the opposite should occur when conflict is about public goods. What do the data say?

1.3.1 Evidence on Heterogeneity and Civil Conflict

Conflicts over public goods and government characteristics are more likely to emerge among groups that belong to the same political jurisdiction and therefore share nonrival and nonexcludable goods and policies by institutional design. Consequently, we can expect that conflict over public goods and policies should play an important role in many (but not all) civil conflicts.

This observation is consistent with empirical work associating ethnic polarization (a measure that captures distance between groups within a country) with conflict over public goods. Of particular note is the empirical study of ethnicity and intrastate conflict by Esteban, Mayoral, and Ray (2012), building on theoretical work by Esteban and Ray (2011). In their theoretical framework, Esteban and Ray (2011) and Esteban, Mayoral, and Ray (2012) also draw a distinction between public goods and private goods. In their model, a central role is played by three indices, measuring polarization, fractionalization, and cohesion.

Formally, polarization P and fractionalization F are defined as follows. There are m groups engaged in conflict. N_i denotes the number of individuals in group i, and N is the total population. The "distance" between group i and group j is denoted by $d(i, j)$. In Esteban, Mayoral, and Ray (2012), this distance is defined in terms of differences between payoffs and is equal to 0 when the two groups share the same ideal policies. Polarization P is defined as

$$P = \sum_{i=1}^{m} \sum_{j=1}^{m} (n_i^2 \times n_j \times d(i, j)), \tag{1.41}$$

while fractionalization F is defined as

$$F = \sum_{i=1}^{m} \sum_{j \neq i} (n_i \times n_j).$$ (1.42)

   Intuitively, the squaring of population shares in P makes group sizes matter above the mere counting of individual heads used to calculate F, while P also takes into account intergroup distance. In contrast, F only captures the probability that two individuals, randomly taken from the population, would belong to different groups, irrespective of their distance. Thus, polarization increases as the distance between groups increases. Holding distance between groups constant, polarization is maximized when there are two groups of equal size, while fractionalization keeps increasing as one adds more small groups. In general, there is a nonmonotonic relationship between polarization and fractionalization. For example, for a given distance between groups and assuming for simplicity that all groups are of equal size, at $m=1$ we have $F=P=0$ by definition. As we move to $m=2$, both F and P become positive. As we increase the number of groups to $m=3, 4, \ldots$ and so on, F continues to increase. In contrast, P is maximized at $m=2$ and decreases with m for all $m>2$. In fact, consistent with this intuition, the empirical correlation between measures of fractionalization and polarization is positive at low levels of fractionalization but negative at high levels of fractionalization—for example, see figure 1 on p. 802 in Montalvo and Reynal-Querol (2005). For a discussion of the relationship between fractionalization and polarization, see also Alesina et al. (2003, 177–179).

   In Esteban, Mayoral, and Ray (2012), the weight of these two indices P and F in explaining conflict intensity depends on the particular nature of each conflict. When group cohesion is high, polarization increases conflict if the prize is public, and fractionalization increases conflict if the prize is private. In their empirical analysis, Esteban, Mayoral, and Ray use measures of ethnolinguistic polarization based on linguistic distances between groups, building on Fearon (2003), and find that linguistic polarization increases civil conflict over public goods. Such measures can be interpreted in terms of our theoretical model, because linguistic trees capture long-term relations between populations and are correlated with measures of historical and cultural relatedness (see Spolaore and Wacziarg 2016b). We will return to these measures of linguistic distance and their connection with other measures of cultural distance when discussing our own empirical work. Overall, the effects of linguistic distance and polarization found by Esteban, Mayoral, and Ray (2012) are entirely consistent with the implications of our basic hypothesis that less closely related groups are more likely to fight over the control of public goods.

Desmet, Ortuño-Ortín, and Wacziarg (2012) also find that linguistic diversity has a significant impact on civil conflict. In their empirical estimates, more linguistic diversity within a country is associated with more civil conflict and worse outcomes regarding the provision of public goods, governance, and redistribution. Their analysis is focused on detecting the effects of heterogeneity at different levels of linguistic aggregation. Interestingly, they find that deep cleavages, originating thousands of years ago, are better predictors of conflict across linguistically heterogeneous groups that share the same country compared to more superficial linguistic distinctions that appeared more recently. These findings strongly support the central hypotheses of this chapter. Desmet, Ortuño-Ortín, and Wacziarg (2017) show that civil conflict is more likely when ethnic divisions are reinforced by cultural cleavages, such as differences in preferences, values, and norms as revealed in the World Value Survey. This evidence also is consistent with our model, where differences in preferences drive the positive relationship between genealogical relatedness and the likelihood of civil conflict.

Long-term measures of diversity within populations, based on genetic data, are at the center of a study by Arbatli, Ashraf, and Galor (2015). Using genetic diversity within each country, they find that populations that are more diverse are more likely to engage in civil conflict. These results are consistent with our theoretical framework insofar as civil conflict among people with preferences that are more diverse is about public goods and policies rather than about rival goods.

In sum, recent studies have found significant empirical evidence linking long-term measures of diversity to civil conflict, especially over public goods and policies. This evidence strongly supports the hypothesis illustrated in our conceptual framework.

It must be noted, however, that evidence of a positive relationship between heterogeneity and civil conflict does not imply that, in general, cultural and ethnic distance should always be associated with a lower probability of civil conflict, independent of what the conflict is about. In principle, groups engaged in civil and ethnic conflict may also fight over rival goods. Then, according to our conceptual framework, groups that are more similar would be expected to fight more with each other, and heterogeneity of traits and preferences could in principle have a pacifying effect. In general, our framework predicts that, insofar as civil conflicts are about a complex mix of disputes over rival and public goods, one should expect ambiguous effects of heterogeneity on civil conflict, depending on the extent to which specific civil conflicts are about rival goods or nonrival goods (public goods). This theoretical ambiguity can shed some light on the ongoing debate on the role of ethnic divisions in causing conflict within countries—for example, see the pathbreaking contributions by Fearon and Laitin (2003) and Montalvo and Reynal-Querol (2005).

That said, the more recent evidence on the determinants of civil conflict provided by Esteban, Mayoral, and Ray (2012), Desmet, Ortuño-Ortín, and Wacziarg (2012), and Arbatli, Ashraf, and Galor (2015) suggest two observations. First, when civil conflict seems to be mainly about public goods, more heterogeneity tends to be associated with more conflict, as predicted by our analytical framework. Second, more heterogeneity—measured for instance by greater ethnolinguistic distance—seems to be empirically associated with increased civil conflict and worse political economy outcomes within each country. In other words, in the observed historical record, the net impact of long-term cultural heterogeneity on the propensity for civil conflict seems positive: more heterogeneity, more conflict. In light of our framework, we can interpret this empirical regularity as being consistent with a large role for conflict over public goods and policies. In other words, when heterogeneous groups fight with each other within a country, chances are that they are disagreeing about the fundamental traits and characteristics of their common government and common policies. More research is necessary, however, to measure the extent to which different civil conflicts happen to be about public goods or rival goods, and the consequences of this distinction when estimating the impacts of different measures of heterogeneity on civil conflict.

1.3.2 Evidence on Heterogeneity and International Conflict

In the case of civil conflict, more heterogeneity is typically (but not always) associated with more conflict, but what do the data say about international conflict? In principle, international conflict could involve both rival and nonrival goods. However, in contrast to the case of civil conflict, the importance of a "public-goods effect" is likely to be much lower, or even entirely absent, when sovereign states fight with each other. Even though disagreements about the provision of public goods and policies may also emerge among different governments—that is, how to address international terrorist threats, global climate change, or financial instability—historically, interstate militarized conflicts have been mostly about control of rival and excludable goods, such as territories, cities, and natural resources. The view that international conflict is closely linked to disputes over territories and resources is emphasized, for instance, by Caselli, Morelli, and Rohner (2014), who cite the results in Tir et al. (1998) and Tir (2003) that 27 percent of all territorial changes between 1816 and 1996 involved full-blown military conflict, and 47 percent of territorial transfers involved some level of violence. Caselli, Morelli, and Rohner (2014) also cite Weede's (1973, 87) statement that "the history of war and peace is largely identical with the history of territorial changes as results of war."

In our empirical work on international conflict, we found that the evidence unambiguously supports the hypothesis that populations that are more culturally similar fight more with each other—that is, the opposite of what would be implied by a "Clash of Civilizations" hypothesis. In what follows, we discuss some of the empirical findings reported in Spolaore and Wacziarg (2016a) in light of the conceptual framework presented in this chapter.

1.3.2.1 Measures of cultural distance between populations How can we measure distance in cultural traits and preferences between societies? In our empirical analysis, we use a genealogical approach to heterogeneity, consistent with the insights of the model presented earlier. Specifically, we use genetic distance, which captures the length of time since two populations became separated from each other. The basic idea behind the use of genetic distance as a way to measure cultural distance between populations is that human traits—not only biological but also cultural—are mostly transmitted from one generation to the next, with variation. Therefore, the longer two populations have drifted apart, the greater the differences in cultural traits and preferences between them.

Genetic distance is not the only measure that captures distance in intergenerationally transmitted traits. A closely related measure is linguistic distance, which is also based on a trait that is mostly transmitted from one generation to the next over time, even though individuals and entire populations have sometimes changed their language because of conquest or other factors. Another cultural trait that is mostly transmitted intergenerationally is religion—although in this case also, people can change their religious beliefs. In sum, linguistic and religious distances provide alternative measures of differences in cultural traits that are transmitted with variation from one generation to the next. Another class of distance between populations can be constructed directly by measuring specific differences in cultural traits, values, norms, and attitudes, as revealed by surveys such as the World Values Survey (WVS). All these different traits are in large part transmitted intergenerationally over time, so we should expect that the various classes of measures based on these traits (genetic distance, linguistic distance, religious distance, cultural distance based on surveys), while distinct from each other, will be positively correlated. This is indeed what we find in Spolaore and Wacziarg (2016b), where we further elaborate on the complex links between various measures of historical and cultural distance between populations and analyze the empirical relationships between them.

In our empirical study of international conflict (Spolaore and Wacziarg 2016a), we used three measures of genealogical and cultural distance between countries, based respectively on genetic distance, linguistic distance, and religious distance, to analyze the determinants of interstate conflict. Here, we briefly describe the construction of these three measures. They are discussed in more detail in Spolaore and Wacziarg (2009, 2013, and 2016b).

The data on genetic distance come from Cavalli-Sforza, Menozzi, and Piazza (1994). The set of world populations from that dataset is matched to ethnic groups from Alesina et al. (2003). In order to account for the fact that modern countries include groups with different ancestries and ethnic origins, we constructed a measure of weighted genetic distance.[14] Assuming that country i is composed of populations $m = 1 \ldots M$ and country j is composed of populations $n = 1 \ldots N$, and denoting by s_{im} the share of population m in country i (similarly for country j) and d_{mn} the distance between populations m and n, the weighted F_{ST} genetic distance (GD_{ij}) between countries i and j is defined as

$$GD_{ij} = \sum_{m=1}^{M} \sum_{n=1}^{N} (s_{im} \times s_{jn} \times gd_{mn}), \qquad (1.41)$$

where s_{km} is the share of group m in country k, and gd_{mn} is the F_{ST} genetic distance between groups m and n.

To address concerns that current genetic distance may be endogenous with respect to past wars, as well as possible bias resulting from errors in matching populations to countries for the current period, we also matched countries to their populations in the year 1500, before the great migrations following European explorations and conquests. For instance, for 1500, Australia is matched to the Australian Aborigines rather than to the English. We employ this measure of genetic distance based on the 1500 match as an instrument for current genetic distance. We are therefore assuming that the only way that 1500 genetic distance affects current conflict is through its effect on current genetic distance.[15]

To measure linguistic distance between countries, following Fearon (2003), we use linguistic trees from Ethnologue. We compute the number of common linguistic nodes between languages in the world, a measure of their linguistic similarity. The linguistic tree in this dataset involves up to 15 nested classifications, so two countries with populations speaking the same language will share 15 common nodes.[16] Using data on the distribution of each linguistic group within and across countries, from the same source, we compute a measure of the number of common nodes shared by languages spoken by plurality groups within each country in a pair. Again, to take into account the presence of groups speaking different languages within a country, we computed a weighted measure of linguistic similarity, representing the expected number of common linguistic nodes between two randomly chosen individuals, one from each country in a pair, analogous to the formula for weighted genetic distance in equation (1.41). Finally, these measures of linguistic similarity are transformed in an index of linguistic distance (LD_{ij}):

$$LD_{ij} = \sqrt{\frac{15 - \text{\# Common Linguistic Nodes}}{15}}. \qquad (1.42)$$

To measure religious distance, we use a family tree of world religions analogous to the family tree of languages used to compute linguistic distance. The religious nomenclature is obtained from Mecham, Fearon, and Laitin (2006). In the tree, we start with three separate branches, one for the monotheistic religions of Middle Eastern origin, one for Asian religions, and a third for a residual category. Then, each branch is subdivided into finer groups—for example, Christians, Muslims, and Jews for the first group, and so on. The number of common classifications—up to five in this dataset—captures religious similarity. We match religions to countries using Mecham, Fearon, and Laitin's (2006) data on the prevalence of religions by country. The data about common religious nodes are transformed, analogous to what we did for linguistic distance in equation (1.42). Therefore, we obtain a measure of religious distance (RD_{ij}) between countries:

$$RD_{ij} = \sqrt{\frac{5 - \text{\# Common Linguistic Nodes}}{5}}. \qquad (1.43)$$

Correlations between measures of genetic, linguistic, and religious distance are positive but not very large, as each reflects a different set of traits that are transmitted intergenerationally with variation. In our dataset of country pairs, weighted genetic distance GD_{ij} bears a correlation of 0.201 with weighted linguistic distance LD_{ij} and 0.172 with weighted religious distance RD_{ij}, while the correlation between weighted LD_{ij} and weighted RD_{ij} is 0.449.

1.3.2.2 Empirical results The data on interstate conflict is an 1816–2001 panel from the Correlates of War Project (Jones Bremer, and Singer 1996; Faten, Palmer, and Bremer 2004). In any given year, the indicator of conflict between pairs (dyads) of states takes on a value from 0 for no militarized conflict to 5 for an interstate war involving more than 1,000 total battle deaths (the indicator is defined symmetrically across dyads: if the indicator is x between state i and state j, it is also x between state j and state i). As in several other contributions in the literature on interstate conflict, we define a dummy variable equal to 1 if the intensity of militarized conflict between a pair of states is equal to or greater than 3 and 0 otherwise. In our cross-sectional analysis, we look for pairs that were ever involved in a conflict over the time period 1816–2001. Our baseline cross-sectional regression specification is

$$C_{ij} = \text{ß}_1 X_{ij} + \text{ß}_2 GD_{ij} + T_{ij}, \tag{1.44}$$

where the vector X_{ij} contains controls such as a contiguity dummy, measures of geodesic distance, longitudinal and latitudinal distance, several other indicators of geographic isolation, and dummy variables indicating whether the countries in a pair were ever part of the same polity and were ever in a colonial relationship. The equation is estimated using probit, clustering standard errors at the country-pair level. We present results in terms of marginal effects, evaluated at the mean of the independent variables. In addition to these marginal effects, we also report the standardized magnitude of the effect of genetic distance: the effect of a one standard deviation change in genetic distance as a percentage of the mean probability of conflict. To improve readability, the coefficients are multiplied by 100 in all tables.

Table 1.1 presents estimates of the coefficients in equation (1.44) using various specifications. Column 1, the univariate regression, shows a strong negative relationship between weighted genetic distance and the incidence of international conflict. In terms of magnitude, a one standard deviation change in genetic distance (0.068) is associ-

Table 1.1
Effect of genetic distance on international conflict.

	(1) Conflict, univariate specification	(2) Conflict, baseline specification	(3) Conflict, baseline specification IV	(4) Conflict, noncontiguous pairs only	(5) War, baseline specification	(6) War, baseline specification IV
Genetic distance (GD), weighted	−57.3760** (−17.800)	−19.8786** (−9.317)	−30.6802** (−8.843)	−18.5357** (−9.379)	−6.3389** (−7.478)	−8.6043** (−5.746)
Log geodesic distance		−1.6281** (−5.567)	−1.0182** (−3.090)	−1.4809** (−5.065)	−0.2929* (−2.505)	−0.1728 (−1.349)
Log absolute difference in longitude		0.1424 (0.731)	−0.0677 (−0.336)	0.1629 (0.842)	−0.0197 (−0.254)	−0.0629 (−0.787)
Log absolute difference in latitude		−0.1130 (−0.887)	−0.1312 (−1.002)	−0.0729 (−0.614)	−0.1314** (−2.612)	−0.1366** (−2.660)
1 for contiguity		15.4610** (10.095)	16.2256** (5.465)	−	0.8262** (2.701)	0.9060 (1.856)
Number of landlocked countries in the pair		−2.6247** (−9.471)	−2.6311** (−9.566)	−2.4127** (−8.927)	−0.6406** (−5.531)	−0.6500** (−5.635)
Number of island countries in the pair		0.8212** (2.923)	0.8762** (3.005)	0.6967** (2.755)	0.4118** (3.828)	0.4439** (3.711)

1 if pair shares at least one sea or ocean		1.9440**	1.9935**	1.9930**	-0.0154	-0.0199
		(4.909)	(3.799)	(5.181)	(-0.128)	(-0.161)
Log product of land areas in square kilometers		0.8940**	0.9045**	0.7960**	0.3132**	0.3201**
		(18.992)	(17.145)	(18.528)	(17.452)	(9.755)
1 for pairs ever in colonial relationship		7.3215**	7.6147**	8.6303**	0.9013*	0.9754
		(5.094)	(3.175)	(6.004)	(2.099)	(1.463)
1 if countries were or are the same country		1.9512	2.2217	1.6352	1.0952*	1.1373
		(1.846)	(1.541)	(1.229)	(2.424)	(1.564)
Number of observations	13,175	13,175	13,175	12,928	13,175	13,175
Pseudo-R^2	0.075	0.275	—	0.202	0.236	—
Standardized effect (%)	-68.81	-23.84	-36.79	-27.34	-20.57	-27.92

Source: Spolaore and Wacziarg (2016a), table 3.

Notes: Probit or IV probit estimator. Dependent variable: dummy for whether a country pair was ever involved in a conflict or war between 1816 and 2001. Robust t statistics in parentheses. The standardized magnitude refers to the effect of a one standard deviation increase in genetic distance as a percentage of the mean probability of conflict or war for the sample used in each regression. The table reports probit marginal effects. All coefficients are multiplied by 100 for readability.
* significant at 5%; ** significant at 1%.

ated with a 68.81 percent decline in the percentage probability of conflict between 1816 and 2001. Needless to say, this estimate is likely to be tainted by omitted variables bias.

In column 2, we introduce eight geographic controls (capturing potential geographic barriers to militarized conflict) and two measures of colonial past. The estimated effects of these measures usually have the expected signs (more distance, less conflict). While the effect of genetic distance is reduced by the inclusion of these controls, it remains negative and highly significant both statistically and economically: a one standard deviation increase in genetic distance reduces the probability of conflict by 23.84 percent relative to the mean.

Column 3 addresses endogeneity and measurement error by instrumenting for modern genealogical distance using genetic distance between populations as of the year 1500. Matching countries to genetic groups is much more straightforward for 1500, while genetic distance in 1500 is unlikely to be causally affected by conflicts between 1816 and 2001. The IV results are even stronger: the standardized effect of genealogical distance rises to 36.79 percent compared to the estimate in column 2. The effect of genetic distance also remains significant in column 4, where we limit the analysis to countries that are not geographically contiguous to further control for geographic factors affecting conflict.

Finally, columns 5 and 6 show the determinants of full-blown wars. That is, here the dependent variable is equal to 1 if and only if the pair ever experienced a conflict of intensity equal to 5, corresponding to violent conflicts with more than 1,000 total battle deaths over the sample period.[17] As before, we find that a greater genetic distance has a pacifying effect: a one standard deviation increase in genetic distance reduces the probability of ever having experienced a war by 20.57 percent of this variable's mean. As shown in column 6, the standardized magnitude of the effect rises when we instrument using genetic distance in the year 1500. In Spolaore and Wacziarg (2016a), we further explored the robustness of these results to the inclusion of additional geographic controls in the regression, finding that the baseline results discussed here were not affected.

Table 1.2 includes the effects of linguistic distance and religious distance. We start in column 1 with the baseline estimates using the new sample for which all variables are available (we lose about 24 percent of the sample because of unavailable data on linguistic and religious distances). These baseline estimates are similar to those reported in table 1.1. When adding linguistic distance and religious distance, the coefficient on genetic distance does not change much.

Table 1.2
Adding the effects of linguistic distance (LD) and religious distance (RD).

	(1)	(2)	(3)	(4)
	Baseline specification	Add linguistic distance	Add religious distance	Add religious and linguistic distances
Genetic distance (GD), weighted	−29.3281** (8.872)	−29.1266** (8.792)	−27.1691** (8.369)	−27.4118** (8.484)
Log geodesic distance	−2.4924** (5.374)	−2.4971** (5.379)	−2.4498** (5.315)	−2.4268** (5.291)
1 for contiguity	22.5037** (10.375)	22.3377** (10.308)	21.4007** (10.161)	21.7116** (10.155)
Linguistic distance (LD), weighted	–	−0.8099 (0.659)	–	2.3819 (1.778)
Religious distance (RD), weighted	–	–	−5.1999** (5.013)	−5.9958** (5.281)
Pseudo-R^2	0.250	0.250	0.255	0.255
Standardized effect (%)	−28.050	−27.857	−25.985	−26.217

Source: Spolaore and Wacziarg (2016a), table 5.
Notes: Probit estimator. Dependent variable: dichotomous indicator of conflict. Robust t statistics in parentheses. The standardized magnitude is the effect of a one standard deviation increase in genetic distance as a percentage of the mean probability of conflict. The table reports probit marginal effects. All coefficients are multiplied by 100 for readability; 10,021 observations were used in all columns. Controls: In addition to reported coefficients, all regressions include controls for log absolute difference in longitude, log absolute difference in latitude, number of landlocked countries in the pair, number of island countries in the pair, dummy for pairs sharing at least one sea or ocean, log product of land areas in square kilometers, dummy for pairs ever in colonial relationship, dummy for countries that were or are the same country.
* significant at 5%; ** significant at 1%.

Linguistic distance is not significant when controlling for genetic distance, while religious distance has a negative and significant effect on conflict. The effect of religious distance is consistent with our hypothesis that populations that are more similar are more likely to fight with each other. Religion is an important trait that is transmitted intergenerationally and makes populations more or less related to each other. Populations that share religions that are more similar are also more likely to care about the same holy sites and territories (e.g., Jerusalem) and therefore are more likely to fight with each other.

Table 1.3 presents direct evidence in support of the hypothesis that countries that are more similar are more likely to fight over rival goods. In column 2, we document a negative interaction between genetic

Table 1.3
Fighting over rival goods (oil, temperate climate, and fertile soil).

	(1)	(2)	(3)	(4)	(5)	(6)
	Baseline (oil sample)	Oil	Baseline (temperate climate sample)	Temperate climate	Baseline (fertile soil sample)	Fertile soil
	1945–2001	1945–2001	1816–1900	1816–1900	1816–1900	1816–1900
Genetic distance weighted	-11.8279** (-6.933)	-7.1885** (-3.184)	-2.0078** (-5.470)	-0.1500 (-0.549)	-1.0450** (-5.396)	-0.0079 (-0.054)
Log geodesic distance	-1.0813** (-5.185)	-1.1553** (-5.361)	-0.0853 (-1.455)	0.0136 (0.331)	-0.0750* (-2.571)	-0.0339 (-1.697)
Interaction of oil producer dummy and genetic distance		-9.6647** (-3.124)				
Dummy for at least one country in the pair being a major oil producer		1.3988** (3.833)				
Interaction of temperate climate and genetic distance				-1.2588** (-2.886)		
Dummy for one or more country in the pair with >60% land in temperate zone				0.6627** (8.386)		
Interaction of fertile soil dummy and genetic distance						-0.8456** (-4.069)

						0.1381** (7.510)
Dummy for one or more country in the pair with >40% fertile soil						
Number of observations	13,175	13,175	10,216	10,216	13,033	13,033
Pseudo-R^2	0.280	0.284	0.261	0.313	0.289	0.322
Standardized effect [a]	−19.690	−28.050	−15.470	−10.850	−8.632	−7.050

Source: Spolaore and Wacziarg (2016a), table 6.

Notes: Dependent variable: dummy for whether a country pair was ever in conflict in the period specified in row 3. Robust z statistics in parentheses. The standardized magnitude refers to the effect of a one standard deviation increase in genetic distance as a percentage of the mean probability of conflict or war for the sample used in each regression. Controls: Additional controls included (estimates not reported) log absolute difference in longitude, log absolute difference in latitude, dummy = 1 for contiguity, number of landlocked countries in the pair, number of island countries in the pair, dummy = 1 if pair shares at least one sea or ocean, log product of land areas in square kilometers, dummy = 1 for pairs ever in colonial relationship, dummy = 1 if countries were or are the same country.

[a] With interaction effects, the standardized magnitude reported here is the total standardized effect of genetic distance when the endowment dummy equals 1. The table reports probit marginal effects. All coefficients are multiplied by 100 for readability.

* $p < 0.05$; ** $p < 0.01$.

distance and a dummy for oil (1 if at least one of the countries has oil, 0 otherwise), showing that countries that are more similar were more likely to fight over oil between 1945 and 2001.[18] Analogous effects are documented in columns 4 and 6 for temperate climate and fertile soil. Those effects hold for conflicts that took place between 1816 and 1900, when agriculture still played a more central role in the world economy.

In sum, the evidence on the determinants of international conflict strongly supports a central role for conflict over rival goods between populations that are culturally more similar. The evidence also suggests an interaction between the two effects highlighted in our conceptual framework. In addition to a direct effect stemming from conflict over rival goods, international conflict (or lack of it) can be influenced by the fact that rulers anticipate the heterogeneity costs associated with conquering populations that are dissimilar from those they already rule. In other words, rulers may care about "winning the peace" after winning the war, and therefore they may be more likely to fight over territories inhabited by people with whom it would be easier to share common public goods and policies after the war. In contrast, rulers may be more willing to allow populations that are more heterogeneous to become independent without violent conflict. In fact, as shown in Spolaore and Wacziarg (2016a), historically the process of decolonization and independence was more likely to take place peacefully rather than violently when it involved populations that were culturally more distant from the colonial power. Such evidence is consistent with the view that rulers are more likely to fight over a territory when it is inhabited by populations more similar to their own, because populations that are more heterogeneous involve higher costs for providing common public goods and policies.

In an older, working-paper version of Spolaore and Wacziarg (2016a), we also presented a panel data analysis, where we controlled for time-varying variables such as income differences, trade, and differences in political and institutional characteristics (democracy). Interestingly, those variables themselves are partly determined by cultural and genealogical distance, as we have found in our own work on the diffusion of development and institutions (Spolaore and Wacziarg 2009, 2016c). The exploration of the interrelations between conflict, trade, democracy, development, and measures of genealogical and cultural distance is a very promising area for future research.

1.4 Concluding Remarks

At the beginning of this chapter, we mentioned two different views regarding the relationship between heterogeneity and conflict: an optimistic view and a pessimistic (or "primordialist") view. Our theoretical and empirical analysis implies that neither of these views is correct. The optimistic view underplays the risks of conflict and disruption when heterogeneous populations must share common public goods and policies within a given jurisdiction. The evidence strongly suggests that deeply rooted cultural divergence can lead to civil conflict over public goods and government characteristics.

However, there is no reason to believe that heterogeneous populations are always bound to fight with each other. In fact, when they are organized within different political jurisdictions, they are less likely to engage in wars. It is those populations that are more similar, sharing closer preferences over rival goods and resources, that are more likely to fight with each other across national borders.

Interestingly, the historical record also points to significant interactions between conflicts within and across borders. For example, two rulers are more likely to fight over a territory (a rival good) if it is inhabited by people who are more similar to those they already rule, as it would later be easier to provide common public goods and policies. A promising direction for future research is the study of the connections and interactions between measures of cultural and political heterogeneity, domestic and international conflict, and the formation and breakup of countries and other political jurisdictions.

Appendix: Conflict over Rival Goods with Peaceful Bargaining

In our basic model, the two states engage in conflict when both strongly care about the prize. However, conflict is costly, and both states would be better off if they could agree on an allocation of the prize that replicates the expected allocation from conflict without bearing the actual costs from violent confrontation. For instance, if the prize is divisible, the two states would be better off sharing it in proportion to their relative power—that is, state i would obtain a share equal to π_i and state j would obtain a share equal to $(1 - \pi_i)$. If the prize is indivisible, the states could in principle agree to a lottery where each has a probability of winning the prize equal to its probability of winning the war, therefore saving the costs of going to war. However, even abstracting from issues of imperfect information, it might be extremely difficult to implement such a solution ex post (the loser may prefer to go to war after all). Even in the case of a divisible prize, states may have an incentive to unilaterally renege on the bargaining solution, and a war may occur as an equilibrium because each state would be better off fighting than surrendering when the other state fights. In fact, war may be the only equilibrium if each state faces an incentive to go to war unilaterally when the other state has agreed to a peaceful negotiation. In the absence of incentives to deviate unilaterally from peaceful bargaining, multiple equilibria may occur: war and peaceful bargaining.

In the latter case, populations that are more closely related and, hence, may be more similar culturally, linguistically, and in other ways, might be more successful at communicating and coordinating on the efficient equilibrium. If the probability of solving the conflict via peaceful bargaining is indeed higher for populations that are more closely related, this coordination effect could reduce or offset the main effect stemming from similarity in preferences. Then, the net effect of genetic distance on conflict would be ambiguous. However, coordinating on peaceful bargaining in an anarchic international environment, in the absence of credible commitment technologies, might be relatively rare. Moreover, the hypothesis that populations that are more closely related are better at coordination is purely speculative, and one could conceive of reasons why coordination may be harder among people who care more strongly about the same rival and excludable goods. Therefore, it is not clear, ex ante, whether such a coordination effect would reduce or eliminate the main effect of relatedness highlighted in our model. As we saw in section 1.4, the empirical evidence is consistent with the main effect in our model dominating any countervailing effect from coordination on peaceful bargaining. These ideas are formalized here with a simple extension of our basic model of conflict over rival goods.

Consider an extension of the basic model, where peaceful bargaining can follow the choice of actions {C, F}—which are now reinterpreted as {challenge, respond to challenge} rather than {challenge, fight}. Assume that if state j challenges and state i responds to the challenge, each player can choose whether to bargain (B) or go to war (W). If both choose "bargain," the prize is divided peacefully between the two states, and the two states obtain benefits equal to $\pi_i b_i$ and $(1 - \pi_i) b_j$, respectively. That is because we assume that a state's bargaining power depends on its strength should negotiations break down (peaceful bargaining takes place "under the shadow of war").[19] If both states choose W, war follows, with the same payoffs as in the basic model. If state i chooses W while state j chooses B, war also follows, but with the payoffs

$$U_i\{W, B\} = (1+\xi)\pi_i b_i - c_i \tag{1.45}$$

and

$$U_j\{W, B\} = [1 - (1+\xi)\pi_i]\, b_j - c_j, \tag{1.46}$$

where

$$0 < \xi \le \frac{1}{\pi_i} - 1. \tag{1.47}$$

The parameter ξ captures the increased probability of winning that results from being the initiator of the conflict, in the tradition of Schelling (1960).[20] By the same token, if state i chooses B in the subgame but state j chooses W, the payoffs are

$$U_i\{B, W\} = [1 - (1+\xi)(1-\pi_i)]\, b_i - c_i$$

and

$$U_j\{B, W\} = (1+\xi)(1-\pi_i)\, b_j - c_j. \tag{1.49}$$

Under these assumptions, if one state plays W, the other state is better off playing W rather than B, which implies that {W, W} is a Nash equilibrium of the subgame for all values of the parameters. However, {W, W} may or may not be the unique Nash equilibrium. If {W, W} is the unique Nash equilibrium, the implications of this extension are the same as in the basic model. If {B, B} is also a Nash equilibrium, war may be avoided if both states coordinate on the peaceful equilibrium. Therefore, our model is consistent with Fearon's (1995) discussion of war as emerging from an inability to commit to a Pareto-superior outcome. In our framework, both states would be better off if each could commit to play B, but they can do that credibly only if {B, B} is also a Nash equilibrium. For the symmetric case ($\pi_i = \frac{1}{2}$ and $c_i = c_j = c$), a necessary and sufficient condition for {B, B} to be an equilibrium of the subgame is

$$\xi \le \frac{2c}{\min\{b_i, b_j\}}. \tag{1.50}$$

The intuition for the preceding condition is straightforward: the parameter capturing the unilateral incentives to deviate from bargaining must be small enough for {B, B} to be a Nash equilibrium of the subgame. If {B, B} is a Nash equilibrium of the subgame, it is the unique coalition-proof Nash equilibrium. Three cases are possible: (i) states never coordinate on such an equilibrium even when the condition holds, (ii) states always coordinate on such an equilibrium when available, and (iii) sometimes states coordinate, while at other times they do not (coordination failure). Cases (i) and (ii) do not modify the implications of the basic model regarding the effect of relatedness on conflict.

The effect of relatedness on conflict could in principle be modified in case (iii) if the likelihood of observing a coordination failure happened to depend on relatedness. For instance, coordination failure could be more likely across populations that are genealogically more distant, because their norms, habits, languages, and other factors would tend to be more different, and they might therefore find communication and coordination more difficult. If that were the case, such a "coordination failure effect" would reduce the negative correlation between genetic distance and probability of conflict. However, a priori, and in the absence of a compelling theory of equilibrium selection, there is no strong reason to expect that coordination failure would be less likely among populations that are more closely related. The relationship might even go in the opposite direction: coordination failure could be more likely between populations that are more closely related—for example, because of mistrust and animosity resulting from a history of previous conflicts over other rival goods. In that case, the effect of relatedness on conflict would be strengthened. As we saw in the empirical section, the net effect of genetic distance on conflict is negative. This is consistent with two possibilities: (a) coordination failure is not less likely among populations that are more closely related, or (b) coordination failure is less likely among populations that are more closely related, but this effect is not large enough empirically to offset the main effect of relatedness on conflict highlighted by the basic model.

Notes

1. For recent discussions of the political economy of European integration, stressing the role of heterogeneity costs, see Spolaore (2013, 2015).

2. The qualitative results would not change if we were to assume that the ancestral population is of type A with probability 100 percent or of type B with probability 100 percent.

3. At $\mu = 1/2$, each population would have equal chances of being of either type, independent of the parent population's type, while at $\mu = 1$, each population would be of the same type as their ancestors with 100 percent probability.

4. By dividing both $F(\mu)$ and $G(\mu)$ by μ and rearranging terms, the inequality $F(\mu) - G(\mu) > 0$ can be rewritten equivalently as

$$2 - 10\mu + 16\mu^2 - 8\mu^3 \equiv f(\mu) > 0.$$

It can immediately be verified that this inequality holds, given that $f(\frac{1}{2}) = f(1) = 0$ and the derivative

$$f'(\mu) = 2(-5 + 16\mu - 12\mu^2)$$

is strictly positive for $1/2 < \mu < 5/6$, 0 at $\mu = 5/6$, and negative for $5/6 < \mu \leq 1$.

5. That is, we abstract from the possibility that states may include mixed populations with different preferences. However, in the empirical analysis reviewed in section 1.3, we take into account population heterogeneity within states when computing the distance between states.

6. In the appendix, we present an extension in which peaceful bargaining is possible as an alternative to war when state j challenges and state i responds to the challenge.

7. The choice of specification in this chapter is inconsequential because we treat military capabilities as exogenous. A straightforward extension would be to endogenize military capabilities. The extension could strengthen the link between relatedness and probability of conflict, insofar as states with similar preferences might face similar incentives to invest in military capabilities, all other things being equal.

8. When $U_i > 0$ and $U_j = 0$, two subgame perfect equilibria exist: $\{C, F\}$ and $\{NC, F\}$. When $U_i = 0$ and $U_j > 0$, there are also two subgame perfect equilibria: $\{C, F\}$ and $\{C, NF\}$. When $U_i = U_j = 0$, three equilibria may occur: $\{C, F\}$, $\{C, NF\}$, and $\{NC, F\}$. When $\min\{U_i, U_j\} < 0$, the only subgame perfect equilibria are peaceful. If $U_i < 0$, the only subgame perfect equilibrium is $\{C, NF\}$. If $U_i > 0$ and $U_j < 0$, the only subgame perfect equilibrium is $\{NC, F\}$. Finally, when $U_i = 0$ and $U_j < 0$, there are two (peaceful) equilibria: $\{NC, F\}$ and $\{C, NF\}$.

9. To simplify the analysis, we do not consider the knife-edge cases $c = \frac{1}{2} R$ and $c = \frac{1}{2} R(1 - |t_A - t_B|)$ when it's possible that $\min\{U_i, U_j\} = 0$, implying that one or both states may be indifferent between war and peace, and multiple equilibria may trivially occur, as detailed in the proof to lemma 1.1.

10. In principle, similarities in technology could affect the probability of conflict not only by affecting preferences over rival goods but also, more directly, by affecting military capabilities (populations that are more similar may be more similar in military technologies and hence capabilities, other things being equal).

11. Multiple equilibria, with and without conflict, exist in the knife-edge case $\delta = \delta^*$.

12. For $\delta = 0$, the condition in (1.33) reduces to the condition for war in the case of pure rival goods: $c < \frac{1}{2} R$.

13. In the case $\delta = \gamma = 1$, the condition in (1.36) reduces to the condition for war in the case of pure public goods: $c < \left(|t_A - t_B|\right)\frac{R}{2}$.

14. We also constructed the distance between the plurality ethnic groups of each country in a pair—that is, the groups with the largest shares of each country's population. Genetic distance based on plurality groups is highly correlated with weighted genetic distance (the correlation is 93.2 percent). In our empirical analysis, we prefer to use weighted genetic distance because it is a more precise measure of average genetic distance between countries.

15. For a discussion of the plausibility of this assumption, see Spolaore and Wacziarg (2016a).

16. We have also used a separate measure of linguistic distance, based on lexicostatistics, from Dyen, Kruskal, and Black (1992). This is a more continuous measure than the one based on common nodes, but it is only available for countries speaking Indo-European languages. Using the weighted measure of cognate distance led to effects very similar to those obtained when controlling for the Fearon measure, albeit on a much smaller sample of countries.

17. Only 2.1 percent of the country pairs in our sample ever experienced a war, as defined here, between 1816 and 2001.

18. Details of the empirical strategy are explained in Spolaore and Wacziarg (2016a).

19. This is a common assumption in the literature. For example, see Alesina and Spolaore (2003).

20. Analogous results could be obtained by also assuming that the initiator of the conflict faces lower war costs. We abstract from this possibility to keep the notation simpler.

References

Alesina, A., A. Devleeschauwer, W. Easterly, S. Kurlat, and R. Wacziarg. 2003. "Fractionalization." *Journal of Economic Growth* 8:55–194.

Alesina, A., and E. Spolaore. 2003. *The Size of Nations*. Cambridge, MA: MIT Press.

Arbatli, C. E., Q. Ashraf, and O. Galor. 2015. "The Nature of Civil Conflict." Working paper. Providence, RI: Brown University.

Blattman, C., and E. Miguel. 2010. "Civil War." *Journal of Economic Literature* 48 (1): 3–57.

Caselli, F., M. Morelli, and D. Rohner. 2014. "The Geography of Inter-state Resource Wars." *Quarterly Journal of Economics* 130 (1): 267–315.

Cavalli-Sforza, L. L., P. Menozzi, and A. Piazza. 1994. *The History and Geography of Human Genes*. Princeton, NJ: Princeton University Press.

Desmet, K., I. Ortuño-Ortín, and R. Wacziarg. 2012. "The Political Economy of Ethnolinguistic Cleavages." *Journal of Development Economics* 97 (1): 322–332.

Desmet, K., I. Ortuño-Ortín, and R. Wacziarg. 2017. "Culture, Ethnicity and Diversity." *American Economic Review* 107 (9): 2479–2513.

Deutsch, K. W. 1964. "Communication Theory and Political Integration." In *The Integration of Political Communities*, edited by Philip E. Jacob and James V. Toscano: 46–74. Philadelphia: J. B. Lippincott.

Dyen, I., J. B. Kruskal, and P. Black. 1992. "An Indo-European Classification: A Lexicostatistical Experiment." *Transactions of the American Philosophical Society* 82:1–132.

Esteban, J., L. Mayoral, and D. Ray. 2012. "Ethnicity and Conflict: An Empirical Study." *American Economic Review* 102 (4): 1310–1342.

Esteban, J., and D. Ray. 2011. "Linking Conflict to Inequality and Polarization." *American Economic Review* 101 (4): 1345–1374.

Faten, G., G. Palmer, and S. A. Bremer. 2004. "The MID3 Data Set, 1993–2001: Procedures, Coding Rules, and Description." *Conflict Management and Peace Science* 21:133–154.

Fearon, J. 1995. "Rationalist Explanations for War." *International Organization* 49 (3): 379–414.

Fearon, J. 2003. "Ethnic and Cultural Diversity by Country." *Journal of Economic Growth* 8:195–222.

Fearon, J., and D. Laitin. 2003. "Ethnicity, Insurgency, and Civil War." *American Political Science Review* 97 (1): 75–90.

Garfinkel, M. R., and S. Skaperdas. 2007. "Economics of Conflict: An Overview." In *Handbook of Defense Economics*, vol. 2, edited by K. Hartley and T. Sandler, 649–709. Amsterdam: North-Holland.

Haas, E. B. 1958. *The Uniting of Europe: Political, Social, and Economic Forces, 1950–1957.* London: Stevens.

Haas, E. B. 1964. *Beyond the Nation State: Functionalism and International Organization.* Stanford, CA: Stanford University Press.

Hirshleifer, Jack. 1989. "Conflict and Rent-Seeking Success Functions: Ratio vs. Difference Models of Relative Success." *Public Choice* 63 (2): 101–112.

Huntington, S. 1993. "The Clash of Civilizations." *Foreign Affairs* 72 (3): 22–49.

Huntington, S. 1996. *The Clash of Civilizations and the Remaking of World Order.* New York: Simon and Schuster.

International Institute for Strategic Studies. 2017. *Armed Conflict Survey 2017.* London: International Institute for Strategic Studies.

Jones, D. M., S. A. Bremer, and J. D. Singer. 1996. "Militarized Interstate Disputes, 1816–1992: Rationale, Coding Rules, and Empirical Patterns." *Conflict Management and Peace Science* 15:163–213.

Mecham, R. Q., J. Fearon, and D. Laitin. 2006. "Religious Classification and Data on Shares of Major World Religions." Unpublished manuscript, Stanford University.

Montalvo, J. G., and M. Reynal-Querol. 2005. "Ethnic Polarization, Potential Conflict and Civil War." *American Economic Review* 95 (3): 796–816.

Schelling, T. 1960. *The Strategy of Conflict.* Cambridge, MA: Harvard University Press.

Spolaore, E. 2013. "What Is European Integration Really About? A Political Guide for Economists." *Journal of Economic Perspectives* 27 (3): 125–144.

Spolaore, E. 2015. "The Political Economy of European Integration." In *The Routledge Handbook of the Economics of European Integration*, edited by Harald Badinger and Volker Nitsch, 435–448. London: Routledge.

Spolaore, E., and R. Wacziarg. 2009. "The Diffusion of Development." *Quarterly Journal of Economics* 124 (2): 469–529.

Spolaore, E., and R. Wacziarg. 2013. "How Deep Are the Roots of Economic Development?" *Journal of Economic Literature* 51 (2): 325–369.

Spolaore, E., and R. Wacziarg. 2016a. "War and Relatedness." *Review of Economics and Statistics* 98 (5): 925–939.

Spolaore, E., and R. Wacziarg. 2016b. "Ancestry, Language and Culture." In *The Palgrave Handbook of Economics and Language*, edited by Victor Ginsburgh and Shlomo Weber, 174–211. London: Palgrave Macmillan.

Spolaore, E., and R. Wacziarg. 2016c. "The Diffusion of Institutions." In *Complexity and Evolution: Toward a New Synthesis for Economics*, edited by David S. Wilson and Alan Kirman, 147–166. Cambridge, MA: MIT Press.

Sumner, W. G. 1906. *Folkways*. New York: Ginn.

Tir, J. 2003. "Averting Armed International Conflicts through State-to-State Territorial Transfers." *Journal of Politics* 65:1235–1257.

Tir, J., P. Schafer, P. F. Diehl, and G. Goertz. 1998. "Territorial Changes, 1816–1996: Procedures and Data." *Conflict Management and Peace Science* 16:89–97.

Weede, E. 1973. "Nation-Environment Relations as Determinants of Hostilities among Nations." *Peace Science Society (International) Papers* 20:67–90.

2 Regional Fragility Clusters: State Capacity and Civil Conflicts

Arthur Silve and Thierry Verdier

2.1 Introduction

Civil wars and state failures tend to cluster in time and in space. Between the Great Lakes region in Central Africa, the Horn of Africa, the Balkan countries and Central Asian regions after the fall of the Communist bloc, or more recently the Arab Spring, there is ample anecdotal evidence of the phenomenon. There are two main explanations for this pattern. First, similar geographical or social characteristics, resource endowments, and climatic conditions may favor conflict simultaneously in neighboring countries. Indeed, very extensive empirical literature studies the intrinsic characteristics of countries that prevail in countries marred by civil war and fragility; see Sambanis (2002) and Blattman and Miguel (2010) for detailed reviews of the literature, and Besley and Persson (2011a) for some theoretical approaches generally linking state capacity to conflicts. The second reason for the clustering of civil wars has to do with cross-border contagion effects. This has also been widely documented in political science,[1] as well as in the development policy and international security literature.[2,3,4]

The most frequently cited mechanism for such diffusion effects is the existence of ethnic ties of rebelling groups across "porous" borders.[5] More generally, a bad neighbor may facilitate access to warfare technology, information, and experience by an insurgent group. For instance, Ofcansky (1996) highlights how Idi Amin recruited discharged Sudanese mercenaries to build his army in Uganda; Bakke (2013) points out that the Chechen insurgency was helped by foreign Muslims fighting for a greater Islamist cause; and Hazen and Horner (2007) document how violence in the Niger Delta was fueled by weapons smuggled from Liberia and Sierra Leone. Similarly, Forsberg (2008) and Weidmann (2015) argue in more general terms that cross-border kinship favors the transmission of information on the opportunity and feasibility of conflict, especially when the disorder in the neighboring country stimulates the emergence of armed nonstate actors (militia, mercenaries, and organized crime) that are parties to the diffusion of conflict activities across the region.[6]

One aspect widely documented by the literature as a vector of instability diffusion is the cross-border proliferation of small arms (pistols, rifles, carbines, submachine guns, and light machine guns), which are distinguished from other conventional weapons by their portability. From the Cold War era to the present-day underground economy, the small arms trade has been a lucrative industry, exploiting regional conflicts and porous borders for economic gains. Of the 875 million small arms estimated to be in global circulation, approximately two-thirds are in the hands of private bodies.[7] Importantly, the destabilizing effects of small arms persist across generations because these weapons are portable, durable, and low maintenance, undermining long-term stability in regional areas such as West Africa, Latin America, and Central Asia.

Lack of transparency by major weapons exporters (such as the Russian Federation, China, Pakistan, Belarus, Iran, and South Africa) also facilitates small arms falling into the hands of nonstate actors, unaccountable to international or domestic laws because of their location along porous borders of two territories. Such agents, the "problems without passports" (Picciotto et al. 2005), have been described in the international security literature as important facilitators of cross-border conflict spillover effects (Wolff 2010; Geneva Centre for the Democratic Control of Armed Forces and Geneva Call 2011).

Another important vector of diffusion of conflict in neighboring states is the displacement of populations coming from a conflict zone and refugee movements crossing borders of fragile and weak states. Indeed, the massive arrival of refugees in a country creates huge economic pressures on local resources, significantly altering the ethnic and social structure for communities and exacerbating economic rivalries. Refugees may also extend the networks of rebel groups and enable transnational diffusion of combatants, weapons, and ideologies, reinforcing and complementing the destabilizing effects of other detrimental aspects of porous borders.[8]

Motivated by the previous observations, the purpose of this chapter is to provide a theoretical framework to analyze some central issues on the diffusion of conflicts and their interactions with socioeconomic development. Why are some countries more vulnerable than others to the diffusion of neighboring civil wars? Why is it that some governments seem to succeed in building better institutions in the face of such a threat? Why do we observe regional clusters of state fragility with rampant civil conflicts on both sides of borders?

To discuss these issues, we construct a simple two-country model of civil conflict and repression. In each country, the group in power (the "government") is able to exploit a resource that may be disputed by another group (the "contender"). Fighting over the resource is costly to all parties, and the contender may prefer not to dispute the control of the resource. The government may in turn discourage a rebellion, thanks to two tools: a transfer to the other group, to reward peaceful behavior through "redistribution," and investment in warfare technology, to increase the cost of a possible conflict through "deterrence." The political regime in each country is governed by two parameters of interest: the opportunity cost of fighting for the contender, and the capacity of the government to commit to resource sharing. Conflict cannot be avoided when there are low opportunity costs and low credibility. As either gets higher, the political outcome is likely to turn to peace and the government is likely to favor redistribution over deterrence. A conflict in a neighboring country is assumed to lower the opportunity cost of fighting for the contender. It may therefore affect the domestic political regime.

This model provides several layers of results. First, this framework generates the usual categories of political regimes: "redistributive," "repressive" (where the transfer is used jointly with investment in warfare technology to discourage a rebellion), and finally civil war.

Second, the possibility of diffusion of civil conflict across borders induces a basic regional complementarity between governments choosing their own national political regime. The incentive for one national government to choose a peaceful internal social settlement with its contender group is positively affected by the choice of neighboring governments to do the same with their own opposition. This leads naturally to the possibility of multiple regional political regime equilibria, one where both countries are at peace and the other where they are both in a civil war. This observation highlights the importance of regional institutions to coordinate national policies in order to avoid regional clusters of civil conflicts.

Third, if the state has the possibility of investing in "state capacity" (its institutional capacity to credibly commit to a certain policy regime), it may avoid the fate of its warring neighbor. In other words, the model predicts a second possible spillover from a civil war abroad. Large spillovers of civil conflicts abroad result in negative incentives to invest in domestic state capacity (i.e., negative spillovers). Interestingly, however, small regional conflict spillovers eventually lead a national government to increase its own level of state capacity as a defense mechanism to avoid a civil war regime at home (i.e., positive spillovers).

Section 2.2 examines the related literature. Section 2.3 develops our basic framework of analysis and uncovers the various feasible political regimes in the case of one isolated country. Section 2.4 naturally extends the analysis to the case of two countries interconnected by the possibility of contagion of civil conflict from abroad. Section 2.5 considers the issue of institutional investment in state capacity, ensuring some degree of policy credibility. Section 2.6 illustrates some of the predictions by using the case of the "Arab Spring" and the civil unrest in Morocco. Section 2.7 presents our conclusions.

2.2   Related Literature

The features of the model provide a framework that combines several strands of the literature.

In the initial setup of the model, described in section 2.3, conflicts are determined by two parameters: the opportunity cost of conflict for the contender, and the credibility of the government. A wealth of works support the role of these parameters. To capture opportunity costs, empirical studies have compared the contrasting impacts of price shocks and available resources on conflict. Arguably, the significance of the former is evidence of the role of opportunity costs in triggering conflict. For instance, Chassang and Padró i Miquel (2009) argue that while negative economic shocks adequately account for a lower opportunity cost of fighting, poverty does not. Much evidence indeed supports the role of negative economic shocks as triggers for civil conflict (Besley and Persson 2009a; Brückner and Ciccone 2007; Collier and Hoeffler 2004; Dube and Vargas 2013; Miguel, Satyanath, and Sergenti 2004). However, these results remain disputed in the literature. For instance, Bazzi and Blattman (2014) and Ciccone (2013) reach the opposite conclusion, that economic shocks are not significant predictors of conflict. De Soysa and Fjelde (2010) use a different approach. They argue that institutions that reward investment are favorable to peace. The issue is not settled, and for all the empirical difficulties involved in accounting for the opportunity costs of fighting, we think that, as a first pass, it remains a reasonable and plausible mechanism of transmission of civil conflicts across borders. As such, it is therefore worth investigating its implications for institutional clustering.

The second key parameter of the model is the credibility of the government. In line with McBride, Milante, and Skaperdas (2011), we abstract from distinguishing between the various concepts or dimensions that define a government's ability to commit: the credibility of its promises, its good governance, the institutional structure of checks and balances and constraints on the executive, the state's administrative capacity, and even its implicit bureaucratic norms and social capital. For our purposes, these terms can be used interchangeably as a general notion of "state capacity." State capacity has been identified as an important determinant of conflict by many scholars, such as Braithwaite (2010), Fearon and Laitin (2003), Fjelde and De Soysa (2009), Hendrix (2010), Keefer (2008), and McBride, Milante, and Skaperdas (2011). Several of these works include military capacity as an element of state capacity. Here, for definitional purposes, we use the term "state capacity" to refer only to the government's credibility, and we define its "military capacity" as a separate dimension.

The role of state capacity remains disputed in the literature as much as that of the opportunity cost of conflict. Sobek (2010) and Thies (2010) both argue in favor of reverse causality: while state capacity does not affect the probability of conflict, conflict indeed affects state capacity. Interestingly, the literature is not conclusive as to this reverse causality either, though it mostly focuses on a narrow definition of state capacity as the capacity to raise taxes. Tilly (1985), Levi (1988), and Brewer (1989) all argue that war was key in the development of the fiscal capacity of Europe, while Besley and Persson (2008, 2009b, 2010) provide models of the investment in state capacity where the risk of a civil war is a negative determinant of state capacity. Again, we still believe that the pacifying effect of the state's ability to commit is a reasonable assumption for our model.

Based on these two parameters, the model predicts the existence of three different regimes. The state can use transfers only to maintain social peace (redistributive regime) or invest in military capacity (repressive regime), or it may allow a civil war. In our model, the three regimes are associated with decreasing levels of state capacity. This typology and this latter property are in line with the literature, despite typological differences. Besley and Persson (2009c, 2010, 2011b) simply call the redistributive regime "peace," but Taydas and Peksen (2012) provide empirical support in favor of the existence of a redistributive regime. McBride, Milante, and Skaperdas (2011) and Phillips (2015) prefer to call the repressive regime "military."

While contagion of civil conflicts across national borders is a well-established fact, our model predicts another form of conflict spillover as well. Interestingly, our analysis points out that conflict abroad may also provide positive reactive institutional spillovers. Indeed, a national government facing a neighboring country in civil war may be induced to undertake higher investment in institutions whenever this allows the government to avoid falling into a civil war itself. This interesting feature of our model is supported by Braithwaite (2010) and McBride, Milante, and Skaperdas (2011). More generally speaking, though, our analysis argues that the possible contagion of conflict favors a spatial clustering of state capacity institutions as well.

2.3   A Model of Deterrence and Redistribution

Let us first consider an economy composed of two groups, indexed by G and C, for government and contender, respectively. The model assumes that each group behaves as a unitary agent. It accounts for the possibility of conflict between the two groups over a resource R. The groups may engage $M_G \geq 0$ and $M_C \geq 0$ into the conflict. The technology of conflict is described by the probability of the government being overthrown:[9]

$$\prod = 1, \text{ if } \gamma M_C \geq M_G \text{ and } M_G < \overline{M}$$
$$= \pi, \text{ with } 0 < \pi < 1, \text{ if } \gamma M_C \geq M_G > \overline{M} \qquad (2.1)$$
$$= 0, \text{ if } \gamma M_C < M_G.$$

The parameter γ represents the fighting efficiency of group C relative to the government. C is more efficient at fighting than G if $\gamma > 1$ and less efficient otherwise. This parameter characterizes the warfare technology as more favorable to the government or to a guerrilla, the terrain conditions, the degree of political mobilization, or the morale in the army. The parameter $\overline{M}$ captures a scale effect in the defense technology of the government. A minimum defense expenditure is required to avoid being ousted by any challenger. The parameter π captures the probability that conditional on there being a rebellion, it will be successful. A higher π means that if the contender rises against the government, the government has little chance of surviving the conflict, though it says nothing of the likelihood of that conflict. π can also be affected by conditions of the warfare technology and, notably, the capacity of the rebels to access weapons and mercenaries. Note that this way of modeling the conflict technology is akin to the S-shaped probability function assumed by Skaperdas (1992), albeit with discontinuities. These discontinuities allow for a simpler characterization of the various equilibrium types. Given this warfare technology, the government can either fight with the excluded group, threaten to fight, or pay the price of peace, in line with Azam (2001).

The following assumption ensures that the resource level R is large enough to make it worthwhile for both parties to eventually engage in conflict to contest it.

$$R > \overline{M}\left[\frac{1}{\pi}, \frac{1}{1-\pi}\right]. \tag{A.1}$$

Both G and C can allocate the labor endowments N_G and N_C between production and conflict. The output levels of the two groups are very stylized:

$$Y_G = N_G - M_G \text{ and } Y_C = a(N_C - M_C).$$

N_G and N_C are the resources available to each group, and M_G and M_C are the resources they respectively invest in conflict. When not overthrown, the government remains in control of the contestable resource R. If it loses the conflict, the control of the resource R shifts to the other group. It may, for instance, account for mineral resources, whose produce accrues to the group in power. The parameter a represents the productive efficiency of group C relative to the government. C is more efficient at producing if $a > 1$ and less efficient otherwise; a depends on the relative productivity of each group, but also on the relative prices they face, when the government and the contenders face different trade shocks.

The game takes place in four stages, as illustrated in figure 2.1.

1. The government first irreversibly engages $M_G \geq 0$ and offers the other group a "social contract," which consists of a transfer $T \geq 0$ conditional on the other group not entering into conflict, $\Pi = 0$, which comes down to $\gamma M_C < M_G$.

2. The contender engages $M_C \geq 0$.

3. If $\gamma M_C \geq M_G$, a civil war erupts. Otherwise, peace prevails, the transfer promised by the government is effected with probability θ (for now, given exogenously). θ measures the state's capacity to undertake credible commitments.

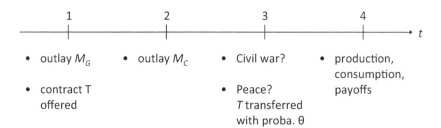

Figure 2.1
Timing of the game.

4. Production and consumption take place, and the two groups derive the following payoffs:

$$\begin{cases} U_G = (N_G - M_G) + (1 - \Pi)R - \theta\chi T \\ U_C = a(N_C - M_C) + \theta\chi T + \Pi R \end{cases}.$$

The parameter χ is an indicator of peace. It is equal to 0 if the two groups fight and equal to 1 if they are at peace.

These payoffs capture in a reduced form the essence of the redistributional stakes for civil conflict in various developing countries endowed with natural resources that are generally under the control of the state. Note as well that θ, our operational notion of state capacity, defined as the credibility of the state's promises of transfers, captures only one dimension of what economists describe as state capacity. In particular, we do not account for other dimensions such as fiscal or legal capacity, as for instance emphasized by Besley and Persson (2009b), and their impact on the economic incentives of the two groups.

The government is subject to a budget constraint (BC). It can never credibly promise more than what it produces in times of peace:

(BC) $N_G + R - M_G - T \geq 0.$

If the other group accepts the contract in stage 2, it does not put any resource in the conflict and $M_C = 0$. If it prefers to enter into conflict, it invests $M_C = M_G/\gamma$. It follows that it accepts the contract iff

$$\theta T \geq \begin{cases} \pi R - \alpha M_G \ \text{ if } M_G \geq \overline{M} \\ R - \alpha M_G \ \ \text{ otherwise.} \end{cases}$$

The left-hand side of this condition is the transfer expected from the government if it accepts the contract. The right-hand side of this condition is the expected gain from civil war. The parameter $\alpha = a/\gamma$ represents the comparative advantage of the contender at producing versus fighting. Intuitively, α is a proxy for the opportunity cost of conflict for group C in terms of the forgone production. Further examination of the conflict technology allows us to simplify this condition thanks to the following lemma.

Lemma 2.1   Under assumption (A.1), $M_G \geq \overline{M}$.

When the value of the contested resource R is large enough, the government always invests in a military capacity at least as large as the minimum deterrent level $\overline{M}$. If it expects a conflict, this reduces the probability of losing the resource from 1 to π. Investing in the same military capacity level also helps achieve a peaceful outcome and deter an unruly group from contesting R.[10]

The incentive constraint (IC) can therefore be simplified as

(IC) $\theta T \geq \pi R - \alpha M_G$.

The transfer necessary to ensure that C accepts the contract is lower for higher values of α and M_G and lower values of π and R. On the one hand, the amount of resources up for grabs R increases the temptation of conflict, and the more likely a rebellion is to succeed π, the more costly it is for the government to discourage it. On the other hand, the higher the opportunity cost of conflict α and the resources invested in warfare technology M_G, the less tempting a conflict is, and the less costly it is for the government to discourage it.

Jointly, (BC) and (IC) define the set of feasible contracts. The optimal "peaceful" contract for the government results from the following program:

$$\max_{M_G,T} N_G - M_G + R - \theta T$$

$$\text{s.t.} \begin{cases} N_G - M_G + R - T \geq 0 \ \text{(BC)} \\ \theta T \geq \pi R - \alpha M_G \ \text{(IC)}. \end{cases}$$

This is a simple linear programming problem. It has the following solution.

Lemma 2.2   Define

$$\overline{\theta}(\alpha) = \frac{\pi R - \alpha \overline{M}}{R + N_G - \overline{M}}. \tag{2.2}$$

Under (A.1), the optimal peaceful contract for the government is characterized as follows:

1. When $\alpha < 1$ and $\theta \geq \bar{\theta}(\alpha)$, then

$$M_G = \overline{M} \text{ and } T = \frac{\pi}{\theta}R - \frac{\alpha}{\theta}\overline{M}.$$

2. When $\pi R/(R + N_G) \leq \alpha < 1$ and $\theta < \bar{\theta}(\alpha)$, then

$$M_G = \frac{(\pi - \theta)R - \theta N_G}{\alpha - \theta} \text{ and } T = \frac{\alpha N_G + (\alpha - \pi)R}{\alpha - \theta}.$$

3. When $\alpha > 1$, then

$$M_G = \max\left[\overline{M}, \frac{\pi}{\alpha}R\right] \text{ and } T = 0.$$

Both the opportunity cost for the government and the benefit for the rebel group of a unit of transfer T is θ because the government may renege with a probability $1 - \theta$. The marginal opportunity cost of military spending for the government is 1, but matching an increase of one unit of military spending M_G would cost the rebel group α. To deter a rebellion, the government would therefore rather resort to transfers when $\alpha < 1$ and to military spending when $\alpha > 1$.

When $\alpha < 1$, the government may not be in a position to credibly replace all military spending by a transfer: it cannot commit beyond the budget constraint (BC). When the state capacity θ is high enough (e.g., $\theta \geq \bar{\theta}(\alpha)$), then any unit of military spending above the minimum $\overline{M}$ can be advantageously replaced by α units of transfer. When the state capacity is not high enough, the state would like to resort to transfers instead of military spending, but it cannot promise transfers beyond its resources. Finally, notice that for $\alpha < \pi R/(R + N_G)$ and $\theta < \bar{\theta}(\alpha)$, there is no feasible contract that can allow the government to achieve a peaceful outcome.

Lemma 2.2 conveniently defines three peaceful regimes. Regime 1 corresponds to a "redistributive" state that ensures peace, relying on a transfer to the other group, for example, $T > 0$, and without having recourse to military deterrence. Thus, military spending is set at its minimum; for example, $M_G = \overline{M}$. This regime under peace is optimal when the opportunity cost of conflict α of the rebel group is low enough (e.g., $\alpha < 1$) and the degree of credibility θ of the government is large enough (e.g., $\theta \geq \bar{\theta}(\alpha)$). Regime 2 corresponds to a "repressive" state that relies on both the transfer (e.g., $T > 0$) and military spending to deter a rebellion (e.g., $M_G > \bar{M}$). It is optimal when the credibility of the government is weak and the opportunity cost of conflict α of the rebel group is low enough (e.g., $\pi R/(R + N_G) \leq \alpha < 1$ and $\theta < \bar{\theta}(\alpha)$). Finally, regime 3 can be described as a "praetorian" regime, relying exclusively on force (e.g., $T = 0$ and $M \geq \bar{M}$) (for a related discussion, see Azam 2006). It is optimal when the rebel's opportunity cost is high (e.g., $\alpha > 1$).

To avoid a tedious taxonomy discussion, in what follows we focus on the case $\alpha < 1$, where the optimal peaceful social contract is a redistributive or a repressive regime. The frontier separating the two regimes, when (BC) becomes binding, is characterized by the frontier $\theta = \bar{\theta}(\alpha)$. $\bar{\theta}$ decreases with α and $\bar{M}$, and increases with R and π. The fact that $\bar{\theta}$ decreases with α illustrates that in that region both the ability of the government to commit and the opportunity cost of fighting are favorable to a redistributive solution. A higher θ may compensate for a lower α, and vice versa. Similarly, an increase in the minimum deterrent military capacity $\bar{M}$ of the government tends to favor the redistribution regime. On the other hand, an increase in the contested stakes R of the conflict reduces the scope for a redistributive regime as a peaceful solution, in line with the evidence in Bazzi and Blattman (2014). Finally, the more likely that a rebellion will be successful (e.g., the higher π), the more likely the government will be to resort to deterrence in order to avoid a conflict. A repressive regime may therefore become the best option for the government.

To determine the conditions for a peace regime, we may compute the indirect payoffs to G in all cases. They are given as follows:

1. Redistributive regime: $V_G = N_G + (1 - \pi)R - (1 - \alpha)\bar{M}$.

2. Repressive regime: $V_G = (1 - \theta)\dfrac{\alpha(N_G + R) - \pi R}{\alpha - \theta}$.

3. Praetorian regime: $V_G = N_G + R - M_G$.

4. Civil war: $V_G = N_G - \bar{M} + (1 - \pi)R$.

A simple comparison of these payoffs reveals that a peaceful regime is always better for the government than civil war when this is implemented either as a redistributive regime or as a praetorian regime. However, it may not always be the case that the repressive regime is preferable to civil war. As a matter of fact, the government prefers a civil war to a repressive regime if and only if

$$\theta < \underline{\theta}(\alpha) = \frac{(1-\alpha)\pi R - \alpha\overline{M}}{(1-\alpha)(N_G + R) - \overline{M}}.$$

$\underline{\theta}(\alpha)$ decreases with α and $\overline{M}$ and increases with R. First, the ability of the government to commit and the opportunity cost of fighting both help the government achieve a peaceful solution. Second, the government's military advantage makes it easier for it to achieve a peaceful outcome. Third, in line with the literature emphasizing the role of "incentive" or "greed," the larger stakes of the civil conflict make it harder to achieve a peaceful outcome.

The following proposition summarizes the preceding discussion.

Proposition 2.1

1. When $\alpha < 1$ and $\theta \geq \overline{\theta}(\alpha)$, the government implements a redistributive regime, with $M_G = \overline{M}$, $M_C = 0$, $T = \pi R/\theta - \alpha\overline{M}/\theta$, and $V_G = N_G + (1-\pi)R - (1-\alpha)\overline{M}$.

2. When $\pi R/(R + N_G) \leq \alpha < 1$ and $\underline{\theta}(\alpha) \leq \theta < \overline{\theta}(\alpha)$, the government implements a repressive regime, with $M_G = ((\pi - \theta)R - \theta\,N_G)/(\alpha - \theta)$, $M_C = 0$, $T = (\alpha\,N_G + (\alpha - \pi)R)/(\alpha - \theta)$ and $V_G = (1-\theta)(\alpha\,N_G + (\alpha - \pi)R)/(\alpha - \theta)$.

3. When $\alpha \geq 1$, the government implements a praetorian regime, with $M_G = \max[\overline{M}, \pi R/\alpha]$, $M_C = 0$, $T = 0$, and $V_G = N_G + R - M_G$.

4. When $\theta < \min[\underline{\theta}(\alpha), \overline{\theta}(\alpha)]$, a civil war erupts, with $M_G = \overline{M}$, $M_C = \gamma\overline{M}$, $T = 0$, and $V_G = N_G - \overline{M} + (1-\pi)R$.

Beyond the analysis of lemma 2.2, notice that civil war erupts simultaneously for low levels of state capacity θ and opportunity cost of conflict α. When state capacity increases (i.e., when the government is increasingly able to commit to transfer resources to the other group), civil war can be more easily avoided. When α is larger, however, deterrence finds some bite against transfers and, thanks to a mix of deterrence and redistribution, the government implements peace through a repressive regime (for intermediate values of θ). As θ grows yet higher, deterrence becomes unnecessary, and a transfer to the other group is all that is needed to prevent the contender from investing in conflict. Figure 2.2 illustrates proposition 2.1.

Also notice that when θ is low enough, starting from an initial state of civil war, an increase in α also allows the state to achieve peace

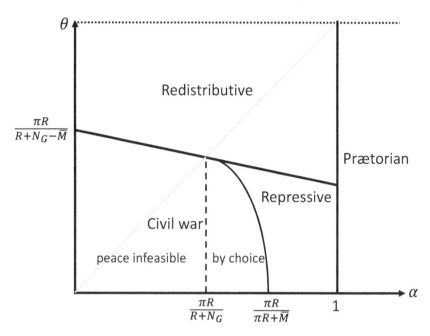

Figure 2.2
Typology of equilibria.

through a repressive regime. As α grows yet higher, the government switches to a praetorian regime. It does not need to share its resource with the other group, whose opportunity cost of conflict is too large to credibly threaten the government.

2.4   Regional Contagion of Civil Conflicts

Now consider two countries, A and B. Whenever we need to differentiate the two countries, we add an A or a B superscript to any variable. Conversely, when we wish to speak of a generic situation, we will omit the superscript. This should leave no room for ambiguities.

There are mutual regional spillover effects of civil conflict between the two countries. Arguably there are several ways through which such spillover effects can materialize. Typically, a conflict in country B will likely make it easier for the contender in country A to access weapons, mercenaries, and other necessities for conflict. The literature also has insisted on the role of war refugees as important vectors of contagion for civil conflicts across regions. For instance, abrupt cross-border movements of populations can create important pressure on local resources and environments, leading to social, ecological, and economic tensions inside the receiving region. We capture these features by simply assuming that a conflict in country B lowers the opportunity cost of conflict in country A from α^A to $\alpha^A - \beta^A$. $\beta^A > 0$ measures the spillover of a conflict in country B on α^A. A large β^A denotes a large domestic impact from having a bad neighbor. Similarly, we can define $\beta^B > 0$. Furthermore, to ensure that our setup allows for contagion, we must have that in at least one of the two countries

$$\alpha < \frac{\pi R}{\pi R + \overline{M}},$$ \hfill (A.2)

while in the other country

$$\alpha - \beta < \frac{\pi R}{\pi R + \overline{M}}.$$ \hfill (A.3)

Equation (A.2) ensures that a conflict is possible in the first country when it has a low state capacity, even without contagion from abroad, while (A.3) ensures that the second country is vulnerable to contagion from abroad (again, for low state capacity). To make the exposition clearer, we will suppose that (A.2) holds in both countries in order to consider the possibility that either country may be the source of the regional destabilization. To clarify, all parameters may be country-specific, so in the end we consider the situation where

$$\begin{cases} \alpha^A < \dfrac{\pi^A R^A}{\pi^A R^A + \overline{M}^A}, \\ \alpha^B < \dfrac{\pi^B R^B}{\pi^B R^B + \overline{M}^B}. \end{cases}$$

The framework is therefore adequate to examine a wealth of symmetric or asymmetric country dyads. Neither, either, or both countries may be resource rich (high R), vulnerable to a coup (high π), or display a different ex ante military deterrence effect for the government (high $\overline{M}$).

Let us further introduce the following convenient notations:

$$\begin{cases} \underline{\theta}_W = \min\left[\overline{\theta}(\alpha - \beta), \underline{\theta}(\alpha - \beta)\right] & \overline{\theta}_W = \overline{\theta}(\alpha - \beta), \\ \underline{\theta}_P = \min\left[\overline{\theta}(\alpha), \underline{\theta}(\alpha)\right] & \overline{\theta}_P = \overline{\theta}(\alpha). \end{cases}$$

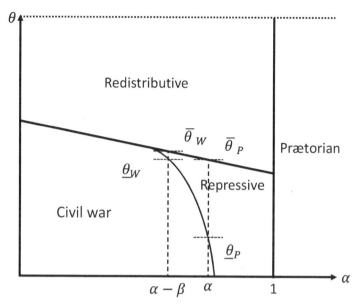

Figure 2.3
(Large) spillovers of civil war.

They account for the respective thresholds for a civil war and for a redistributive regime, with a bad neighbor and with a good neighbor. Notice that if $\alpha - \beta \leq \pi\, R/(R+N_{\mathrm{G}})$, then $\underline{\theta}_{\mathrm{W}} = \overline{\theta}_{\mathrm{W}}$, and if $\alpha \leq \pi\, R/(R+N_{\mathrm{G}})$, then $\underline{\theta}_{\mathrm{P}} = \overline{\theta}_{\mathrm{P}}$. Since $\underline{\theta}$ and $\overline{\theta}$ are both decreasing, $\underline{\theta}_{\mathrm{W}} > \underline{\theta}_{\mathrm{P}}$ and $\overline{\theta}_{\mathrm{W}} > \overline{\theta}_{\mathrm{P}}$: a civil war abroad raises the level of state capacity necessary to implement a redistributive state as well as the state capacity necessary to avoid a civil war itself. A country that would have been at peace without a bad neighbor may be forced into a civil war, and a redistributive regime may be turned into a repressive one. Possibly, when the spillover is large enough, such as when $\overline{\theta}_{\mathrm{P}} < \underline{\theta}_{\mathrm{W}}$, a redistributive regime may even be forced into a civil war by a nearby conflict. Figure 2.3 illustrates these considerations.

Again, this is assumed to be true of both countries, with the appropriate superscripts. This provides the following characterization of the regional system of political regimes.

Proposition 2.2

1. Country A is at peace while B is at war if and only if $\theta^{A} \geq \underline{\theta}_{\mathrm{W}}^{A}$ and $\theta^{B} < \underline{\theta}_{\mathrm{P}}^{B}$ (and vice versa).

2. Regional peace is an equilibrium when $\theta \geq \underline{\theta}_P$ in both countries.
3. Regional conflict is an equilibrium when $\theta < \underline{\theta}_W$ in both countries.

Since a bad neighbor lowers a country's opportunity cost of conflict, civil war in any country may diffuse over to the whole region. A weakly institutionalized country, such that $\theta < \underline{\theta}_P$, cannot escape a civil war, regardless of what happens in neighboring countries. Conversely, if the government has a high ability to commit, such that $\theta \geq \overline{\theta}_W$, it is immune to contagion from a civil war in a neighboring country. Therefore, civil war and peace may only coexist in a single region that has very disparate abilities to commit. When countries have comparable levels of state capacity, clusters of conflict and peace are likely to appear (item 1 of proposition 2.2).

For comparable levels of state capacity, the two countries are either both at peace (item 2) or both in a civil war (item 3). The negative spillovers of a neighboring civil war are felt at intermediate levels of institutional development, such as when a country has $\underline{\theta}_P \leq \theta < \underline{\theta}_W$. In that range, a country is vulnerable and can be destabilized by a neighboring conflict. With good neighbors, it will manage to remain peaceful, too, but a weakly institutionalized neighbor that is involved in a civil conflict itself would be enough to destabilize it.

Interestingly, when both countries have an intermediate level of institutional credibility, two equilibria may emerge: both countries may be at peace simultaneously, or they may both suffer from their own internal strife. Which equilibrium emerges depends on how the different countries coordinate their expectations about each other's institutional stability. Under pessimistic expectations about each other's neighbor's capacity to implement a peaceful regime within its own national territory, both governments may be ready to accept civil war domestically. Conversely, under optimistic expectations about the institutional stability of the region, each country may succeed in avoiding civil conflict. Figure 2.4 illustrates proposition 2.2.

While the model cannot account for which regional equilibrium might emerge, it does account for the pattern of clustering of civil wars. It also suggests that there are parameter configurations for which the institutional stability of a region is highly sensitive to small extrinsic factors not directly related to observable economic fundamentals. Indeed, the possibility of multiple equilibria when both countries display intermediate values of institutional development suggests some considerations for policy. First, it might be difficult to predict ex ante the regime

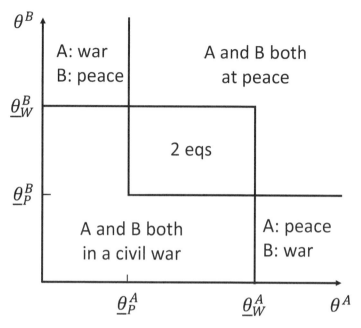

Figure 2.4
Regional equilibria with spillovers.

in which countries may end up. Second, a specific regional situation at a given point in time may be vulnerable to shifts in expectations by the different regional agents and quickly lead to a much different situation because of diffusion effects. Third, international exchange of information and communication at the governmental level can be useful for coordinating expectations on the peaceful regional equilibrium.

The previous discussion focuses on civil war versus peace. A more careful consideration of peaceful equilibria, namely redistributive and repressive, uncovers a few additional mechanisms. Notice as well that when the regional spillovers are small, such as when $\bar{\theta}_P \approx \bar{\theta}_W > \underline{\theta}_W$, then whenever there are multiple equilibria, the peaceful equilibrium must be repressive. The choice is between an equilibrium where both countries are in their own civil war and an equilibrium where both countries are deterring conflict through demonstrations of police strength. On the contrary, when spillovers are large, such as when $\bar{\theta}_P < \underline{\theta}_W$, then the peaceful equilibrium does not necessarily entail repression. Indeed, when the state capacity $\theta \geq \bar{\theta}_P$, the peaceful equilibrium will be redistributive.

Interestingly, this analysis yields yet one more type of fragility diffusion. When $\underline{\theta}_W, \bar{\theta}_P \leq \theta < \bar{\theta}_W$, then a country that alone would have been in a redistributive regime is forced into a repressive regime by a bad neighbor. To summarize, an open conflict may diffuse across borders. Conflict may also diffuse by lack of coordination, even though the region could otherwise have been at peace. Finally, conflict may induce repression in a neighbor country. Later on, when we allow the state to invest in its own capacity, yet another type of spillover will emerge.

Comparative statics. Economic shocks in one country may have repercussions for the region's stability. For instance, consider a country whose institutions are good enough to immunize it against contagion ($\theta \geq \underline{\theta}_W$). An increase in the price of the resource controlled by the government R would result in a higher $\underline{\theta}_W$, thus possibly taking away that country's immunity. The country would find itself vulnerable to contagion but would not necessarily be a source of instability itself ($\underline{\theta}_P \leq \theta < \underline{\theta}_W$). A further increase in the value of R would, however, possibly destabilize the country. In that case, the country would become a source of instability for the region ($\theta < \underline{\theta}_P$).

A change in the government's military incumbent advantage $\overline{M}$ has the converse effect. Such an effect may derive from several sources. The military technology to quell rebellions may be made cheaper, or there may be externalities from the state's defense expenditures. Foreign military assistance may also provide a disproportionate advantage to a government facing rebels. A restless group may be discouraged from starting a civil war if the government gains a higher military advantage $\overline{M}$. An increase in $\overline{M}$ may therefore turn a country from a source of instability for the region ($\theta < \underline{\theta}_P$) into a country where conflict could happen if it spilled over from outside ($\underline{\theta}_P \leq \theta < \underline{\theta}_W$) and even further into a country immune to contagion ($\theta \geq \underline{\theta}_W$).

Cross-border rebel networks. A factor often emphasized as a major driver of regional instability is the existence of cross-border ethnic groups and communities whose territories cross over porous borders that cannot be effectively monitored by national governments (Checkel 2014).[11] Through the use of their cross-border social networks, members of a rebel group in a given country may then enjoy substantial coordination, protection, and support from fellow members located on the other side of the border. This feature naturally creates an important channel for regional spillovers of conflict across weakly institutionalized states.

Moreover, when such cross-border rebel connections interact with other conflict spillovers, one may get a spiraling destabilization effect in the whole region that would not have happened absent the existence of these networks. One simple way to capture this in our model is to assume that the contender group C^A in country A is part of the same ethnic group as the contender group C^B in country B and that the groups can jointly decide their actions across national borders. In particular, the two groups can freely hire resources from the other side of the border and share the spoils on the captured resources if successful. Given this and the free mobility of resources across the network, the opportunity cost of conflict for a contender group in a given country is then simply given by the smallest opportunity cost of conflict across the two countries $\alpha = \min[\alpha^A, \alpha^B]$. To fix ideas, assume without loss of generality that $\alpha^A < \alpha^B$. Then the existence of a cross-border ethnic network between country A and country B clearly creates a negative spillover from country A on country B. Specifically, when country B's institutional capacity θ^B is such that $\underline{\theta}^B(\alpha^B) < \theta^B < \underline{\theta}^B(\alpha^A)$, the existence of a cross-border rebel network brings that country B into open conflict, which would not have happened without the existence of the cross-border network. Interestingly, this outcome may occur when the neighboring country A has enough institutional capacity to prevent a domestic civil conflict with members of its own contender group (e.g., when $\underline{\theta}^A(\alpha^A) < \theta^A$). Importantly, however, the civil conflict triggered in country B may in turn generate a negative spillover effect β^A on country A such that $\theta^A < \underline{\theta}^A(\alpha^A - \beta^A)$. In such a case, country A will also be affected by a civil conflict because of the feedback effect of the civil conflict induced by the rebel network on the neighboring country B. Ironically, while country A may in isolation have enough institutional capacity θ^A to be immune to a conflict emanating directly from its own contender group, it could still be driven into a civil conflict because of the feedback effect from the conflict that members from that very group have induced on the neighboring country B through cross-border networks. Cross-border rebel networks then tend to magnify other contagion spillovers and increase the likelihood of regional clusters of fragility and conflicts even more.

2.5 State Capacity Building and Cross-Border Contagion

2.5.1 A Simple Model of State Capacity Building

So far, we have assumed that the institutional state capacity θ of each country is exogenous. Now consider that the government can invest in its capacity to credibly commit θ at a cost $C_i(\theta)$. Let us first consider the case of a country in isolation. Thanks to proposition 2.1, we can write

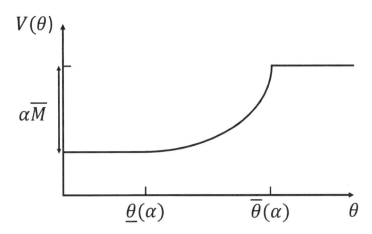

Figure 2.5
The government's indirect payoffs.

the indirect payoffs to the government depending in particular on the parameters α and θ:

$$V(\theta) = \begin{cases} N_G - \overline{M} + (1-\pi)R & \text{when } \theta < \underline{\theta}(\alpha), \\ \dfrac{1-\theta}{\alpha - \theta}(\alpha(N_G + R) - \pi R) & \text{when } \underline{\theta}(\alpha) \leq \theta < \overline{\theta}(\alpha), \text{ and} \\ N_G + (1-\pi)R - (1-\alpha)\overline{M} & \text{when } \overline{\theta}(\alpha) \leq \theta. \end{cases}$$

The government does not benefit from a higher θ either when the country is in a civil war or when it implements a redistributive regime. In the intermediate, repressive stage, the government's payoff is increasing and convex in θ. These properties are illustrated in figure 2.5.

The government then sets θ_{opt} so as to maximize $V(\theta) - C_1(\theta)$. Under the most simple framework possible, the cost of better institutions is linear:

$$C_1(\theta) = s\theta. \tag{A.4}$$

The parameter s is the marginal cost of investing in state capacity. In that context, the state's optimization program results in the following lemma.

Lemma 2.3 Define

$$\underline{\alpha} = \frac{s\pi R}{\overline{M}(R + N_G - \overline{M} + s)}.$$

Under (A.4), the optimal investment in state capacity is

$$\theta_{\text{opt}} = \begin{cases} \overline{\theta}(\alpha) & \text{if } \alpha \geq \underline{\alpha} \\ 0 & \text{otherwise.} \end{cases}$$

This lemma states that the government does not bother to invest in institutions if the opportunity cost of conflict of the contender is too low. In that case, the propensity of that group to go to conflict is too high for the government to contain it. The government realizes its best option is to allow a civil conflict, which makes institutions useless. Conversely, if the opportunity cost of conflict is high enough (e.g., α over the threshold $\underline{\alpha}$), then it is profitable for the government to invest in institutions.[12] Again, the parameters may all be country-specific, which would be accounted for by the appropriate superscripts on s, π, N_G, $\overline{M}$, and $\underline{\alpha}$. Conditional on investing in state capacity, the government sets $\theta_{\text{opt}} = \overline{\theta}(\alpha)$. This is the minimum level of commitment that allows it to implement a redistributive regime. Recall that $\overline{\theta}$ decreases with α and $\overline{M}$ and increases with R and π. A higher opportunity cost of conflict α or a higher military advantage $\overline{M}$ allows a lower investment in state capacity. Conversely, higher stakes R of the conflict or a higher likelihood π that a rebellion would be successful would give the government an incentive to invest in stronger institutions.

Investment in state capacity is nonmonotonic in α. The intuition is as follows. For low enough levels of $\alpha < \underline{\alpha}$, the government prefers to allow a civil war and has no interest in developing state capacity. Conversely, above a certain threshold, such as for $\alpha \geq \underline{\alpha}$, it prefers peace. However, as the opportunity cost of conflict α rises, the contender is likely to accept a lower level of commitment from the government. As a result, θ_{opt} decreases. This is illustrated in figure 2.6.

$\underline{\alpha}$ increases with s, π, and R and decreases with $\overline{M}$.[13] First, a higher cost s of state capacity building makes it less profitable to accommodate the "marginal" contender, such as the contender characterized by an opportunity cost of conflict α close to $\underline{\alpha}$. However, conditional on providing institutions, their provision $\overline{\theta}$ does not depend on s.[14]

Second, a higher likelihood π that a rebellion would be successful would also make it less profitable to accommodate the marginal contender. The threshold $\underline{\alpha}$ over which the government does so anyway rises, and conditional on providing institutions, their provision $\overline{\theta}$ also rises.

Third, a higher value R of the contested resources raises the stakes of a civil war. To accommodate the contender, the government must

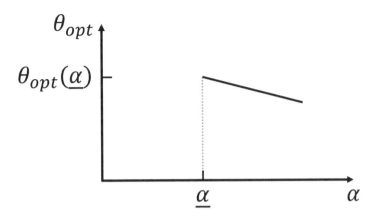

Figure 2.6
Investment in state capacity.

improve the redistribution of this resource. This is no longer profitable for the marginal contender: $\underline{\alpha}$ rises. However, the same reasoning applies, and as long as the government still provides institutions, their provision rises with R.

Fourth, an increase in the military advantage $\overline{M}$ of the government means it is actually easier to accommodate a contender, even with fewer institutions. As a result, the government can accommodate contenders with lower opportunity costs of conflict α, and the threshold $\underline{\alpha}$ over which there is investment in state capacity decreases.

2.5.2   Regional State Capacity Clusters
It is now time to reintroduce the two-country setup and extend it to account for regional patterns of state capacity building. Remember that having a bad neighbor lowers the opportunity cost of conflict α by an amount β. We have the following proposition.

Proposition 2.3

1. When $\alpha \geq \underline{\alpha} + \beta$, the government avoids contagion from a civil war abroad by investing in better institutions.

2. When $\underline{\alpha} \leq \alpha < \underline{\alpha} + \beta$, the country would not be able to avoid contagion from a civil war abroad. When the condition holds in two countries, they are either both at peace or both in a civil war.

3. When $\alpha < \underline{\alpha}$, the country is in a civil war regardless of its neighbors.

In the previous sections, we examined contagion in the absence of any institutional response from the government. This section introduces the first layer of policy response, in the form of state capacity building. With the possibility of investing in better institutions, the state is able to withstand a larger shock on the opportunity cost of conflict. Figure 2.7 highlights the equilibrium pattern of state capacity building at the regional level, depending on the structure of the opportunity cost of conflicts across countries. Recall that superscripts are used to clarify which country a variable refers to.

Comparative statics. When the opportunity costs of conflict are very asymmetric within a region, it may happen that a civil war erupts in country A but that country B is still in a position to avoid contagion (and vice versa). The civil war in A still lowers the opportunity cost of conflict in B, not enough to discourage the government from implementing a peaceful regime but enough to force it to improve its institutions. To ensure the participation of the contender, the government indeed implements $\theta_{\mathrm{opt}}^{B}(\alpha^{B}-\beta^{B})>\theta_{\mathrm{opt}}^{B}(\alpha^{B})$. In country B, this case results either from an inherently high level of stability (high α^{B}) or from small spillovers β^{B} from the civil war in country A. Since country B is not a source of instability for country A, country A is in a civil war only if it is inherently unstable (low α^{A}). Even if country A has some degree of intermediate stability, the absence of instability in the region would

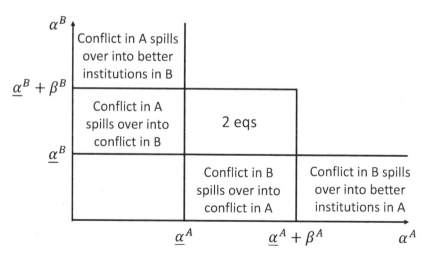

Figure 2.7
The spillovers of conflict and regional patterns of state capacity.

allow it to remain peaceful. To summarize, strong regional asymmetries in α result in even stronger asymmetries in state capacity. The risk of contagion from neighboring civil wars may be an incentive to invest in even better institutions (item 1 of proposition 2.3). Generally, we expect that countries at the frontier of regional clusters of civil conflict should be characterized by higher, rather than lower, levels of state capacity.

When the asymmetries are less pronounced, the model predicts not only regional clusters of civil wars but also clusters of state capacity. Unless country B is inherently very stable and spillovers are not too large, its government may prefer to allow a neighboring civil war to spread instead of investing in state capacity. A civil war in country A would then spill over into a civil war in country B, and both countries would end up with no state capacity (and vice versa).

For intermediate levels of α in both countries, the spatial correlation is made especially obvious. Both countries may be at peace and invest in state capacity, or both may be at war and don't invest in state institutions. Once again, the model does not predict which equilibrium emerges but only predicts that the contagion of civil war results in regional clusters of state capacity (item 2 of proposition 2.3).

Finally, for low levels of α, a country is in a civil war regardless of what happens in the region. This may spill over into other countries through two possible mechanisms: either it spills over into civil war for the vulnerable neighbor or, interestingly, it may spill over into better institutions for more resilient neighbors that do not get into civil conflicts (item 1 of proposition 2.3). Morocco and the wave of the Arab Spring discussed in the next section provide vivid examples consistent with the latter situation.

2.6   The Arab Spring Example

The Arab Spring started on December 17, 2010, with the Tunisian Revolution, and then spread throughout many Arab League countries and their neighbors. Major insurgencies happened in Syria, Libya, and Yemen, civil uprisings occurred in Egypt and Bahrain, large street demonstrations were held in Algeria, Iraq, Jordan, Kuwait, Morocco, and Oman, and there were even minor protests in Saudi Arabia.

In a region with significant potential spillovers, the countries touched by the Arab Spring wave displayed a large variety of political trajectories. Indeed, while the first wave of revolutions and protests faded by mid-2012, some led to the fall of past incumbent regimes (Tunisia, Libya, and Egypt), others to large-scale ongoing civil conflicts in the Middle East (Syria, Libya, and Iraq). In Syria, for instance, the civil war that erupted in March 2011 favored the emergence of jihadi militant groups, most notoriously the Islamic State of Iraq and the Levant (ISIL), also known as ISIS or Daesh. These political trajectories across North Africa and the Middle East present some characteristics that are reassuringly consistent with some implications of our model.

First, the clustering of fragility and conflicts that resulted in the toppling of several governments in the region (Libya, Egypt, Syria, and Iraq) suggests the existence of institutional complementarities at the regional level, as outlined by our framework. Meanwhile, some countries succeeded in maintaining some degree of peace and stability after the initial shock (Tunisia, Algeria, and Morocco). One country indeed made the transition to a constitutional democracy (Tunisia), and Morocco stands out as a rare example of immunity to the spread of the Arab Spring. This contrast between the Maghreb on the one hand and the rest of the Arab world on the other is interestingly consistent with the multiplicity of equilibrium outcomes highlighted in proposition 2.2.

Second, Morocco is an interesting example in suggesting increased incentives for state capacity building when neighboring countries become more unstable (as illustrated in our discussion of proposition 2.3). Civil unrest did occur in Morocco, in 2011–2012. However, when it did, King Mohammed VI agreed to constitutional reform to avoid outright riots and did not have to request foreign military assistance or institutional support. The model predicts that to avoid contagion a state has to invest in θ, the credibility of the revenue-sharing agreement. Indeed, the 2011 constitutional reforms illustrate that exact mechanism. The reforms were mainly concerned with transfers of power as well as symbolic and substantial gestures toward minorities. On the first count, the king renounced several key discretionary powers in favor of the parliament. For instance, the prime minister must now be named from within the largest party in the parliament and presides over the executive branch of government. The judiciary system is independent from the two other branches of the government. On the second count, the reforms grant new rights to women. The constitution recognizes Berber as an official language and protects Hassaniya Arabic as a national cultural heritage.

2.7   Conclusion

Civil wars and weak state institutions tend to cluster regionally. In this chapter, we proposed a theoretical framework that explains this pattern. We highlighted a basic regional complementarity between governments choosing their own national political regimes. When civil conflict can indeed diffuse across borders, the incentives for one government to choose a particular internal social settlement with domestic contender groups depends crucially on how neighboring governments address their own internal conflicts. This feature leads naturally into the possibility of multiple regional political equilibria and provides a convincing explanation for the clustering of civil wars and of peaceful countries. Furthermore, if government can invest (or not) in state capacity building, the regional externalities also explain the regional clustering of institutional fragility. Interestingly, the spillover effects of weak neighbors on one's own incentives to invest in state capacity institutions may not always be negative.

While we think that our model captures essential features of the regional political economy of conflicts and state fragility, it also opens up a number of interesting areas for future research.

First, in our setup, civil conflicts spill across borders by lowering the opportunity cost of conflict for rebels in neighboring countries. We took this as given and investigated its implications for regional policy regimes. It would be interesting to open this black box and provide explicit microfoundations for this mechanism. One line of research would be to explicitly model migration flows of refugees and their consequences on the regional economies and the opportunity costs of engaging in local conflicts. Another possibility would be to model the emergence of nonstate actors, such as warlords, terrorist organizations, organized crime, weapon trafficking, and intermediaries, that emerge at the porous border between two territories. Such agents, the "problems without passports" (Picciotto et al. 2005), have been abundantly described in the international security literature as important facilitators of cross-border conflict spillover effects (Wolff 2010; Geneva Centre for the Democratic Control of Armed Forces and Geneva Call 2011).

Also, our model suggests a number of regional coordination and external issues at the regional and international levels. This leads to important policy questions such as the construction of regional institutions to resolve such problems or the foreign policy incentives of a specific country to choose to intervene (militarily or institutionally) to "stabilize" a neighboring country, and the adequate policy responses of the international community to address the issue of halting the spread of regional conflicts.

While addressing these questions (and others) is clearly beyond the scope of this chapter, we hope that the framework we presented here paves the way for these future extensions.

Notes

1. See, for instance, Anselin and O'Loughlin (1992), Bara (2014), Black (2013), Braithwaite (2005, 2006), Gleditsch (2002, 2007), Hegre and Sambanis (2006), Most and Starr (1980), Starr and Most (1983), and Ward and Gleditsch (2002).

2. Some of the most indicative works in this international security literature are Lemke (2002), Buzan and Waever (2003), Rubin (2002, 2006), Mincheva (2005), and Ansorg (2011). See also the recent book edited by Olowu and Chanie (2016).

3. In the policy literature, see Vallings and Moreno-Torres (2005) for a discussion of fragility. Also see Moreno-Torres and Anderson (2004) for a discussion of the regional dimension of state fragility in West Africa or the case study by the OECD on peace-building and development in the Democratic Republic of Congo (Organisation for Economic Cooperation and Development 2004).

4. Economists also emphasized the regional dimension of fragility spillover cost effects. Looking at how low-income countries under stress (LICUS) generate spillover costs for their neighbors, Chauvet and Collier (2004) showed, for instance, that the typical neighbor of a LICUS country tends to lose about 1.6 percentage points of its annual growth rate in income per capita.

5. See Bara (2014), Buhaug and Gleditsch (2008), Cederman, Girardin, and Gleditsch (2009), Cederman, Gleditsch, and Buhaug (2013), Forsberg (2008), Gleditsch (2007), and Salehyan (2011).

6. See, for instance, Geneva Centre for the Democratic Control of Armed Forces and Geneva Call (2011) for a recent review of such actors in regional conflicts.

7. For an analysis of changing trends in small arms from 2001 to 2010, see, for instance, http://www.smallarmssurvey.org/publications/by-type/yearbook.html.

8. See Salehyan and Gleditsch (2006), Adelman (1998), Rufin (1999), Salehyan (2007), Atzili (2006), and Rüegger (2013b). A good recent survey of the literature is Ansorg (2011). Also see Rüegger (2013a) for a recent analysis of refugee camps and their connections to transnational rebels.

9. This technology of conflict and several features of the model are inspired by Azam (2006).

10. The proof of lemma 2.1 is as follows. In the case of a civil war, the government maximizes $N_G - M_G + (1 - \Pi) R$ with $\Pi = 1$ if $M_G < \overline{M}$, and $\Pi = \pi$ otherwise. In the case of peace, the government maximizes $N_G - M_G + R - \theta T$ subject to the incentive constraint. Since $(1 - \pi)R \geq \overline{M}$, it is worth investing $M_G \geq \overline{M}$ in both cases. Even in the case of peace, the government invests at least $\overline{M}$ in the conflict, to deter a rebellion.

11. See also Isoke (2015) for a case study on Uganda, and see Rüegger (2013a) for a survey.

12. The proof of lemma 2.3 is obtained by comparing the corner payoffs of the government at $\theta = 0$ and $\theta = \bar{\theta}(\alpha)$ or $V(0) = N_G - \overline{M} + (1 - \pi)R$ to $V(\bar{\theta}(\alpha)) = N_G + (1 - \pi)R - (1 - \alpha)\overline{M} - s\bar{\theta}(\alpha)$. Therefore, investment occurs at $\theta = \bar{\theta}(\alpha)$ if and only if $\alpha\overline{M} \geq s\bar{\theta}(\alpha)$, which is equivalent to the condition expressed in lemma 2.3.

13. The only nontrivial comparative static is for $\overline{M}$, but it is easy to see that $\dfrac{s\pi R}{\overline{M}[R + N_G - \overline{M} + s]}$ is decreasing in $\overline{M}$ when $R > \dfrac{\overline{M}}{\pi} > \overline{M}$ and $N_G > \overline{M}$.

14. This is because our cost function for investment in state capacity is linear in θ.

References

Adelman, H. 1998. "Why Refugee Warriors Are Threats." *Journal of Conflict Studies* 18 (1): 49–69.

Anselin, L., and J. O'Loughlin. 1992. "Geography of International Conflict and Cooperation: Spatial Dependence and Regional Context in Africa." In *The New Geopolitics*, edited by Michael D. Ward, 39–75. Philadelphia: Gordon and Breach.

Ansorg, N. 2011. "How Does Militant Violence Diffuse in Regions? Regional Conflict Systems in International Relations and Peace and Conflict Studies." *International Journal of Conflict and Violence* 5 (1): 173–187.

Atzili, B. 2006. "When Good Fences Make Bad Neighbors: Fixed Borders, State Weakness, and International Conflict." *International Security* 31 (3): 139–173.

Azam, J.-P. 2001. "The Redistributive State and Conflicts in Africa." *Journal of Peace Research* 38 (4): 429–444.

Azam, J.-P. 2006. "The Paradox of Power Reconsidered: A Theory of Political Regimes in Africa." *Journal of African Economies* 15 (1): 26–58.

Bakke, K. M. 2013. "Copying and Learning from Outsiders? Assessing Diffusion from Transnational Insurgents in the Chechen War." In *Transnational Dynamics of Civil War*, edited by J. T. Checkel, 31–62. Cambridge: Cambridge University Press.

Bara, C. 2014. "Incentives and Opportunities: A Complexity-Oriented Explanation of Violent Ethnic Conflict." *Journal of Peace Research* 51 (6): 696–710.

Bazzi, S., and C. Blattman. 2014. "Economic Shocks and Conflict: Evidence from Commodity Prices." *American Economic Journal: Macroeconomics* 6 (4): 1–38.

Besley, T., and T. Persson. 2008. "Wars and State Capacity." *Journal of the European Economic Association* 6 (2–3): 522–530.

Besley, T., and T. Persson. 2009a. "The Incidence of Civil War: Theory and Evidence." STICERD—Economic Organisation and Public Policy Discussion Papers Series 5. London: Suntory and Toyota International Centres for Economics and Related Disciplines, London School of Economics and Political Science.

Besley, T., and T. Persson. 2009b. "The Origins of State Capacity: Property Rights, Taxation, and Politics." *American Economic Review* 99 (4): 1218–1244.

Besley, T., and T. Persson. 2009c. "Repression or Civil War?" *American Economic Review* 99 (2): 292–297.

Besley, T., and T. Persson. 2010. "State Capacity, Conflict, and Development." *Econometrica* 78 (1): 1–34.

Besley, T., and T. Persson. 2011a. "Fragile States and Development Policy." *Journal of the European Economic Association* 9 (3): 371–398.

Besley, T., and T. Persson. 2011b. "The Logic of Political Violence." *Quarterly Journal of Economics* 126 (3): 1411–1445.

Black, N. 2013. "When Have Violent Civil Conflicts Spread? Introducing a Dataset of Substate Conflict Contagion." *Journal of Peace Research* 50 (6): 751–759.

Blattman, C., and E. Miguel. 2010. "Civil War." *Journal of Economic Literature* 48 (1): 3–57.

Braithwaite, A. 2005. "Location, Location, Location ... Identifying Hot Spots of International Conflict." *International Interactions* 31 (3): 251–273.

Braithwaite, A. 2006. "The Geographic Spread of Militarized Disputes." *Journal of Peace Research* 43 (5): 507–522.

Braithwaite, A. 2010. "Resisting Infection: How State Capacity Conditions Conflict Contagion." *Journal of Peace Research* 47 (3): 311–319.

Brewer, J. 1989. *The Sinews of Power: War, Money and the English State, 1688–1783*. London: Unwin Hyman.

Brückner, M., and A. Ciccone. 2007. "Growth, Democracy, and Civil War." CEPR Discussion Papers 6568. London: Centre for Economic Policy Research.

Buhaug, H., and K. S. Gleditsch. 2008. "Contagion or Confusion? Why Conflicts Cluster in Space." *International Studies Quarterly* 52 (2): 215–233.

Buzan, B., and O. Waever. 2003. *Regions and Power: The Structure of International Security*. Cambridge: Cambridge University Press.

Cederman, L.-E., L. Girardin, and K. S. Gleditsch. 2009. "Ethnonationalist Triads: Assessing the Influence of Kin Groups on Civil Wars." *World Politics* 61 (3): 403–437.

Cederman, L.-E., K. S. Gleditsch, and H. Buhaug. 2013. *Inequality, Grievances, and Civil War*. Cambridge Studies in Contentious Politics. Cambridge: Cambridge University Press.

Chassang, S., and G. Padró i Miquel. 2009. "Economic Shocks and Civil War." *Quarterly Journal of Political Science* 4 (3): 211–228.

Chauvet, L., and P. Collier. 2004. *Development Effectiveness in Fragile States: Spillovers and Turnarounds*. Technical report. Oxford: Center for the Study of African Economies.

Checkel, J. T. 2014. "Transnational Dynamics of Civil War." In *Transnational Dynamics of Civil War*, edited by J. T. Checkel, 3–30. Cambridge: Cambridge University Press.

Ciccone, A. 2013. "Estimating the Effect of Transitory Economic Shocks on Civil Conflict." *Review of Economics and Institutions* 4 (2): 1–14.

Collier, P., and A. Hoeffler. 2004. "Greed and Grievance in Civil War." *Oxford Economic Papers* 56 (4): 563–595.

De Soysa, I., and H. Fjelde. 2010. "Is the Hidden Hand an Iron Fist? Capitalism and Civil Peace, 1970–2005." *Journal of Peace Research* 47 (3): 287–298.

Dube, O., and J. F. Vargas. 2013. "Commodity Price Shocks and Civil Conflict: Evidence from Colombia." *Review of Economic Studies* 80 (4): 1384–1421.

Fearon, J. D., and D. D. Laitin. 2003. "Ethnicity, Insurgency, and Civil War." *American Political Science Review* 97 (1): 75–90.

Fjelde, H., and I. De Soysa. 2009. "Coercion, Co-optation, or Cooperation? State Capacity and the Risk of Civil War, 1961—2004." *Conflict Management and Peace Science* 26 (1): 5–25.

Forsberg, E. 2008. "Polarization and Ethnic Conflict in a Widened Strategic Setting." *Journal of Peace Research* 45 (2): 283–300.

Geneva Centre for the Democratic Control of Armed Forces (DCAF) and Geneva Call. 2011. *Armed Non-state Actors: Current Trends and Future Challenges*. Technical Report 5. Geneva: Geneva Centre for the Democratic Control of Armed Forces.

Gleditsch, K. S. 2002. *All International Politics Is Local: The Diffusion of Conflict, Integration, and Democratization*. Ann Arbor: University of Michigan Press.

Gleditsch, K. S. 2007. "Transnational Dimensions of Civil War." *Journal of Peace Research* 44 (3): 293–309.

Hazen, J. M., and J. Horner. 2007. "Small Arms, Armed Violence, and Insecurity in Nigeria: The Niger Delta in Perspective." Occasional Paper 20. Geneva: Small Arms Survey.

Hegre, H., and N. Sambanis. 2006. "Sensitivity Analysis of Empirical Results on Civil War Onset." *Journal of Conflict Resolution* 50 (4): 508–535.

Hendrix, C. S. 2010. "Measuring State Capacity: Theoretical and Empirical Implications for the Study of Civil Conflict." *Journal of Peace Research* 47 (3): 273–285.

Isoke, H. 2015. "The Dilemma of Porous Frontiers: Uganda's Experience in Combating Terrorism." Master's thesis, Naval Postgraduate School, Monterey, CA.

Keefer, P. 2008. "Insurgency and Credible Commitment in Autocracies and Democracies." *World Bank Economic Review* 22 (1): 33–61.

Lemke, D. 2002. *Regions of War and Peace*. Cambridge: Cambridge University Press.

Levi, M. 1988. *Of Rule and Revenue*. California Series on Social Choice and Political Economy. Berkeley: University of California Press.

McBride, M., G. Milante, and S. Skaperdas. 2011. "Peace and War with Endogenous State Capacity." *Journal of Conflict Resolution* 55 (3): 446–468.

Miguel, E., S. Satyanath, and E. Sergenti. 2004. "Economic Shocks and Civil Conflict: An Instrumental Variables Approach." *Journal of Political Economy* 112 (4): 725–753.

Mincheva, L. G. 2005. "Dissolving Boundaries between Domestic and Regional / International Conflict." *New Balkan Politics* 9: 24–44.

Moreno-Torres, M., and M. Anderson. 2004. "Fragile States: Defining Difficult Environments for Poverty Reduction." Poverty Reduction in Difficult Environments (PRDE) Team Working Paper 1. London: UK Department for International Development.

Most, B. A., and H. Starr. 1980. "Diffusion, Reinforcement, Geopolitics, and the Spread of War." *American Political Science Review* 74 (4): 932–946.

Ofcansky, T. P. 1996. *Uganda: Tarnished Pearl of Africa*. Boulder, CO: Westview Press.

Olowu, D., and P. Chanie, eds. 2016. *State Fragility and State Building in Africa: Cases from Eastern and Southern Africa*. United Nations University Series on Regionalism 10. Cham, Switzerland: Springer.

Organisation for Economic Cooperation and Development (OECD). 2004. *DAC Experts Meeting on Peace-Building and Development in the Democratic Republic of Congo in the Context of the Region of Central Africa*. Technical report. Paris: Organisation for Economic Cooperation and Development.

Phillips, B. J. 2015. "Civil War, Spillover and Neighbors' Military Spending." *Conflict Management and Peace Science* 32 (4): 425–442.

Picciotto, R., C. Alao, E. Ipke, M. Kimani, and R. Slade. 2005. *Striking a New Balance: Donor Policy Coherence and Development Cooperation in Difficult Environments*. London: The International Policy Institute at Kings College London and The Global Policy Project.

Rubin, B. R. 2002. *The Fragmentation of Afghanistan*. New Haven, CT: Yale University Press.

Rubin, B. R. 2006. "Peace Building and State-Building in Afghanistan: Constructing Sovereignty for Whose Security?" *Third World Quarterly* 27 (1): 175–185.

Rüegger, S. 2013a. "Conflict Actors in Motion: Refugees, Rebels and Ethnic Groups." PhD thesis, ETH Zürich.

Rüegger, S. 2013b. "Refugee Flows, Transnational Ethnic Linkages and Conflict Diffusion: Evidence from the Kosovo Refugee Crisis." Technical report. Paper prepared for presentation at the Regional Research Promotion Programme Annual Conference, Belgrade, Serbia, May 24–26, 2013.

Rufin, J.-C. 1999. *Les Causes Perdues*. Paris: Gallimard.

Salehyan, I. 2007. "Transnational Rebels: Neighboring States as Sanctuary for Rebel Groups." *World Politics* 59 (2): 217–242.

Salehyan, I. 2011. *Rebels without Borders: Transnational Insurgencies in World Politics*. Ithaca, NY: Cornell University Press.

Salehyan, I., and K. S. Gleditsch. 2006. "Refugees and the Spread of Civil War." *International Organization* 60 (2): 335–366.

Sambanis, N. 2002. "A Review of Recent Advances and Future Directions in the Quantitative Literature on Civil War." *Defence and Peace Economics* 13 (3): 215–243.

Skaperdas, S. 1992. "Cooperation, Conflict, and Power in the Absence of Property Rights." *American Economic Review* 82 (4): 720–739.

Sobek, D. 2010. "Masters of Their Domains: The Role of State Capacity in Civil Wars." *Journal of Peace Research* 47 (3): 267–271.

Starr, H., and B. A. Most. 1983. "Contagion and Border Effects on Contemporary African Conflict." *Comparative Political Studies* 16 (1): 92–117.

Taydas, Z., and D. Peksen. 2012. "Can States Buy Peace? Social Welfare Spending and Civil Conflicts." *Journal of Peace Research* 49 (2): 273–287.

Thies, C. G. 2010. "Of Rulers, Rebels, and Revenue: State Capacity, Civil War Onset, and Primary Commodities." *Journal of Peace Research* 47 (3): 321–332.

Tilly, C. 1985. "War Making and State Making as Organized Crime." In *Bringing the State Back In*, edited by P. B. Evans, D. Rueschemeyer, and T. Skocpol, 149–191. Cambridge: Cambridge University Press.

Vallings, C., and M. Moreno-Torres. 2005. "Drivers of Fragility: What Makes States Fragile?" Poverty Reduction in Difficult Environments (PRDE) Team Working Paper 7. London: UK Department for International Development.

Ward, M. D., and K. S. Gleditsch. 2002. "Location, Location, Location: An MCMC Approach to Modeling the Spatial Context of War and Peace." *Political Analysis* 10 (3): 244–260.

Weidmann, N. B. 2015. "Communication Networks and the Transnational Spread of Ethnic Conflict." *Journal of Peace Research* 52 (3): 285–296.

Wolff, S. 2010. "The Regional Dimensions of State Failure." *Review of International Studies* 37 (3): 951–957.

3 The Cost of Sanctions: Estimating Lost Trade with Gravity

Julian Hinz

3.1 Introduction

Economic sanctions are a frequently used tool of foreign policy. Targeting the sanctioned country's economy through restrictions or bans on the trade of certain goods and services, severance of financial ties, or an all-out embargo, the measures are used when diplomacy fails but military options appear too drastic. However, sanctions also affect the countries that are not directly targeted, including the *sanctioning* country itself. Erecting new trade barriers makes the cross-border transfers of goods and money more costly for all exporters and importers—directly or indirectly.

The aim of this chapter is to study the consequences of three recent sanction cases on international trade. The three case studies are instructive in their own respects:

1. The international sanctions against Iran in response to its nuclear program, in particular those by Western countries, are virtually unprecedented in their severity. The financial sanctions introduced effectively cut off the country from the international financial system and seriously restricted trade, while the ban on imports of crude and refined oil has added to Iran's dire economic situation.

2. Sanctions against the Russian Federation in response to its involvement in the political and military crisis in Ukraine and the annexation of Crimea after the "Maidan Revolution" were less severe compared to the Iran sanctions (albeit they intensified over time) but hit a country that had strong economic ties in the period preceding the events.

3. The sanctions against Myanmar (Burma) are instructive in that they represent a case of lifted sanctions. While presanction trade ties with the

country were less important and the overall severity of the measures less harsh than in the two other cases, the recovery of trade flows (or lack thereof) can be instructive for other cases.

I analyze the impact of these three sanction regimes on bilateral trade between sanctioned, sanctioning, and nonimplicated countries using a structural gravity setup that allows me to perform a general equilibrium counterfactual exercise. Using quarterly trade data from 48 countries from the beginning of 2010 until the end of 2015, the analysis provides an estimate of the "cost of sanctions." The results highlight the heterogeneous impact of the three sanction regimes by the different sanctioned and sanctioning countries involved.

The use of sanctions as a tool of foreign policy has seen a sustained increase over time, in particular since the end of the Cold War. Figure 3.1 shows the number of sanction cases active in a given year since 1945. Naturally, the use and effect of sanctions as a foreign policy tool has attracted substantial literature in both political science and economics. The bulk of the existing work has shed light on the determinants of the success or failure of such policies and the effect of sanctions on the *target* economy through which the intended outcome—a change of certain policies—is supposed to work. Drezner (1999), van Bergeijk

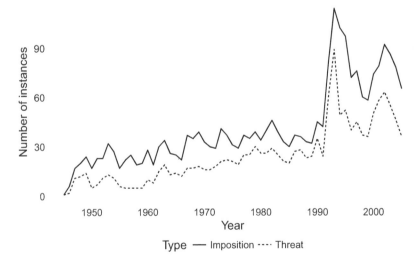

Figure 3.1
Number of sanctions active in a given year, based on data from Morgan, Bapat, and Krustev (2009).

(2009), and Hufbauer, Schott, and Elliott (2009) provide instructive overviews of the state of research in this respect. Rosenberg et al. (2016) and Drezner (2011) provide analyses of the currently fashioned "smart sanctions," the use of targeted travel bans and asset freezes against implicated individuals. For empirical analyses, Hufbauer, Schott, and Elliott (2009) also provide a thorough record of sanction cases, with an emphasis on American- and European-imposed sanctions. The TIES database by Morgan, Bapat, and Krustev (2009) provides a second and very detailed source for sanctions encompassing more sender and target countries. Both datasets provide quantitative measures of the scope and intensity of applied measures and attempt to judge their success or failure with respect to their political aims. Caruso (2003) estimates the average effects of sanctions in the second half of the twentieth century in a simple *naive* gravity setup on aggregate trade flows.

A number of papers have looked at the economic impact of sanctions in *sender* countries. The case of the Embargo Act of 1807 is particularly well studied, as it provided the first use of sanctions and embargoes in the modern era. Frankel (1982), Irwin (2005), and O'Rourke (2007) found effects in the range of 4–8 percent of US GDP by looking at trade losses and commodity price changes. Hufbauer and Oegg (2003) looked at macroeconomic effects of sanctions in place in the 1990s and found that the total effect on US GDP hovered around a much lower 0.4 percent. Crozet and Hinz (2016) is most closely related to the present chapter. The authors studied the case of the Russia sanctions in depth along two dimensions, at the country and firm levels. They distinguished between those goods that were directly affected by the Russian embargo and those that were not, finding substantial "collateral damage." The general equilibrium framework in this chapter borrows their methodology in estimating "lost trade" resulting from the sanctions in place.

Other studies looked at the economic impact on the *target* economy. Dreger et al. (2015) evaluated the economic impact of the sanction regime between Western countries and the Russian Federation, estimating the consequences of the sanctions on the Russian macroeconomic performance. Dizaji and van Bergeijk (2013) studied the macroeconomic and political impacts on Iran while aiming to quantify the effectiveness of the sanctions' regime. Also looking at the case of the Western-imposed sanctions on Iran, Haidar (2017) studied the impact of sanctions using firm-level data.

This chapter is also related to the literature studying the link between conflict and trade. Martin, Mayer, and Thoenig (2008a, 2008b) analyze the prevalence and severity of interstate and civil wars through the lens of trade economists. They show that multilateral trade openness increases the probability of escalation with another country, while direct bilateral trade deters it. Similarly, small-scale civil wars are shown to be fueled by trade openness, while trade openness decreases the probability of large-scale strife. Glick and Taylor (2010) show the disruptive effects of war on international trade and economic activity in general. Their approach relies on a gravity setup, and they quantify the losses by accounting for changes in bilateral and multilateral resistance.[1]

Another strand of the literature analyzes changes in consumer preferences following political shocks. Fuchs and Klann (2013) show that high-level meetings with the Dalai Lama are costly for the hosting country, in the sense that bilateral trade with China is significantly reduced in the following year. Michaels and Zhi (2010) show that the diplomatic clash between France and the United States over the Iraq War in 2003 significantly reduced trade between the two countries during a short period of time. Pandya and Venkatesan (2016) exploit scanner data to reveal that sales in the US market of brands marketed to appear French while not necessarily imported from France were affected by this conflict. Heilmann (2016) studied the impacts of various boycott campaigns, among them the boycott of Danish products in some Muslim-majority countries in 2006 by using a synthetic control group methodology.

This chapter's contribution is to assess the effect of recent sanction regimes using quarterly aggregate export data from ITC Trade Map in a structural gravity framework. I find the overall trade lost by using this tool of foreign policy totaled more than US$50 billion in 2014, about 0.4 percent of world trade. The bulk of this lost trade is carried by a few countries, with the sanctioned countries Russia and Iran unsurprisingly being hit hardest (in 2014, US$8.2 billion and US$12.2 billion, respectively). At the same time, major exporting economies such as Germany, France, and Italy are bearing a large share as well (in 2014, US$12.2 billion, US$3.3 billion, and US$2.8 billion, respectively).

The chapter is structured as follows. Section 3.2 provides a brief overview of the three major sanction regimes that affected global trade flows in recent years. In section 3.3, I describe the methodology for the structural gravity estimation and subsequent general equilibrium exercise. I present the results in section 3.4. Section 3.5 gives concluding remarks.

3.2 Recent Sanction Episodes

I analyze the cost of sanctions for three recent cases of sanctions that are particularly instructive: Iran, Russia, and Myanmar. Each of the sanction episodes is insightful in its own way. The sanctions levied on Iran can be considered the most severe, as they essentially entailed cutting off the country from the international financial infrastructure. The case of Russia is unique because of the strong presanction ties between the sanctioning and sanctioned countries. The case of Myanmar is instructive because sanctions were first suspended in 2012 and then lifted in 2013, after having been in place for almost half a decade. In the following, I provide a brief overview of the three cases to provide some background information. For the remainder of this study, I denote as "sanctioning" and "sender" countries those countries that enacted economic sanctions against the respective "sanctioned" or "target" country, such as the Russian Federation, the Islamic Republic of Iran, and Myanmar.

Case 1: Iran
Most Western sanctions against the Islamic Republic of Iran have been in response to its nuclear program as well as human rights abuses. The United States has had various forms of sanctions in place since the Iranian Revolution in 1979 and the subsequent hostage crisis.[2] The United Nations first placed sanctions on Iran in response to its noncooperation with regard to UN Security Council Resolution 1696 from July 2006, in which it demanded Iran halt its uranium enrichment program. After Iran's failure to address the UN concerns, Resolution 1737 was passed, which introduced measures that restricted exports of possible nuclear-related technology and material to Iran, as well as levying asset freezes on certain individuals and companies.[3] Subsequent resolutions further toughened these measures, most notably Resolution 1747, which imposed an arms embargo and expanded the freeze on Iranian assets; Resolution 1803, which called on states to monitor the activities of Iranian banks, inspect Iranian ships and aircraft, and monitor the movements of individuals involved with the program through their territory; and Resolution 1929 in June 2010, which banned trade in further military and dual-use goods, introduced travel bans, and mandated UN member states to actively inspect Iranian vessels and aircraft.[4]

In response to insufficient cooperation by the Iranian authorities, in January 2012, the European Union moved to introduce separate, more severe sanctions on Iran.[5] The measures included further asset freezes and travel bans; most importantly, however, an import embargo on Iranian oil was declared.[6] The next and ultimate escalation of the sanction regime was then put forward in March 2012, where banks identified to be in violation of previous sanctions regarding trade restrictions were disconnected from SWIFT, the global hub for electronic financial transactions, effectively cutting off Iran from the global financial system.[7] After a period of rapprochement between Iran and Western countries, sanctions were lifted as part of the "Joint Comprehensive Plan of Action" that was agreed on in July 2015, adopted in November of the same year, and implemented after being greenlighted by the International Atomic Energy Agency in January 2016.[8] In the empirical analysis, I estimate the effect of the financial and trade sanctions by the European Union and allied countries (next to those by the United Nations on military and dual-use material) that were initially put in place in the first quarter of 2012.

Case 2: Russia
The Western sanctions against the Russian Federation and Russia's countersanctions are rooted in the simmering conflict in eastern Ukraine and Crimea. Following the Russian annexation of Crimea and its support of separatists in the eastern part of Ukraine, the European Union and allied Western countries, most prominently the United States, imposed the first sanctions against the Russian Federation in mid-March 2014. This first wave of sanctions from Western countries, dubbed smart sanctions, focused on implicated political and military personnel as well as select Russian financial institutions (Ashford 2016). A second wave in the weeks to follow expanded the list of sanctioned individuals and entities.[9]

The first and second waves of EU sanctions consisted of travel bans and asset freezes on several officials and institutions from Russia and Ukraine, which were implemented through Council Decision 2014/145/CFSP and Council Regulation (EU) 269/2014 in March 2014 and amounted to an "EU-wide asset freeze and travel ban on those undermining the territorial sovereignty or security of Ukraine and those supporting or doing business with them." The list of targeted individuals and entities was further amended over the course of the spring of 2014. The measures imposed by the United States, implemented by executive orders 13660, 13661, and 13662, also consisted of asset freezes and travel bans. It was also progressively extended over the course of 2014 to a growing list of persons and entities, including major Russian financial institutions with close links to the Kremlin (Baker and Mc-Kenzie 2014). Other countries allied with the European Union and the United States followed a similar path and introduced comparable measures at around the same time.[10] These lists of individuals and entities were successively appended over the spring and summer of 2014.[11] The Russian Federation condemned the measures and reciprocated by issuing travel bans on influential Western politicians and officials.[12]

After the crash of a civilian airplane (Malaysian Airlines flight MH17), shot down over the separatist region of Donbass with the alleged implication of pro-Russian insurgents, trade sanctions were levied and existing financial restrictions expanded further. This so-called third wave of EU sanctions went beyond previous measures in depth and scope. Not only were Russian individuals and entities targeted, but European entities were restricted from exporting certain goods and buying certain Russian assets (Dreger et al. 2015). These new restrictions were enacted through Council Decision 2014/512/CFSP and Council Regulation (EU) 833/2014 at the end of July 2014. Exporting firms in Western countries were still mostly affected indirectly, as only a small number of industries' exports were directly targeted: those firms that export products and technology intended for military and dual use and some equipment for the oil industry.[13] The United States had implemented its own measures in mid-July 2014, stating that the US Treasury Department had "imposed sanctions that prohibit U.S. persons from providing new financing to two major Russian financial institutions ... and two Russian energy firms ..., limiting their access to U.S. capital markets," as well as "eight Russian arms firms, which are responsible for the production of a range of materiel that includes small arms, mortar shells, and tanks."[14] Other Western countries reciprocated the measures taken by the United States and European Union and enacted similar trade sanctions and financial restrictions (Dreger et al. 2015; Dreyer et al. 2015). The Swiss government enacted legislation that was meant to prevent circumvention of existing sanctions while continuing to refrain from imposing direct sanctions on the Russian Federation and as such was not affected by Russian countersanctions (Reuters 2014).[15]

The Russian side, unsurprisingly, retaliated and enacted sanctions on European and other sanctioning countries. In early August 2014, the Russian Federation imposed a ban on imports of certain raw and processed agricultural products as an "application of certain special economic measures to ensure the security of the Russian Federation."[16] The embargoed products were select agricultural products, raw materials, and foodstuffs originating from the European Union, the United States, Canada, Australia, and Norway.[17] In the empirical analysis, I assume that trade relations were impacted by the diplomatic tensions and sanction measures since the first quarter of 2014.

Case 3: Myanmar

Some form of economic sanction against Myanmar has been in place for decades, mostly in response to human rights issues in the (now former) military dictatorship.[18] In the wake of the transition from a military to a civil government, coupled with the release of political prisoners, the European Union and United States first suspended most sanctions in the first half of 2012 and then lifted them in 2013. The European Union suspended sanctions with Council Regulation (EU) 409/2012 and then repealed Council Regulation (EC) 194/2008, which had first enacted the measures.[19] The United States followed in May 2012 and the following months by suspending parts of the "Burmese Sanctions Regulations" enforced by the Treasury Department's Office of Foreign Assets Control (OFAC).[20] Further restrictions were lifted in September 2016.[21] While the Southeast Asian nation had not been well integrated into the world economy—likely in large part because of the political and economic reclusiveness pursued by the military junta and externally enforced by the sanctions in place—the case provides insights into the dynamics of trade when lifting sanctions. In the following empirical analysis, I mark the second quarter of 2012 as the beginning of sanction-free trade between previously "treated" country pairs.

3.3   Computing the Cost of Sanctions with Gravity

I analyze the impact of the sanctions' regimes against Iran, Russia, and Myanmar using quarterly trade data and relying on the methodology introduced by Crozet and Hinz (2016). Their methodology complements recent advances in the estimation of general equilibrium gravity models—and their application to counterfactual simulations. Two prominent recent works are by Adao, Costinot, and Donaldson (2017), who develop a nonparametric counterfactual methodology, and Anderson, Larch, and Yotov (2018), who use the properties of the PPML estimator, following Santos Silva and Tenreyro (2006) and Fally (2015), to "estibrate" theory-consistent counterfactual flows in the spirit of Dekle, Eaton, and Kortum (2007, 2008). Crozet and Hinz's procedure closely follows that of Anderson, Larch, and Yotov but does not rely on any data besides observable trade flows, by fully relying on estimated fixed effects. This makes the estimations consistent with theory and immune to data collection issues, and additionally it does not impose an a priori structure on how sanctions impacted trade flows.

In the current context, the different sets of sanctions imposed by the European Union and other countries against Iran, Russia, and Myanmar enter as a *bilateral* trade cost. As such, the approach is similar to that of Hufbauer, Schott, and Elliott (2009) but improves on the theoretical foundation of the model, as no structure on the effect of the sanctions is imposed.[22] I quantify the "lost trade" resulting from the sanctions episodes as the difference between observed trade and those flows predicted in the general equilibrium counterfactual framework.

3.3.1 Theoretical Framework

In order to calculate the lost trade caused by the various sanctions measures put in place, I use the methodology of Crozet and Hinz (2016), which extends the previous works by Dekle, Eaton, and Kortum (2007, 2008) and Anderson, Larch, and Yotov (2018). The main idea is that by using information embedded in observed trade flows, hypothetical trade flows between "treated" countries can be constructed. Therefore, suppose that bilateral trade flows X_{odt} between origin country o and destination country d at time t are described by

$$X_{odt} = \frac{Y_{ot}}{\Omega_{ot}} \cdot \frac{X_{dt}}{\Phi_{dt}} \cdot \tau_{odt},$$

$$(3.1)$$

where $Y_{ot} = \Sigma_d X_{odt}$ is the value of production in the origin country o, $X_{dt} = \Sigma_o X_{odt}$ is the value of expenditures in the destination country d, and

$$\Omega_{ot} = \sum_d \frac{X_{dt}\tau_{odt}}{\Phi_{dt}} \text{ and } \Phi_{dt} = \sum_o \frac{Y_{ot}\tau_{odt}}{\Omega_{ot}}$$

are the respective outward and inward multilateral resistance terms. I assume that sanctions enter as a component of bilateral trade costs such that sanction S_{odt} affects trade through changes in $\tau_{odt} = \varphi_{odq}e^{\delta S_{odt}}$. φ_{odq} is an exporter-importer quarter-specific characteristic.

Usually, one could now go ahead and estimate the *average partial effect* of sanctions, δ, by specifying S_{odt} as a dummy variable that turns

1 for a "treated" country pair at a time of sanctions. This, however, imposes a certain structural form on how sanctions affect bilateral trade. Instead, following the method by Crozet and Hinz (2016), I proceed differently here in a way that permits me to be agnostic about the impact. Following Santos Silva and Tenreyro (2006), I estimate equation (3.1) as

$$X_{odt} = \exp\left(\Xi_{ot} + \Theta_{dt} + \varphi_{odq}\right) + \varepsilon_{odt} \tag{3.2}$$

using a Poisson estimator and explicitly *excluding* observations that are treated with sanctions. Ξ_{ot}, Θ_{dt}, and φ_{odq} are fixed effects capturing all exporter × time, importer × time, and exporter × importer × quarter characteristics. I let the latter vary quarterly (i.e., Q1, Q2, etc.) in order to control for bilateral seasonal variations, very present in quarterly trade data.

The rationale behind excluding treated observations is the following. Having data for all country pairs (including those "treated") before or after the period in which the sanctions were enforced, all fixed effects can still be estimated. Hence, given a reference exporter × time fixed effect as well as reference exporter × importer × quarter fixed effects,[23] I obtain values for all Ξ_{ot}, Θ_{dt}, and φ_{odq}.[24]

3.3.2 General Equilibrium Counterfactuals

Using the estimated fixed effects from equation (3.2) allows me to construct counterfactual trade $\hat{X}_{odt}$ in the absence of sanctions by computing

$$\hat{X}_{odt}(\hat{\phi}_{odq}) = \frac{\hat{Y}_{ot}(\hat{\phi}_{odq})}{\hat{\Pi}_{ot}(\hat{\phi}_{odq})^{1-\sigma}} \frac{\hat{E}_{dt}(\hat{\phi}_{odq})}{\hat{P}_{dt}(\hat{\phi}_{odq})^{1-\sigma}} (\hat{\phi}_{odq}).$$

All terms can be recovered and iteratively computed in a manner similar to the procedure described by Anderson, Larch, and Yotov (2018). Current pseudo production and expenditure figures can be retrieved from the estimated fixed effects as

$$\hat{Y}_{ot}^{current} = \sum_{d} \exp(\hat{\Xi}_{ot} + \hat{\Theta}_{dt} + \hat{\phi}_{odq})$$

and analogously

$$\hat{X}_{dt}^{current} = \sum_{o} \exp(\hat{\Xi}_{dt} + \Theta_{dt} + \hat{\phi}_{odq}),$$

while inward and outward multilateral resistance terms can be constructed for any given global trade cost matrix $\hat{\phi}_q$ via a contraction mapping algorithm, iteratively solving the system of matrix equations

$$\widehat{\Pi}_t^{1-\sigma} = \hat{\phi}_t (\hat{X}_t \otimes \hat{P}_t^{-\sigma}),$$

$$\hat{P}_t^{1-\sigma} = \hat{\phi}_t^T (\hat{Y}_t \otimes \widehat{\Pi}_t^{-\sigma}),$$

where $\widehat{\Pi}_t^{1-\sigma}$ and $\hat{P}_t^{1-\sigma}$ are vectors of outward and inward multilateral resistances at time t. $\widehat{\Pi}_t^{-\sigma}$ and $\hat{P}_t^{-\sigma}$ are vectors of elementwise inverses of $\widehat{\Pi}_t^{1-\sigma}$ and $\hat{P}_t^{1-\sigma}$, and $\otimes$ denotes the elementwise product.[25] Changes in the production and expenditures of exporters and importers as a result of the new trade costs are computed using first-order price adjustments, following Anderson, Larch, and Yotov (2018), as

$$\hat{Y}_{ot} = \hat{Y}_{ot}^{current} \cdot \left(\frac{\hat{\Omega}_{ot}}{\hat{\Omega}_{ot}^{current}} \right)^{\frac{1}{1-\sigma}} \text{ and } \hat{X}_{dt} = \hat{X}_{dt}^{current} \cdot \left(\frac{\hat{\Omega}_{dt}}{\hat{\Omega}_{dt}^{current}} \right)^{\frac{1}{1-\sigma}},$$

where σ is the elasticity of substitution, which I set at 5 following Head and Mayer (2014).

The general equilibrium counterfactuals are computed by adjusting production and expenditure figures, as well as the respective inward and outward multilateral resistance terms, iteratively until convergence to new equilibrium flows.

3.4 Estimated General Equilibrium Impact

In the following, I present the results from estimating equation (3.2) and performing the general equilibrium exercise using the estimated fixed effects as detailed earlier. For each case, I calculate the general equilibrium counterfactuals and report the lost trade, the difference between predicted and observed trade flows. For information on observed bilateral trade flows, I rely on quarterly export data from ITC Trade Map (United Nations Statistics Division 2015) from the beginning of 2010 until the end of 2015 between Russia, Iran, and Myanmar and the 48 other largest exporters in the world. Export data for Iran and Myanmar are constructed using mirror flows, *imports* from all other countries. The sample covers 94 percent of world trade. I provide the list of countries and descriptive statistics in table A3.1 in Appendix A.

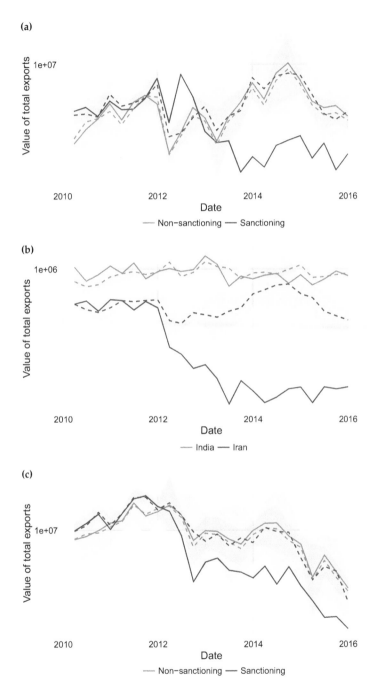

Figure 3.2
(a–c) Predicted versus observed total value of exported goods to and from Iran from sanctioning and nonsanctioning countries. Solid lines display observed trade flows, dashed lines predicted flows; 95 percent confidence intervals in gray.

Case 1: Iran

As described, the European Union and other Western countries introduced *additional* sanctions in early 2012 besides already existing UN restrictions. I therefore removed all bilateral observations between sanctioning countries and Iran for the time period since the first quarter of 2012. The bilateral quarterly fixed effects are therefore estimated from trade flows in the years 2010–2011.

Figure 3.2 shows the predicted and observed flows between sanctioning countries and Iran. Figure 3.2a shows the total exports to Iran over the period 2010–2016. While the immediate impact of the sanctions in 2012 was muted, the dark gray dotted line, the predicted total exports to Iran, visibly diverges from the solid line, the observed flows. The total lost trade over the whole time period—the difference between the dotted and solid lines—amounts to US$31.82 billion. Figure 3.2b shows the same graph for a single exemplary exporter, in this case France. To contrast the results, the light grey lines denote predicted and observed exports to India. The drop in exports is visibly significant already starting in 2012. The lost trade for France amounts to US$6.35 billion or, in relative terms, a decrease of 68 percent compared to predicted exports to Iran. Figure 3.2c shows the same plot for *imports* from Iran by sanctioning and nonsanctioning countries. Unsurprisingly, Iranian exports are hit severely, with total lost trade of US$45.18 billion over the time period.

The impact of the sanctions is very heterogeneous across countries. Figures 3.3a and 3.3b, respectively, display the absolute and relative losses (in terms of total exports) by country. A visible positive outlier is Turkey, which apparently has quite significantly increased its exports to Iran over the sanction period, despite officially sanctioning the country. While in absolute terms Germany, France, and Korea are most affected, in relative terms Sweden is the most severely affected sanctioning country, with a drop in its total exports of 0.39 percent. To put this number in perspective, Iran's total exports are 16 percent lower than they would have been without sanctions. Table B3.1 in Appendix B shows the aggregate lost trade in absolute and relative terms over the whole time period.

Case 2: Russia

As described earlier, the sanctions against the Russian Federation are very instructive in that presanction trade ties between the sanctioning and sanctioned country were very strong. Figure 3.4 shows again the

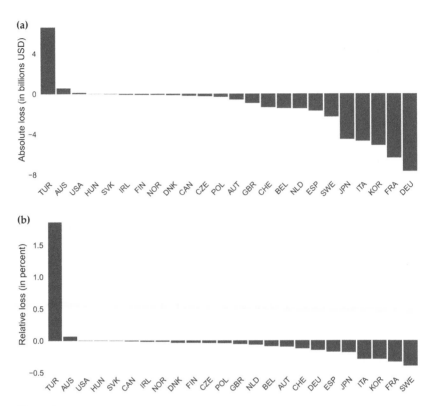

Figure 3.3
(a) Absolute losses (in billions of US$) since 2012. (b) Quarterly relative losses (in percent) since 2012.

predicted and observed flows, here between sanctioning countries and Russia. Figure 3.4a shows the total exports to Russia over the period 2010–2015. Sanctions were first introduced at the end of the first quarter of 2014. The impact is immediately visible. The dark grey dotted line, the predicted total exports to Russia, diverges significantly from the solid line, the observed flows, starting in 2014 and all the way through the end of the sample at the end of 2015. The total lost trade over the time period amounts to US$62.94 billion. Owing to the mentioned presanction strength of ties (and size of the Russian economy), the yearly global lost trade borne by the sanctioning countries is about four times as high as in the case of the Iran sanctions.[26] Figure 3.4b shows the same graph, singling out another exemplary exporter, in this case Germany. The country's predicted and observed exports to the Russian Federation are contrasted with those to Turkey.

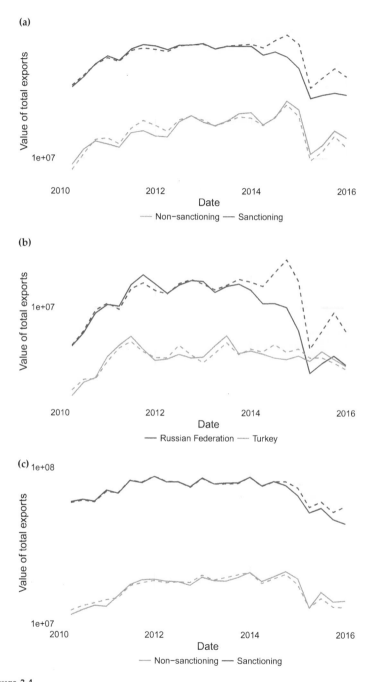

Figure 3.4
(a–c) Predicted versus observed total value of exported goods to and from Russia from sanctioning and nonsanctioning countries. Solid lines display observed trade flows, dashed lines predicted flows; 95 percent confidence intervals in gray.

The drop in exports is visibly significant since the very beginning of the sanctions episode in early 2014. The lost trade for Germany as a result of the Russia sanctions amounts to US$23.22 billion, a 27 percent decrease in relative terms compared to predicted exports to the Russian Federation. Figure 3.4c shows the same plot for *imports* from Russia by sanctioning and nonsanctioning countries. Russian exports are hit severely, with total lost trade of US$35.83 billion over the time period.

As in the case of the Iran sanctions, the impact of the sanctions is very heterogeneous across countries.[27] Figures 3.5a and 3.5b respectively display the absolute losses in billions of US$ and relative losses as a share of predicted total exports by country. In absolute terms, Germany and France (US$4.67 billion) are again most affected, with Poland (US$4.38 billion) following in third. In relative terms, Finland

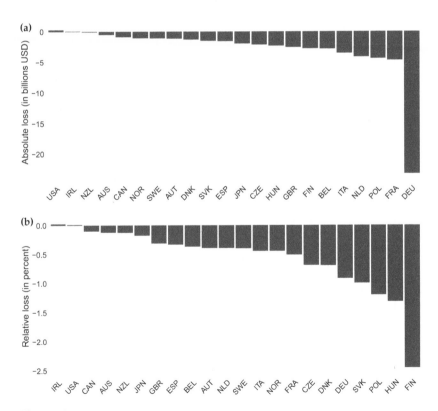

Figure 3.5
(a) Absolute losses (in billions of US$) since 2012. (b) Quarterly relative losses (in percent) since 2012.

Table 3.1
Lost trade resulting from Russia sanctions.

Country	Absolute loss (in billions of US$)	Relative loss (as percentage of total exports)
Russian Federation	−35.83	−5.35
Australia	−0.48	−0.12
Austria	−1.13	−0.39
Belgium	−2.80	−0.36
Canada	−0.87	−0.10
Czech Republic	−2.11	−0.69
Germany	−23.22	−0.91
Denmark	−1.27	−0.69
Spain	−1.53	−0.33
Finland	−2.75	−2.47
France	−4.67	−0.51
United Kingdom	−2.54	−0.31
Hungary	−2.30	−1.32
Ireland	0.05	0.02
Italy	−3.50	−0.44
Japan	−1.95	−0.17
Netherlands	−4.12	−0.39
Norway	−1.05	−0.44
New Zealand	−0.08	−0.13
Poland	−4.38	−1.20
Slovakia	−1.49	−1.00
Sweden	−1.07	−0.39
United States	0.30	0.01
World	−98.77	−0.64

is the most severely affected sanctioning country, with a drop in its total exports of 2.45 percent. This compares with Russia's total exports being 5.32 percent lower than they would have been without the sanctions in place. Table 3.1 shows the aggregate lost trade in absolute and relative terms over the whole time period.

Case 3: Myanmar
The case of Myanmar is different. Although the case is instructive by observing the end of a sanction regime in place as described earlier, econometrically the results are not comparable to those from Iran and Russia. Contrary to the two previous cases, I delete observations from before the *end* of the sanctions. Hence, I effectively compute the "cost" of prolonging the existing sanctions for another quarter or year. Table 3.2 shows the aggregate lost trade in absolute and relative terms over the whole time period.

Table 3.2
Lost trade as a result of Myanmar sanctions.

Country	Absolute loss (in billions of US$)	Relative loss (as percentage of total exports)
Myanmar	−0.34	−1.78
Austria	0.01	0.00
Belgium	−0.00	−0.00
Canada	−0.02	−0.00
Czech Republic	−0.00	−0.00
Germany	−0.08	−0.00
Denmark	−0.00	−0.00
Spain	−0.00	−0.00
Finland	−0.01	−0.01
France	−0.09	−0.01
United Kingdom	−0.02	−0.00
Hungary	−0.01	−0.01
Ireland	−0.00	−0.00
Italy	−0.07	−0.01
Netherlands	−0.01	−0.00
Norway	−0.01	−0.00
Poland	−0.01	−0.00
Slovakia	−0.00	−0.00
Sweden	−0.01	−0.00
United States	−0.13	−0.00
World	−0.82	−0.01

Figure 3.6a again shows the total exports of sanctioning countries to and imports from the sanctioned country—here Myanmar. The sanctions were lifted in the second quarter of 2012. The difference between the predicted and observed exports to Myanmar was relatively constant over time, with US$198 million in 2010, US$199 million in 2011, and US$77 million in the first quarter of 2012. Figure 3.6b shows the flows going the other direction. Myanmar's lost exports, sanctioning countries' forgone imports, however, are not significant. One notable observation can be made: both exports to and imports from the previously sanctioned country did not recover quickly. Aside from a temporary peak in exports to Myanmar in the last quarter of 2012, growth is essentially flat and is outpaced by already much higher trade flows with nonsanctioning countries.

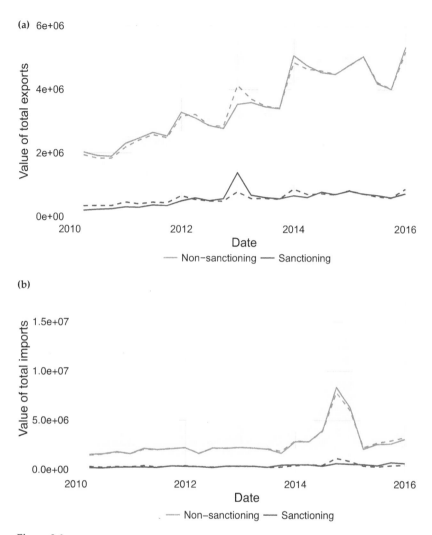

Figure 3.6
Predicted versus observed total value of exported goods to and from Myanmar from sanctioning and nonsanctioning countries. (a) Total exports to Myanmar. (b) Total imports from Myanmar. Solid lines display observed trade flows, dashed lines predicted flows; 95 percent confidence intervals in gray.

3.5   Conclusion

In this chapter, I evaluate and quantify the effects on exports by sanctioning and nonsanctioning countries for the recent sanction episodes with Iran, Russia, and Myanmar. The "lost trade" resulting from the use of this tool of foreign policy is significant in magnitude. I find the overall difference between predicted and observed trade flows totaled more than US$50 billion in 2014, about 0.4 percent of world trade, stemming only from the three most prominent sanctions regimes at that time. The analysis builds on recent advances in the international trade literature on structural gravity equations and performs a general equilibrium counterfactual exercise to predict exports between "treated" country pairs. The methodology rests exclusively on fixed effects and, using quarterly data on bilateral trade flows, allows me to take short-run effects into account.

The aim of this chapter is to quantify the cost of this frequently used tool of foreign policy—not judge its effectiveness in reaching political aims. However, aside from the expected significant economic impact on the side of the *sanctioned* country, I find quantitatively large effects on the part of (some of) the *sanctioning* countries. This impact is shown to be very heterogeneous across countries and sanction episodes. Overall strong presanction ties and severity measures, unsurprisingly, affect the magnitude of the total effect. However, ceteris paribus, the former tend to increase the burden on the *sanctioning* countries, while the latter does so on the *sanctioned* country.

Appendix A: Country-Level Data

Table 3.A.1
Descriptive statistics for exports in 2012.

Country	Mean exports ($US)	Std. deviation of exports ($US)	Total exports ($US)	Exports under sanctions ($US)	Share of exports under sanctions
Australia	1,284,407.69	3,389,033.50	241,468,646.00	446,494.00	0.00
Austria	765,047.10	1,842,084.06	143,828,854.00	274,341.00	0.00
Belgium	2,107,978.54	4,233,773.47	396,299,966.00	403,979.00	0.00
Brazil	1,024,137.39	1,875,442.82	192,537,830.00	0.00	0.00
Canada	2,330,052.39	12,250,191.56	438,049,849.00	113,120.00	0.00
Switzerland	1,450,074.34	2,558,257.66	272,613,976.00	495,337.00	0.00
Chile	379,994.74	775,489.27	71,439,011.00	0.00	0.00

Table 3.A.1 (continued)

Country	Mean exports ($US)	Std. deviation of exports ($US)	Total exports ($US)	Exports under sanctions ($US)	Share of exports under sanctions
China	7,639,164.19	13,756,301.62	1,436,162,868.00	0.00	0.00
Colombia	250,011.71	789,617.84	47,002,202.00	0.00	0.00
Czech Republic	767,248.40	1,867,573.54	144,242,700.00	53,720.00	0.00
Germany	6,670,704.36	8,141,963.61	1,254,092,419.00	3,284,234.00	0.00
Denmark	495,668.72	864,852.80	93,185,720.00	151,922.00	0.00
Ecuador	110,011.72	392,447.63	20,682,204.00	0.00	0.00
Spain	1,203,048.95	2,210,559.80	226,173,203.00	641,549.00	0.00
Finland	314,426.78	459,747.11	59,112,235.00	69,459.00	0.00
France	2,546,188.11	4,210,134.51	478,683,365.00	1,038,588.00	0.00
United Kingdom	2,081,905.73	3,130,950.12	391,398,277.00	156,472.00	0.00
Hungary	444,452.27	981,993.05	83,557,026.00	22,007.00	0.00
Indonesia	910,666.71	1,625,377.46	171,205,342.00	0.00	0.00
India	933,866.63	1,509,172.43	175,566,926.00	0.00	0.00
Ireland	585,322.87	1,256,372.86	110,040,699.00	65,083.00	0.00
Iran, Islamic Republic of	436,948.25	1,201,246.04	78,650,685.00	33,799,630.00	0.43
Israel	268,047.17	649,600.64	50,392,868.00	0.00	0.00
Italy	2,127,176.36	3,300,557.78	399,909,156.00	1,806,732.00	0.00
Japan	3,641,387.97	7,513,229.53	684,580,938.00	654,858.00	0.00
Kazakhstan	395,463.29	847,720.43	74,347,099.00	0.00	0.00
Korea, Republic of	2,314,126.88	5,308,649.02	435,055,854.00	6,295,269.00	0.01
Morocco	94,274.42	216,886.11	17,723,591.00	0.00	0.00
Mexico	1,900,749.02	10,390,334.11	357,340,816.00	0.00	0.00
Myanmar	52,938.44	162,502.19	9,528,920.00	59,058.00	0.01
Malaysia	1,041,485.02	1,911,080.17	195,799,184.00	0.00	0.00
Netherlands	2,934,564.09	6,334,108.81	551,698,049.00	476,230.00	0.00
Norway	813,695.27	1,793,407.53	152,974,710.00	27,524.00	0.00
New Zealand	176,525.88	406,235.76	33,186,866.00	0.00	0.00
Peru	218,223.77	409,894.56	41,026,069.00	0.00	0.00
Philippines	243,342.36	520,692.32	45,748,363.00	0.00	0.00
Poland	853,706.59	1,812,846.44	160,496,838.00	53,890.00	0.00
Qatar	643,568.11	1,672,401.21	120,990,804.00	0.00	0.00
Russian Federation	2,215,408.49	3,532,217.21	398,773,529.00	0.00	0.00
Singapore	1,633,417.40	2,967,687.51	307,082,471.00	0.00	0.00
Slovakia	396,562.75	802,455.01	74,553,797.00	13,280.00	0.00
Sweden	801,858.24	1,122,889.65	150,749,350.00	142,290.00	0.00
Thailand	967,129.68	1,552,568.43	181,820,380.00	0.00	0.00
Turkey	481,249.87	759,981.18	90,474,975.00	9,922,688.00	0.11
Taiwan, Province of China	1,273,280.31	3,202,830.20	239,376,699.00	0.00	0.00
United States	7,067,537.14	13,213,829.50	1,328,696,982.00	258,627.00	0.00
South Africa	306,833.07	513,995.76	57,684,618.00	0.00	0.00
Argentina	330,010.26	648,530.98	62,041,929.00	0.00	0.00

Appendix B: Quantification of Lost Trade by Case

Table 3.B.1
Lost trade resulting from Iran sanctions.

Country	Absolute loss (in billions of US$)	Relative loss (as percentage of total exports)
Iran, Islamic Republic of	−45.18	−16.40
Australia	0.56	0.06
Austria	−0.58	−0.10
Belgium	−1.43	−0.09
Canada	−0.19	−0.01
Switzerland	−1.33	−0.13
Czech Republic	−0.23	−0.04
Germany	−7.67	−0.15
Denmark	−0.13	−0.04
Spain	−1.69	−0.18
Finland	−0.09	−0.04
France	−6.35	−0.34
United Kingdom	−0.92	−0.06
Hungary	0.00	0.00
Ireland	−0.08	−0.02
Italy	−4.68	−0.29
Japan	−4.51	−0.19
Korea, Republic of	−5.11	−0.29
Netherlands	−1.45	−0.07
Norway	−0.10	−0.02
Poland	−0.29	−0.04
Slovakia	−0.01	−0.00
Sweden	−2.27	−0.40
Turkey	6.59	1.85
United States	0.11	0.00
World	−77.03	−0.23

Notes

I thank the participants of the CESifo Venice Summer Institute for fruitful discussions and comments.

1. Head and Mayer (2014) remark that this does not in fact constitute the general equilibrium impact, as it does not account for changes to production and expenditures. Head and Mayer (2014) and Anderson and Yotov (2010) call this the *modular trade impact* or *conditional* general equilibrium effect. In my analysis, I explicitly do account for changes in production and expenditure figures, following and extending approaches by Dekle, Eaton, and Kortum (2007, 2008) and Anderson, Larch, and Yotov (2016).

2. See Hufbauer et al. (2009) for reference.

3. See, for example, http://news.bbc.co.uk/2/hi/middle_east/6205295.stm.

4. See, for example, http://www.bbc.com/news/10276276 and https://www.white house.gov/the-press-office/fact-sheet-new-un-security-council-sanctions-iran.

5. See http://www.consilium.europa.eu/uedocs/cms_data/docs/pressdata/EN/foraff /127446.pdf.

6. See http://www.bbc.com/news/world-europe-16674660. Existing oil contracts were allowed to be honored until July 2012.

7. See Bashir and Lorber (2016) and http://www.bbc.com/news/business-17390456.

8. See, for example, http://www.bbc.co.uk/news/world-middle-east-35335078.

9. See also Crozet and Hinz (2016) for a detailed timeline and description of sanctions and countersanctions.

10. For a list of sanctioned individuals by the respective countries, see https://en.wiki pedia.org/wiki/List_of_individuals_sanctioned_during_the_Ukrainian_crisis.

11. Compare, for example, Ashford (2016) and Dreger et al. (2015).

12. See http://archive.mid.ru//brp_4.nsf/newsline/1D963ACD52CC987944257CA100 550142 and http://archive.mid.ru//brp_4.nsf/newsline/177739554DA10C8B44257CA1 00551FFE.

13. Products for military use are defined in the so-called *common military list* as adopted through Council Common Position 2008/944/CFSP, and dual-use goods are defined in Council Regulation (EC) 428/2009. See Crozet and Hinz (2016) for a list of the affected HS-8 codes.

14. See https://www.treasury.gov/press-center/press-releases/Pages/jl2572.aspx. Additionally, existing "smart sanctions" were extended to more individuals and entities, including the two Ukrainian breakaway regions "Luhansk People's Republic" and the "Donetsk People's Republic."

15. See also the Swiss Verordnung über Massnahmen zur Vermeidung der Umgehung internationaler Sanktionen im Zusammenhang mit der Situation in der Ukraine, AS 2014 877. As a Schengen member state, all travel bans automatically included travel to Switzerland.

16. See the Russian President's Decree No. 560 of August 6, 2014 and the Resolution of the Government of the Russian Federation No. 830 of August 20, 2014.

17. See Crozet and Hinz (2016) for the specific four-digit HS codes targeted.

18. See Hufbauer, Schott, and Elliott (2009) and https://piie.com/commentary/speeches -papers/case-88-1.

19. See, for example, http://www.bbc.com/news/world-asia-17813656 and http:// www.bbc.com/news/world-asia-22254493.

20. See Strangio (2012) for more details.

21. See, for example, http://www.bbc.com/news/world-africa-37365835.

22. Hufbauer, Schott, and Elliott (2009) employ what Head and Mayer (2014) call a *naive* gravity setup.

23. Which are "dropped," implicitly set to 0.

24. In effect, the estimation is equivalent to estimating $X_{odt} = \log (\Xi_{ot} + \Theta_{dt} + \varphi_{odq} + \beta_{odt} \cdot S_{odt})$.

25. Alternatively, Anderson, Larch, and Yotov (2016) show that the PPML estimator itself can be used to compute multilateral resistance terms with observed trade flows and counterfactual trade costs.

26. Notice also that even for nonsanctioning countries exports decrease in early 2015 because of the tumbling oil price and ruble (Dreger et al. 2015).

27. See also Crozet and Hinz (2016) for a further disaggregation into embargoed and nonembargoed goods.

References

Adao, R., A. Costinot, and D. Donaldson. 2017. "Nonparametric Counterfactual Predictions in Neoclassical Models of International Trade." *American Economic Review* 107 (3): 633–689.

Anderson, J. E., M. Larch, and Y. V. Yotov. 2018. "GEPPML: General Equilibrium Analysis with PPML." *World Economy* 41 (10): 1–33.

Anderson, J. E., and Y. V. Yotov. 2010. "The Changing Incidence of Geography." *American Economic Review* 100 (5): 2157–2186.

Ashford, E. 2016. "Not-So-Smart Sanctions." *Foreign Affairs* 95 (1): 114–123.

Baker and McKenzie. 2014. "EU and US Expand Sanctions against Russia. Russia Retaliates." Baker and McKenzie Client Alert.

Bashir, O. S., and E. Lorber. 2016. "Unfreezing Iran." *Foreign Affairs*, March 1. https://www.foreignaffairs.com/articles/iran/2016-03-01/unfreezing-iran.

Caruso, R. 2003. "The Impact of International Economic Sanctions on Trade: An Empirical Analysis." *Peace Economics, Peace Science and Public Policy* 9 (2): 1–29.

Crozet, M., and J. Hinz. 2016. "Friendly Fire—The Trade Impact of the Russia Sanctions and Counter-sanctions." Kiel Working Paper 2059. Kiel, Germany: Kiel Institute for the World Economy (IfW).

Dekle, R., J. Eaton, and S. Kortum. 2007. "Unbalanced Trade." *American Economic Review* 97 (2): 351–355.

Dekle, R., J. Eaton, and S. Kortum. 2008. "Global Rebalancing with Gravity: Measuring the Burden of Adjustment." Working Paper 13846. Cambridge, MA: National Bureau of Economic Research.

Dizaji, S. F., and P. A. G. van Bergeijk. 2013. "Potential Early Phase Success and Ultimate Failure of Economic Sanctions." *Journal of Peace Research* 50 (6): 721–736.

Dreger, C., J. Fidrmuc, K. Kholodilin, and D. Ulbricht. 2015. "The Ruble between the Hammer and the Anvil: Oil Prices and Economic Sanctions." DIW Berlin Discussion Paper 1488. Berlin: DIW Berlin, German Institute for Economic Research.

Dreyer, I., J. Luengo-Cabrera, S. Bazoobandi, T. Biersteker, R. Connolly, F. Giumelli, C. Portela, S. Secrieru, P. Seeberg, and P. A. van Bergeijk. 2015. *On Target?: EU Sanctions as Security Policy Tools.* Paris: European Union Institute for Security Studies.

Drezner, D. W. 1999. *The Sanctions Paradox: Economic Statecraft and International Relations.* Cambridge: Cambridge University Press.

Drezner, D. W. 2011. "Sanctions Sometimes Smart: Targeted Sanctions in Theory and Practice." *International Studies Review* 13 (1): 96–108.

Fally, T. 2015. "Structural Gravity and Fixed Effects." *Journal of International Economics* 97 (1): 76–85.

Frankel, J. A. 1982. "The 1807–1809 Embargo against Great Britain." *Journal of Economic History* 42 (2): 291–308.

Fuchs, A., and N.-H. Klann. 2013. "Paying a Visit: The Dalai Lama Effect on International Trade." *Journal of International Economics* 91 (1): 164–177.

Glick, R., and A. M. Taylor. 2010. "Collateral Damage: Trade Disruption and the Economic Impact of War." *Review of Economics and Statistics* 92 (1): 102–127.

Haidar, J. I. 2017. "Sanctions and Export Deflection: Evidence from Iran." *Economic Policy* 32 (90): 319–355.

Head, K., and T. Mayer. 2014. "Gravity Equations: Workhorse, Toolkit, and Cookbook." In *Handbook of International Economics*, vol. 4, edited by G. Gopinath, E. Helpman, and K. Rogoff, 131–195. Amsterdam: Elsevier.

Heilmann, K. 2016. "Does Political Conflict Hurt Trade? Evidence from Consumer Boycotts." *Journal of International Economics* 99: 179–191.

Hufbauer, G. C., and B. Oegg. 2003. "The Impact of Economic Sanctions on US Trade: Andrew Rose's Gravity Model." Policy Brief PB03–04. Washington, DC: Peterson Institute for International Economics.

Hufbauer, G. C., J. J. Schott, K. A. Elliott, and B. Oegg. 2009. *Economic Sanctions Reconsidered*, 3rd ed. (paper). Washington, DC: Peterson Institute for International Economics.

Irwin, D. A. 2005. "The Welfare Cost of Autarky: Evidence from the Jeffersonian Trade Embargo, 1807–09." *Review of International Economics* 13 (4): 631–645.

Martin, P., T. Mayer, and M. Thoenig. 2008a. "Civil Wars and International Trade." *Journal of the European Economic Association* 6 (2–3): 541–550.

Martin, P., T. Mayer, and M. Thoenig. 2008b. "Make Trade Not War?" *Review of Economic Studies* 75 (3): 865–900.

Michaels, G., and X. Zhi. 2010. "Freedom Fries." *American Economic Journal: Applied Economics* 2 (3): 256–281.

Morgan, T. C., N. Bapat, and V. Krustev. 2009. "The Threat and Imposition of Economic Sanctions, 1971–2000." *Conflict Management and Peace Science* 26 (1): 92–110.

O'Rourke, K. H. 2007. "War and Welfare: Britain, France, and the United States 1807–14." *Oxford Economic Papers* 59:i8–i30.

Pandya, S. S., and R. Venkatesan. 2016. "French Roast: Consumer Response to International Conflict—Evidence from Supermarket Scanner Data." *Review of Economics and Statistics* 98 (1): 42–56.

Reuters. 2014. "Swiss Expand Ban on Defense Sales to Russia, Ukraine." http://www.reuters.com/article/us-ukraine-crisis-switzerland-idUSKBN0GD1MM20140813.

Rosenberg, E., Z. K. Goldman, D. Drezner, and J. Solomon-Strauss. 2016. "The New Tools of Economic Warfare: Effects and Effectiveness of Contemporary U.S. Financial Sanctions." Technical report. Washington, DC: Center for a New American Security.

Santos Silva, J. M. C., and S. Tenreyro. 2006. "The Log of Gravity." *Review of Economics and Statistics* 88 (4): 641–658.

Strangio, S. 2012. "What Obama Wants from Myanmar." *Foreign Affairs*, November 19. https://www.foreignaffairs.com/articles/burma-myanmar/2012-11-19/what-obama-wants-myanmar.

United Nations Statistics Division. 2015. "UN Comtrade." http://comtrade.un.org/.

Van Bergeijk, P. A. 2009. *Economic Diplomacy and the Geography of International Trade*. Cheltenham: Edward Elgar.

4 Sticks and Stones: Sanction Threats, Impositions, and Their Effect on International Trade

Tristan Kohl and Chiel Klein Reesink

4.1 Introduction

Economic sanctions have been used throughout modern history and are usually accompanied or preceded by war (Elliott, Hufbauer, and Oegg 2008).[1] It was only after the horrors of World War I that US president Woodrow Wilson put sanctions on the agenda as a substitute for military aggression. From this moment on, history witnessed an increase in the use of economic sanctions by nation-states and supranational institutions, such as the United Nations, to attain foreign policy goals. According to Kobayashi (2013), the number of sanctions has doubled every decade between 1971 and 2000. By far, the state that has utilized the sanction policy tool the most is the United States: "In most instances in the post-WWII period where economic pressure was brought to bear against the exercise of military power, the United States played the role of international policeman" (Hufbauer, Schott, and Elliott 1990, 5).

The increasing frequency with which nations use economic sanctions as a policy instrument calls for a better understanding of their economic consequences. However, the effect that sanctions have on bilateral trade flows has received relatively little attention in recent years, despite significant advances in the analytical toolkit commonly applied to this type of research. Moreover, most studies of economic sanctions only assess the impact of sanctions actually imposed (Lacy and Niou 2004), thereby ignoring how *threatening* to impose sanctions may alter economic agents' actions.

This chapter measures the impact of sanction threats, in addition to sanction impositions, on bilateral trade flows. We show that threats, while often discussed in the media and causing uncertainty for economic agents, do not have a significant impact on international trade. Sanctions, once imposed, do have detrimental effects on international trade, but the magnitude of these effects is a fraction of what has been documented in the literature.

The remainder of this chapter is structured as follows. Section 4.2 surveys the literature on the impact of economic sanctions on international trade. Recent improvements to the gravity model of international trade are reviewed in section 4.3, along with details of our empirical strategy. Section 4.4 presents the results and sensitivity analyses. Section 4.5 discusses our key findings and concludes with pointers for future research.

4.2   Literature

4.2.1   Economic Sanctions

Morgan, Bapat, and Kobayashi (2014, 2) define economic sanctions as "actions that one or more countries take to limit or end their economic relations with a target country in an effort to persuade that country to change its policies." Therefore, a sanction must (a) involve one or more sender states and a target state and (b) be implemented by the sender(s) in order to change the behavior of the target state.[2] Actions taken by states that restrict economic relations with other countries solely for domestic economic policy reasons do not qualify as sanctions.[3]

Economic sanctions are built on two basic premises (van Bergeijk 2009). First, sanctions are meant to deprive the target country of (part of) the gains it experiences from international trade and investment. Second, this (threat of) disutility will affect the target's behavior. In other words, economic sanctions reduce welfare in the target country in order to force a change in its behavior. Sanctions can take many forms: tariffs, export controls, embargoes, import bans, travel bans, asset freezes, aid cuts, and blockades, all of which (with the exception of blockages) are legal barriers to trade.

Three general categories of sanctions can be discerned: boycotts, embargoes, and financial sanctions (Barber 1979; Caruso 2003). A boycott is a restriction on imports of one or more goods from the target country. It is meant to lower demand for the product from the target country. In addition, the import restriction attempts to reduce the foreign exchange earnings of the target country and thus its ability to purchase goods in international markets. These measures are usually deemed ineffective because of the ease with which target countries can circumvent the import restrictions by finding other trading partners or setting up triangular schemes to sell their products.

A sender country may also restrict its own exports to a target country, which is called an embargo. These exports often comprise goods that are of strategic importance to the target country. An example is the 2014 situation in Ukraine, which led the European Union to restrict the export of arms and related materials, technology for military use, energy-related equipment and technology, and oil exploration services to Russia (European Union 2015). Financial sanctions are meant to cut off lending and investment in the target country through the international credit markets but also to freeze the target country's foreign assets.

An economic sanction is an action by state A against state B in order to bring state B's "behavior" in line with state A's view of what that behavior should be. Economic sanctions therefore usually have a desired outcome, namely a change in the behavior or policies of the target state. Whether real outcomes meet desired outcomes is questioned, and thus economic sanctions are a constant subject of debate (Kaempfer and Lowenberg 1988). Likewise, sanctions have been the subject for a rich body of literature of scientific inquiry owing to the mixed findings regarding their effectiveness in yielding the "desired" outcomes (see, e.g., van Bergeijk 1989; Hufbauer, Schott, and Elliott 1990; Pape 1997; Drezner 2000).

4.2.2   Datasets on Sanctions

Research on economic sanctions has progressed significantly ever since Hufbauer, Schott, and Elliott published their work and corresponding dataset (hereafter referred to as HSE) in 1990. Prior to their research, most work focused on a single sanction case and tried to explain why sanctions did or could not work (Galtung 1967; Hoffmann 1967; Baer 1973; Schreiber 1973; Olson 1979; von Amerongen 1980; Wallensteen 1983).

Since the release of Hufbauer, Schott, and Elliott (1990), research has explored the effects of economic sanctions on foreign direct investment (Biglaiser and Lektzian 2011), human rights (Peksen 2009), the level of democracy (Peksen and Drury 2010), jobs and wages (Hufbauer et al. 1997), and the impact that sanctions have on international trade (Caruso 2003). A related line of inquiry deals with third-country effects or sanction busting, the situation in which a sanctioned state reroutes its trade to other trading partners that are not taking part in sanctioning it, thus eliminating the effect of the sanction (Early 2009; Yang et al. 2009).

Morgan, Bapat, and Krustev (2009) introduced a new dataset on economic sanctions, called Threat and Imposition of Economic Sanctions (hereafter referred to as TIES). The largest advantage of the TIES dataset is that it contains far more cases than the HSE dataset. This suggests that the use of this new dataset might very well change what is currently understood about the impacts of economic sanctions (Morgan, Bapat, and Krustev 2009). For example, research conducted using TIES has given valuable new insights into multilateral sanctions. When using the TIES dataset, Bapat and Morgan (2009) found that, in contrast to the results that were produced with the HSE dataset, multilateral sanctions are more effective than unilateral sanctions. Theory suggested this outcome long before the TIES dataset was created; however, it could not be proved with the HSE dataset.

A comparison of both datasets reveals that the TIES dataset has several advantages over the HSE dataset. TIES contains far more cases than HSE—1,412 compared to 204—and it includes information about sanction threats as well (of the 1,412 cases, 567 cases constitute threats and 845 are impositions. In HSE, all 204 cases refer to impositions only). Also, the United States is the primary sender in 60 percent of the cases in HSE, compared to 48 percent in TIES. This means that HSE is more biased toward the United States than TIES is. Moreover, the mean duration of the cases in TIES is far shorter (2.43 years) than those in HSE (6.6 years), which indicates that HSE severely underestimates the number of relatively short sanction episodes.

4.2.3   Effects of Imposed Sanctions on International Trade

For the purposes of this chapter, impact is defined as the change in bilateral trade flows brought on by the threat or imposition of an economic sanction. The gravity model of international trade has long been used by international economists to empirically examine the determinants of bilateral trade flows (Tinbergen 1962). While many recent methodological improvements have been made to determine the impact of economic integration on international trade (see, e.g., Baier and Bergstrand 2007), they have yet to be applied in the context of disruptive policies such as economic sanctions.

Hufbauer et al. (1997) and Caruso (2003) have applied a gravity model to delve into the impact that economic sanctions have on international trade. Hufbauer et al. (1997) contemporaneously searched for effects on jobs and wages. Yang et al. (2004) applied a gravity model to investigate the impact of US sanctions on US trade with target countries and on third countries.

Hufbauer et al. (1997) was one of the first studies that aimed to empirically measure the impact of US economic sanctions on bilateral trade flows. The authors investigated three years—1985, 1990, and 1995—and 88 countries. Sanctions were categorized into three types: limited, moderate, and extensive. Minor financial, export, cultural, or travel sanctions were labeled as "limited" sanctions. Broader trade or financial sanctions were classified as "moderate." The authors considered comprehensive trade and financial sanctions or a combination of moderate sanctions to be "extensive." Other scholars have used this categorization of sanctions as well (Elliott and Hufbauer 1999; Caruso 2003; Wood 2008; Peksen 2009). Hufbauer et al. (1997) show that extensive US sanctions can reduce bilateral trade by up to 90 percent. The results on limited and moderate sanctions are not as robust as the results on extensive sanctions, but they show an average reduction of about 30 percent.

In his work, Caruso (2003) utilizes the HSE dataset on economic sanctions to reveal the impact the imposition of US economic sanctions has had on international trade. He shows that the imposition of extensive economic sanctions by the United States reduces bilateral trade with the United States by up to 89 percent, depending on the country pair. For limited and moderate sanctions, he finds a small positive, yet insignificant, effect on trade. Caruso also shows that extensively sanctioning other G7 nations induces a disruption of trade for countries other than the United States as well, which he calls negative network effects.

Yang et al. (2004) also employ a gravity model to investigate the impact of US economic sanctions on US trade with target countries and on third countries. Their results are similar to those of the previously mentioned studies. Extensive and comprehensive sanctions have large negative impacts through bilateral trade reductions, while the impact of limited and moderate sanctions seems weak or absent.

Previous research on the impact of economic sanctions suggests that extensive and comprehensive sanctions have a larger negative impact than for limited and moderate sanctions, and that this impact is very high (reductions in bilateral trade flows of up to 90 percent). However, as will be argued, these results are significantly biased owing to (i) limited data on sanctions and (ii) researchers' theoretically inconsistent specification of the gravity equation of international trade.

Table 4.1 provides an overview of the main results so far that are relevant for this literature review. Limited or moderate sanctions typically include partial economic embargoes, import restrictions, export restrictions, the termination of foreign aid, and travel bans. Examples of extensive sanctions include total economic embargoes, blockades,

Table 4.1
Overview of results in the literature.

	Hufbauer et al. (1997)	Caruso (2003)	Yang et al. (2004)
Years studied	1985, 1990, 1995	1960–2000	1980, 1985, 1990, 1995
Number of countries studied	88	50	225
Focus	Impact on US trade	Impact on US trade	Impact on US trade
Dataset used	HSE	HSE	HSE
Threats/impositions	Impositions only	Impositions only	Impositions only
Effect found	LM: −30%* X: −90%*	LM: +13% X: −89%*	LM: +34% X: −78%*

Notes: Effects are averages of multiple parameter estimates. LM is for limited or moderate sanctions, X is for extensive or comprehensive sanctions.
* Indicates statistically significant parameter estimates.

asset freezes, suspension of economic agreements, and composite sanctions combining several types of sanctions.

4.2.4   Effects of Sanction Threats on International Trade

A phenomenon that scholars have only been able to research relatively recently is economic sanction threats. The imposition of economic sanctions has been widely researched for decades; however, only since the inception of the TIES dataset has there been data available on sanction threats. Because of data restrictions, authors chose to focus on a single case such as the United States threatening to sanction China because of the Tiananmen Square massacre in 1989 (Li and Drury 2004; Drury and Li 2006). Sanction threat cases are situations in which a sender state threatens to implement sanctions against a target state if the target does not comply with the sender's demands. Usually, these demands, much as in an imposition case, entail policy changes or a different standpoint on a political matter.

So far, the question when it comes to sanction threats has been whether threats are as effective as sanction impositions. Most recent research has focused on this question and looked solely at the effectiveness of threats (Lacy and Niou 2004; Drury and Li 2006). A threat is effective when the outcome of the threat case is equal to the desired outcome. Therefore, effectiveness is more concerned with the success rate for changing policy rather than the economic consequence (i.e., change in trade flows).

To our knowledge, the impact that sanction threats might have on trade flows has not yet been examined empirically. One of the few papers offering theoretical guidance in this regard is by Lacy and Niou (2004), who present their model as a multistage game of two-sided incomplete information between a sender and a target. The authors state that the threat stage of a case is critical to understanding the outcome of the sanction: "The model reveals that the threat of sanctions can be as potent a policy tool as the imposition of sanctions" (Lacy and Niou 2004, 38). This chapter suggests that threats are just as capable of changing a target's behavior as actual impositions.

Regarding the impact of sanction threats, two scenarios are possible. Let us assume that the government of the sender state has become displeased with the policies adopted by the target. The sender threatens to impose economic sanctions on the target. Firms in these states witness the struggle their governments are in and act according to what they deem fit. In both scenarios, firms expect an economic sanction to follow the sanction threat. However, it is the reaction to the threat that differs in each scenario. In the first scenario, firms expect a sanction episode and anticipate this by pulling out of deals with firms in the target. This line of events would negatively impact the countries' bilateral trade flows. The alternative scenario expects firms to expedite business deals with firms in the target state in order to fully reap the benefits of trade "while they still can." In this situation, a rise in trade between sender and target should be witnessed.

Looking at it this way, it becomes clear that a threat case is significantly different from a case in which a sender actually imposes a sanction on a target, since no definite harm has yet been done. Until now, this aspect of sanction threats has not been tested. We therefore use the TIES dataset to determine empirically how threatening to impose economic sanctions affects international trade.

4.3   Methodology

4.3.1   Gravity Model

For the purposes of this chapter, we follow the literature by applying a gravity equation of international trade. The basic gravity model explains bilateral trade flows by using a log-linear equation

$$\ln \text{TRADE}_{ijt} = \beta_0 + \beta_1 \ln \text{GDP}_{it} + \beta_2 \ln \text{GDP}_{jt} + \beta_3 \ln \text{DISTANCE}_{ij} + \beta_4 \text{TA}_{ijt} + \beta_5 \text{THREAT}_{ijt} + \beta_6 \text{IMPOSITION}_{ijt} + e_{ijt}, \tag{4.1}$$

where $TRADE_{ijt}$ denotes bilateral trade between state i and state j at time t, GDP_{it} and GDP_{jt} represent their gross domestic products, respectively, and $DISTANCE_{ij}$ is the physical distance between states. TA_{ij} is a binary variable, which is 1 if both countries in a given dyad year have a trade agreement and 0 otherwise. $THREAT_{ijt}$ is a binary variable that takes the value 1 when a sanction threat is active between countries i and j in year t and 0 if not. The same goes for $IMPOSITION_{ijt}$; however, in this case it involves a sanction imposition. e_{ijt} is the random error term.

To date, empirical analyses on the trade impacts of sanctions have relied on this very basic version of the gravity equation (Hufbauer, Schott, and Elliott 1990; Caruso 2003; Yang et al. 2004). However, since then, the gravity equation has undergone several significant improvements (for an overview of how the methodology has evolved, see Kohl 2014). The most important advances are (i) (time-varying) multilateral resistance terms and (ii) accounting for endogeneity bias (cf. Baier and Bergstrand 2007).

In 2003, "multilateral resistance terms" (MRTs) entered the gravity model (Anderson and van Wincoop 2003) to take into account that trade between two countries is also affected by their bilateral trade barrier relative to their average trade barriers vis-à-vis all of their other trade partners. Feenstra (2004) demonstrates that these unobserved price indices can be controlled for by adding importer and exporter fixed effects to equation (4.1), which yields

$$\begin{aligned} \ln TRADE_{ijt} = \beta_0 + \beta_1 \ln GDP_{it} + \beta_2 \ln GDP_{jt} \\ + \beta_3 \ln DISTANCE_{ij} + \beta4\ TA_{ijt} + \beta_5\ THREAT_{ijt} \quad\quad (4.2) \\ + \beta_6\ IMPOSITION_{ijt} + F_i + F_j + F_t + e_{ijt}, \end{aligned}$$

where F_i represents fixed effects for the importing country and F_j those for the exporting country. Year effects (F_t) deal with common trends and shocks. Changes in trade costs on one bilateral route can influence trade flows on all other routes because of relative price effects; this is picked up in the model (4.2). Because the multilateral resistance terms, which are correlated with trade costs, are not included in the basic model, this model suffers from omitted variables bias.

The model as shown in equation (4.2) only offers a partial solution to the problem of modeling multilateral trade resistance terms in panel data. From work by Baier and Bergstrand (2007), it follows that in a panel setting "Anderson and van Wincoop's (2003) multilateral resistance terms are actually time-varying, which means that the importer and exporter effects also need to be time-varying to fully capture the

MRT" (Kohl 2014, 8). When country fixed effects are not interacted with time, they control for average trade resistance over time. However, key elements of trade resistance may be time-varying. Without accounting for time-varying MRTs, the results are likely to suffer from an omitted variables bias (Baier and Bergstrand 2007). If we adjust our model for this, the result is a time-varying fixed-effects version of the gravity equation,

$$
\begin{aligned}
\ln \text{TRADE}_{ijt} = \beta_0 &+ \beta_1 \ln \text{GDP}_{it} + \beta_2 \ln \text{GDP}_{jt} \\
&+ \beta_3 \ln \text{DISTANCE}_{ij} + \beta_4 \text{TA}_{ijt} + \beta_5 \text{THREAT}_{ijt} \\
&+ \beta_6 \text{IMPOSITION}_{ijt} + F_{it} + F_{jt} + F_{ij} + e_{ijt},
\end{aligned}
\tag{4.3}
$$

where F_{it} and F_{jt} denote importer-year and exporter-year effects, respectively. This equation represents a time-varying form of equation (4.2). F_{ij} controls for unobserved circumstances that may be correlated with both a country pair's level of trade and factors related to the dyad experiencing a sanction episode. In other words, the dyad fixed effect controls for any endogeneity concerns related to a country pair's bilateral trade and inclination to (threaten to) impose a sanction.

Notice that the country-year fixed effects are perfectly collinear by definition with country-specific time-varying dependent variables. As is by now common in the literature, we will therefore estimate the following structural gravity equation with ordinary least squares (OLS):

$$
\begin{aligned}
\ln \text{TRADE}_{ijt} = \beta_0 &+ \beta_1 \text{TA}_{ijt} + \beta_2 \text{THREAT}_{ijt} \\
&+ \beta_3 \text{IMPOSITION}_{ijt} + F_{it} + F_{jt} + F_{ij} + e_{ijt}.
\end{aligned}
\tag{4.4}
$$

One drawback of estimating the gravity equation in its log-linear form is that zero trade flows are ignored, which may severely bias our parameter estimates (see Santos Silva and Tenreyro 2006). Zero trade flows can be incorporated by estimating the following equation with a Poisson pseudo-maximum likelihood (PPML) estimator:

$$
\begin{aligned}
\text{TRADE}_{ijt} = \beta_0 &+ \beta_1 \text{THREAT}_{ijt} + \beta_2 \text{IMPOSITION}_{ijt} \\
&+ \beta_3 \text{TA}_{ijt} + F_{it} + F_{jt} + F_{ij} + e_{ijt}.
\end{aligned}
\tag{4.5}
$$

We estimate equations (4.4) and (4.5) with high-dimensional fixed-effects Stata packages for OLS (reghdfe) and PPML (ppml_panel_sg), respectively (see Correia 2017; Larch et al. 2017). Armed with these latest advances from the gravity literature, our empirical strategy adds to the literature a model that incorporates time-varying multilateral resistance terms, controls for potential endogeneity bias, and accounts for zero trade flows.

4.3.2 Data

The panel dataset is arranged by country pair and year. Each pair occurs twice, once as importer-exporter (ij) and once as exporter-importer (ji). Nominal bilateral trade flows are from the IMF Direction of Trade Statistics database (International Monetary Fund 2013) and GDP from the World Bank Development Indicators (World Bank 2013). Data on distances are from Mayer and Zignago (2011) and trade agreements from Kohl (2014). Following Baldwin and Taglioni (2007), $\ln(\text{TRADE}_{ijt}) = \ln[\text{IMPORTS}_{ijt} * \text{EXPORTS}_{ijt}]^{\wedge}(1/2)]$. For PPML, trade is simply the sum of imports and exports, where missing values are assumed to be zero. Table 4.2 lists all countries (223) covered in the dataset, even if only for a limited time.

Table 4.2
List of countries.

Afghanistan	Bulgaria	Estonia
Albania	Burkina Faso	Ethiopia
Algeria	Burundi	Faeroe Islands
American Samoa	Cambodia	Falkland Islands
Andorra	Cameroon	Fiji
Angola	Canada	Finland
Anguilla	Cape Verde	France
Antigua and Barbuda	Cayman Islands	French Polynesia
Argentina	Central African Republic	French Southern Territories
Armenia	Chad	Gabon
Aruba	Chile	Gambia
Australia	China	Georgia
Austria	Colombia	Germany
Azerbaijan	Comoros	Ghana
Bahamas	Cook Islands	Gibraltar
Bahrain	Costa Rica	Greece
Bangladesh	Croatia	Greenland
Barbados	Cuba	Grenada
Belarus	Cyprus	Guam
Belgium	Czech Republic	Guatemala
Belize	Democratic Republic of	Guinea
Benin	the Congo	Guinea-Bissau
Bermuda	Denmark	Guyana
Bhutan	Djibouti	Haiti
Bolivia	Dominica	Honduras
Bosnia and Herzegovina	Dominican Republic	Hong Kong
Botswana	Ecuador	Hungary
Brazil	Egypt	Iceland
British Indian Ocean	El Salvador	India
Territory	Equatorial Guinea	Indonesia
Brunei	Eritrea	Iran

Table 4.2 (continued)

Iraq	Myanmar	Somalia
Ireland	Namibia	South Africa
Israel	Nauru	South Korea
Italy	Nepal	Spain
Ivory Coast	Netherlands	Sri Lanka
Jamaica	Netherlands Antilles	St. Helena
Japan	New Caledonia	St. Kitts and Nevis
Jordan	New Zealand	St. Lucia
Kazakhstan	Nicaragua	St. Pierre-Miquelon
Kenya	Niger	St. Vincent and Grenadines
Kiribati	Nigeria	Sudan
Kosovo	Niue	Suriname
Kuwait	North Korea	Swaziland
Kyrgyzstan	Norway	Sweden
Laos	Oman	Switzerland
Latvia	Pakistan	Syria
Lebanon	Palau	Taiwan
Lesotho	Palestinian Authority	Tajikistan
Liberia	Panama	Tanzania
Libya	Papua New Guinea	Thailand
Liechtenstein	Paraguay	Timor-Leste
Lithuania	Peru	Togo
Luxembourg	Philippines	Tonga
Macao	Pitcairn	Trinidad and Tobago
Macedonia	Poland	Tunisia
Madagascar	Portugal	Turkey
Malawi	Qatar	Turkmenistan
Malaysia	Republic of Congo	Tuvalu
Maldives	Romania	Uganda
Mali	Russia	Ukraine
Malta	Rwanda	United Arab Emirates
Marshall Islands	Samoa	United Kingdom
Mauritania	San Marino	United States
Mauritius	Sao Tome and Principe	Uruguay
Mayotte	Saudi Arabia	Uzbekistan
Mexico	Senegal	Vanuatu
Micronesia	Serbia and Montenegro	Venezuela
Moldova	Seychelles	Vietnam
Mongolia	Sierra Leone	Virgin Islands
Montenegro	Singapore	Wallis and Futuna
Montserrat	Slovak Republic	Yemen
Morocco	Slovenia	Zambia
Mozambique	Solomon Islands	Zimbabwe

Sanction data come from the Threat and Imposition of Economic Sanctions (TIES) project. This dataset contains data for both economic sanctions imposed (impositions) and sanction threats. Note that a case may contain multiple types of threats or impositions. Should a sender state convert a sanction threat into an actual imposition, then the case is split into a threat case and an imposition case. The TIES dataset contains 1,412 cases, of which 845 (60 percent) are cases in which sanctions were imposed and 567 (40 percent) are cases involving threats (Morgan, Bapat, and Kobayashi 2014). The period covered is 1948–2005.

Given the richness of the TIES dataset, we can also seek to understand how international trade is affected by different types of threats and impositions. Following the literature, we refine the binary THREAT and IMPOSITION variables to distinguish between "Limited or moderate" and "extensive" threats and impositions, respectively. "Limited or moderate" threats and impositions refer to events where governments threatened to impose, or in fact imposed, partial economic embargoes, import restrictions, export restrictions, termination of foreign aid, or travel bans. We consider "extensive" threats or impositions as including total economic embargoes, asset freezes, suspension of economic agreements or protocols, and multiple types of cases in a given year (based on the authors' calculations). Note that TIES also identifies a few threats or impositions as "other," which were recoded as "missing" so as to be entirely excluded from our analysis. Note that estimating regressions for specific types of threats and impositions is inadvisable because of large asymmetries in the number of observations per type of threat or imposition. For example, we only observe 6 times that a sender has threatened to freeze assets, while threats to impose import restrictions were observed 900 times. We observed 29 times that a sender threatened to impose travel bans, while threats to terminate foreign aid were observed 1,492 times.

4.4   Results

The main results are reported in table 4.3. Column 1 shows the parameter estimates of model 2, which is a naive gravity equation with importer, exporter, and year fixed effects. The coefficients for GDP, distance, and trade agreements are in line with the literature (for an overview, see Head and Mayer 2014).

For threats and impositions, first we simply include both variables in column 1, and we find that threats do not have a significant effect

Table 4.3
Main results with binary threat and imposition variables.

	(1)	(2)	(3)	(4)	(5)	(6)
	Eq. (4.2)	Eq. (4.2) with interaction	Eq. (4.2) with interactions	Eq. (4.4)	Eq. (4.4) with interaction	Eq. (4.4) with interactions
ln(GDP) importer	1.136***	1.136***	1.136***			
	(0.0368)	(0.0368)	(0.0368)			
ln(GDP) exporter	1.172***	1.172***	1.172***			
	(0.0329)	(0.0329)	(0.0329)			
ln(Distance)	-1.359***	-1.359***	-1.359***			
	(0.0202)	(0.0202)	(0.0202)			
Trade agreement	0.686***	0.686***	0.686***	0.392***	0.392***	0.391***
	(0.0320)	(0.0320)	(0.0320)	(0.0212)	(0.0212)	(0.0212)
Threat	0.0264	0.0544	0.0543	0.0753**	0.00297	0.00435
	(0.0483)	(0.0590)	(0.0591)	(0.0277)	(0.0348)	(0.0348)
Imposition	0.0955*	0.108*	0.108*	-0.168***	-0.201***	-0.225***
	(0.0454)	(0.0495)	(0.0532)	(0.0311)	(0.0342)	(0.0369)
Threat * Imposition		-0.0795	-0.0801		0.200***	0.226***
		(0.0791)	(0.0825)		(0.0490)	(0.0513)
Threat * Imposition$_{[t+1]}$			-0.00495			0.162***
			(0.0577)			(0.0364)
F_i, F_j, F_t	Yes	Yes	Yes	No	No	No
F_{it}, F_{jt}, F_{ij}	No	No	No	Yes	Yes	Yes
N	333,898	333,898	333,898	333,898	333,898	333,898
Adjusted R^2	0.761	0.761	0.761	0.916	0.916	0.916

Notes: Estimated with ordinary least squares (OLS). Dependent variable: ln(trade). Robust standard errors (clustered by country pair) in parentheses. Parameter estimates for fixed effects omitted for brevity.
* $p<0.05$; ** $p<0.01$; *** $p<0.001$.

on trade. Surprisingly, impositions have a small positive effect on trade. Recall that previous studies found that sanctions (impositions) decrease trade by around 90 percent. We explain this difference by pointing out that previous studies did not use gravity equations with extensive sets of fixed effects. Moreover, these datasets were more restrictive in terms of country and period coverage, and, importantly, the number of impositions recorded.

A possible limitation to our first specification is that our data are on an annual basis, but threats and impositions could easily occur in the same year. We therefore deem it sensible to include an interaction term so that we can isolate for a given year the effect of threats only, impositions only, and threats in combination with impositions.

As reported in column 2, the interaction term is negative—suggesting that threats followed by impositions in the same year have a negative effect on trade—but the parameter estimate is not statistically significant. What about sanctions that were only imposed in the year following a sanction threat? We construct a binary indicator variable to account for such cases. Similar to column 2, the coefficient in column 3 shows that threats followed by impositions in the following year also have a negative trade impact, albeit not a significant one.

As discussed earlier, a main drawback of equation (4.2) is that the set of fixed effects does not properly account for time-varying multilateral resistance terms or control for potential endogeneity bias. The remainder of table 4.3 therefore repeats the steps reported in columns 1–3 with equation (4.4) in columns 4–6.

First, notice that the coefficient for trade agreements drops substantially—consistent with the literature (see Kohl 2014). Interestingly, the theoretically consistent gravity equation estimated in column 4 shows that threats have a positive and significant effect on trade (approximately 7 percent), while impositions decrease trade (by approximately 15 percent).[4]

However, the inclusion of the interaction terms in column 5 and 6 overturns this finding. Specifically, threats without impositions do not affect trade—at least not for trade flows recorded at an annual level. In contrast, impositions that were not preceded by any type of threat show a decrease in trade of about 20 percent. However, this reduction in trade was almost entirely reversed if the sanction had been "announced" by means of a threat (because the interaction terms are positive and of a similar magnitude).

Two main preliminary conclusions can be drawn from table 4.3. First, earlier estimates of how sanctions affect international trade were overestimated. We find that the effect of sanctions (impositions) on trade is about −20 percent, around one-fifth of the estimate typically found in the literature. In our view, this difference results from the substantial coverage of sanctions in the TIES dataset (compared to the HSE dataset) and our theoretically consistent specification of the gravity equation with time-varying multilateral resistance terms and country-pair fixed effects to control for endogeneity bias. Second, while sender states' threats to impose sanctions could have an economic impact on trade, this positive effect only materializes if sanctions are imposed. Threats alone are of no significant consequence for trade.

To further understand how threats and impositions affect trade, we now proceed to distinguish various *types* of threats and impositions. The setup of table 4.4 is exactly the same as in table 4.3. The only difference is that we now replace the binary THREAT (IMPOSITION) variable with a categorical variable, which is 1 if the sanction threatened (imposed) is classified as being of limited or moderate scope, 2 if it is extensive, and 0 otherwise.

Table 4.4 sheds some light on how the extensiveness of a sanction (threat) affects trade. For example, the point estimates for extensive threats tend to be smaller (negative) than those of limited or moderate threats (while not being significant). Columns 4–6 also show that extensive impositions have the largest negative (and significant) effect on trade compared to impositions that are of a limited or moderate nature.

As with table 4.3, inclusion of the interaction terms suggests that trade responds more negatively to sanctions that were only implemented without preceding threats, compared to threats that led to sanction impositions. Yet, in contrast to table 4.3, the main effects and interaction effects no longer entirely cancel out—suggesting that the type of sanction threatened and imposed matters for trade. Threats without an actual sanction implemented do not have a significant effect on trade. Our results show that limited or moderate impositions without threats reduce trade by 14 percent, whereas extensive impositions lead to a 27 percent reduction. Combined with the interaction terms, the findings suggest that limited or moderate threats followed by a limited or moderate imposition in the same year decrease trade by 14 percent, whereas an imposition in the following year reduces trade by 4 percent. In contrast, extensive threats followed by extensive

Table 4.4
Main results with categorical threat and imposition variables.

	(1)	(2)	(3)	(4)	(5)	(6)
	Eq. (4.2)	Eq. (4.2) with interaction	Eq. (4.2) with interactions	Eq. (4.4)	Eq. (4.4) with interaction	Eq. (4.4) with interactions
ln(GDP) importer	1.136***	1.136***	1.136***			
	(0.0367)	(0.0367)	(0.0367)			
ln(GDP) exporter	1.172***	1.172***	1.171***			
	(0.0329)	(0.0329)	(0.0329)			
ln(Distance)	-1.359***	-1.359***	-1.359***			
	(0.0202)	(0.0202)	(0.0202)			
Trade agreement	0.686***	0.686***	0.686***	0.392***	0.392***	0.392***
	(0.0320)	(0.0320)	(0.0320)	(0.0212)	(0.0212)	(0.0212)
Threat						
Limited/Moderate	0.0894	0.114	0.114	0.0569	0.0166	0.0181
	(0.0505)	(0.0627)	(0.0627)	(0.0313)	(0.0405)	(0.0405)
Extensive	-0.119	-0.234	-0.234	0.140***	-0.0534	-0.0484
	(0.0782)	(0.126)	(0.126)	(0.0399)	(0.0414)	(0.0414)
Imposition						
Limited/Moderate	0.152*	0.182***	0.193***	-0.131***	-0.138***	-0.153***
	(0.0493)	(0.0541)	(0.0576)	(0.0301)	(0.0334)	(0.0357)
Extensive	0.0522	0.0157	0.0126	-0.228***	-0.296***	-0.319***
	(0.0723)	(0.0842)	(0.0887)	(0.0543)	(0.0650)	(0.0690)

Threat* Imposition

	(1)	(2)	(3)	(4)
Limited/Moderate* Limited/Moderate	−0.214*	−0.203*	0.0514	0.0592
	(0.0866)	(0.0907)	(0.0543)	(0.0564)
Limited/Moderate* Extensive	0.0784	0.115	0.268***	0.257***
	(0.118)	(0.117)	(0.0735)	(0.0759)
Extensive* Limited/Moderate	−0.0118	−0.0197	0.300***	0.297***
	(0.159)	(0.160)	(0.0649)	(0.0649)
Extensive* Extensive	0.258	0.243	0.377***	0.387***
	(0.154)	(0.154)	(0.0811)	(0.0827)
Threat* Imposition$_{[t+1]}$				
Limited/Moderate* Limited/Moderate		−0.0115		0.0948*
		(0.0689)		(0.0404)
Limited/Moderate* Extensive		0.199*		0.128*
		(0.0827)		(0.0561)
Extensive* Limited/Moderate		−0.592***		0.220***
		(0.146)		(0.0656)
Extensive* Extensive		−0.138		0.153*
		(0.0901)		(0.0641)
F_i, F_j, F_t	Yes	Yes	No	No
F_{it}, F_{jt}, F_{ij}	No	No	Yes	Yes
N	333,898	333,898	333,898	333,898
Adj. R^2	0.761	0.761	0.916	0.916

Notes: Estimated with ordinary least squares (OLS). Dependent variable: ln(trade). Robust standard errors (clustered by country pair) in parentheses. Parameter estimates for fixed effects omitted for brevity.

* $p<0.05$; ** $p<0.01$; *** $p<0.001$.

Table 4.5
Extended OLS results with categorical threat and imposition variable and lags.

	(1) Contemporaneous	(2) Lag 1	(3) Lag 2	(4) Lag 3	(5) Lag 4	(6) Lag 5
Trade agreement	0.382*** (0.0234)					
Threat						
Limited/Moderate	0.0106 (0.0305)	0.0591** (0.0218)	−0.0579* (0.0257)	0.0338 (0.0263)	−0.0227 (0.0239)	0.0884** (0.0316)
Extensive	−0.0210 (0.0359)	0.0405 (0.0294)	−0.0342 (0.0344)	−0.0478 (0.0343)	−0.0443 (0.0378)	−0.0480 (0.0414)
Imposition						
Limited/Moderate	−0.0456 (0.0318)	−0.0444* (0.0215)	−0.0178 (0.0230)	−0.0280 (0.0232)	−0.0194 (0.0205)	−0.0454 (0.0294)
Extensive	−0.123* (0.0516)	−0.0193 (0.0355)	−0.0688 (0.0377)	0.0172 (0.0297)	−0.0661* (0.0331)	−0.0598 (0.0459)
Threat* Imposition						
Limited/Moderate* Limited/Moderate	−0.0186 (0.0518)	−0.0141 (0.0419)	0.0672 (0.0438)	0.0320 (0.0464)	0.0713 (0.0494)	0.0176 (0.0704)
Limited/Moderate* Extensive	0.0728 (0.0563)	−0.0782 (0.0474)	0.0938 (0.0481)	0.0273 (0.0435)	0.151* (0.0699)	0.0388 (0.0813)
Extensive* Limited/Moderate	0.134* (0.0566)	0.0719 (0.0541)	0.103 (0.0619)	0.208*** (0.0607)	0.0744 (0.0674)	0.121 (0.113)
Extensive* Extensive	0.102 (0.0634)	0.0370 (0.0556)	0.104 (0.0541)	0.0845 (0.0452)	0.110* (0.0500)	0.0926 (0.0822)

Threat* Imposition[t+1]

Limited/Moderate* Limited/Moderate	0.0397	0.0882	0.00217	-0.0145	-0.0314	0.0655
	(0.0555)	(0.0543)	(0.0592)	(0.0665)	(0.0750)	(0.0499)
Limited/Moderate* Extensive	0.0163	-0.0387	-0.0515	-0.0771	-0.0595	0.0333
	(0.0661)	(0.0689)	(0.0662)	(0.0766)	(0.0793)	(0.0647)
Extensive* Limited/Moderate	0.0770	0.0605	0.0564	0.170	0.0734	0.104
	(0.0783)	(0.0882)	(0.0896)	(0.108)	(0.122)	(0.0917)
Extensive* Extensive	-0.0386	0.0746	0.147*	0.0630	0.0855	0.0556
	(0.0808)	(0.0622)	(0.0646)	(0.0791)	(0.109)	(0.0711)
F_i, F_j, F_t	No					
F_{it}, F_{jt}, F_{ij}	Yes					
N	199,473					
Adjusted R^2	0.937					

Notes: Estimated with ordinary least squares (OLS). Dependent variable: ln(trade). Robust standard errors (clustered by country pair) in parentheses. Parameter estimates for fixed effects omitted for brevity.

* $p < 0.05$; ** $p < 0.01$; *** $p < 0.001$.

Table 4.6
Extended PPML results with categorical threat and imposition variable and lags.

	(1) Contemporaneous	(2) Lag 1	(3) Lag 2	(4) Lag 3	(5) Lag 4	(6) Lag 5
Trade agreement	0.135*** (0.0258)					
Threat						
Limited/Moderate	0.00484 (0.0163)	0.000932 (0.0111)	-0.0182 (0.0102)	0.0148 (0.0110)	0.000477 (0.0112)	0.00177 (0.0159)
Extensive	0.00109 (0.0178)	-0.000289 (0.00993)	-0.00499 (0.00809)	-0.00110 (0.00866)	-0.0134 (0.00783)	-0.051*** (0.0136)
Imposition						
Limited/Moderate	0.0268* (0.0135)	-0.00205 (0.00675)	0.00107 (0.00742)	0.00266 (0.00742)	0.00731 (0.00700)	-0.00393 (0.0139)
Extensive	0.00379 (0.0228)	-0.00405 (0.0112)	-0.00446 (0.0137)	-0.0135 (0.0141)	0.0190 (0.0167)	0.0110 (0.0234)
Threat* Imposition						
Limited/Moderate* Limited/Moderate	-0.0539 (0.0336)	-0.0327 (0.0311)	0.00577 (0.0262)	-0.00318 (0.0288)	0.00663 (0.0239)	-0.00592 (0.0330)
Limited/Moderate* Extensive	0.0536 (0.0314)	0.0324 (0.0198)	0.0746** (0.0254)	0.0481 (0.0257)	0.0217 (0.0297)	0.0139 (0.0346)
Extensive* Limited/Moderate	-0.0221 (0.0243)	0.0154 (0.0167)	0.0116 (0.0201)	0.000596 (0.0182)	-0.0228 (0.0153)	-0.00883 (0.0255)
Extensive* Extensive	0.0188 (0.0276)	0.0412* (0.0182)	0.0369* (0.0172)	0.00378 (0.0172)	-0.00684 (0.0187)	0.00498 (0.0313)

Threat* Imposition[t+1]

Limited/Moderate* Limited/Moderate	-0.00001	0.00297	-0.00680	-0.0113	-0.0444	-0.0366
	(0.0349)	(0.0297)	(0.0305)	(0.0262)	(0.0298)	(0.0214)
Limited/Moderate* Extensive	-0.00681	-0.0494	-0.0887*	-0.0228	0.00159	-0.00622
	(0.0272)	(0.0349)	(0.0381)	(0.0316)	(0.0364)	(0.0223)
Extensive* Limited/Moderate	-0.0379	-0.00355	0.00739	0.0819*	0.0123	-0.0332
	(0.0401)	(0.0395)	(0.0385)	(0.0396)	(0.0418)	(0.0386)
Extensive* Extensive	-0.0447	-0.0292	-0.0154	-0.0371	-0.0403	-0.0666*
	(0.0304)	(0.0261)	(0.0297)	(0.0262)	(0.0347)	(0.0281)
F_{it}, F_{jt}, F_{ij}	Yes					
N	1,098,984					
R^2	0.9981					

Notes: Estimated with Poisson pseudo-maximum likelihood (PPML). Dependent variable: trade. Robust standard errors (clustered by country pair) in parentheses. Parameter estimates for fixed effects omitted for brevity.
* $p<0.05$; ** $p<0.01$; *** $p<0.001$.

impositions in the same year increase trade by 20 percent, but those imposed in the following year reduce trade by11 percent.

The magnitude and instability of the coefficients suggest that sanction impositions may have a delayed effect on trade flows. In other words, trade might only gradually respond to changes in sanction-imposed trade costs, akin to trade only gradually responding to decreases in trade costs resulting from trade agreements over the course of 5–10 years. We augment our model to include annual lags for up to five years to explore the extent to which delayed effects might affect trade flows.

The results for this *one* single regression are presented in table 4.5 for OLS and in table 4.6 for PPML. Note that, for each table, columns 2–6 provide the parameter estimates of THREAT, IMPOSITION, and the interaction terms, all of which have been lagged by one to five years. Strikingly, while the bulk of the parameter estimates have the expected (negative) sign, they tend to be small on average and not statistically significant. Re-estimating our models after excluding the top five senders (i.e., United States, Canada, Russia, United Kingdom, and India) from the sample or excluding all senders except the top five does not give rise to substantially different results (not reported for brevity).

4.5   Discussion and Conclusion

We set out to answer whether results from earlier economic sanction research stood the test of time, since developments in the field have been numerous in recent years. By including an extensive dataset on sanctions—both threats and impositions—and employing a theoretically consistent gravity equation, we find that sanctions are hardly as harmful as indicated in the previous literature. Where Hufbauer et al. (1997), Caruso (2003), and Yang et al. (2004) found decreases of up to 90 percent in bilateral trade, our findings suggest—if anything—a reduction of around 20 percent, owing to greater data coverage and improvements in the econometric strategy.

From our results, it follows that there is a difference between threatening to sanction a target state and actually sanctioning that state. Threats alone do not affect trade, while actual impositions decrease trade. The rich nature of the sanctions dataset provided by Morgan, Bapat, and Kobayashi (2014) provides several ways to further explore how sanction mechanisms may be effective in altering modes of international exchange. We now highlight several such avenues for future research.

A topic that has fallen outside the scope of this chapter but generated mixed results in the past is unilateral versus multilateral sanctions. Elliott, Hufbauer, and Oegg (2008) found that multilateral sanctions were less effective than unilateral sanctions, yet this result is counterintuitive and contrasts sharply with work by Bapat and Morgan (2009). Caruso (2003) found no significant difference in impact between unilateral and multilateral sanctions. An application with a state-of-the-art gravity equation is advisable.

Our findings do not indicate that sanction threats impact international trade. To some extent, we have argued that there could be good reasons to expect that markets anticipate future changes in trade policy and respond immediately when threats are issued. However, threats are not issued in a vacuum, and having a better understanding of the context may be important for capturing the pure effect of sanction threats on trade. For example, media coverage of the Crimea crisis was so extensive, and the event so significant, that it should not seem surprising that many observers expected the European Union and United States to impose sanctions even before the respective governments formally announced that they would consider imposing sanctions on Russia. In other cases, however, a government's announced threats may be less expected, even if only because of limited media coverage. Therefore, a refined measure of media coverage of events leading to sanctions being threatened and/or imposed, combined with novel measures of economic uncertainty (see Baker, Bloom, and Davis 2016), could improve the empirical setup employed in this chapter.

Another avenue for further research is to use monthly trade data and/or product-level data, rather than the annual aggregate data used in this chapter. The TIES dataset is sufficiently rich for it to be used to explore the impact of sanctions on a product level, yet such a project would be very data intensive. Furthermore, monthly data could provide a more fine-grained picture of how trade responds to announced threats and news of sanctions actually imposed.

One more issue that deserves further attention is the period following a sanction episode. We know that impositions decrease trade, but what happens when the sanctions are lifted? It would be interesting to find out how long it takes before trade returns to the level that existed before the episode to determine whether there is a "rebound effect." Perhaps trade does not recover for a longer period after the sanctions are already lifted, which would mean that the damage done by sanctions may be more substantial than we expect.

While research has studied the effect of sanctions on international trade, sanction data call into question whether impact studies should mainly be concerned with international trade flows. Travel bans, asset freezes, and cuts in foreign aid, for instance, may be more important for foreign direct investment (FDI) than for international trade. As the quality of data on bilateral FDI improves, future research may shed more light on how sanctions impact modes of international economic exchange in a broader sense than only international trade.

More generally, the question is whether sanctions should ultimately be perceived to have an effect on international trade at all. Ideally, sanctions incentivize targets to adopt a change in policy desired by the sender. From a policy perspective, the effectiveness of sanctions should therefore consider not the impact on economic exchange but rather the impact on changes in targets' policies. A challenge for applied research would be to construct consistent, time-varying, and transparent measures of government policy.

Economic sanctions will most likely remain in the arsenal of policymakers for the foreseeable future, and therefore scholars should continue to scrutinize them. This chapter calls into question whether sanctions or the threat to impose them really affect international trade to the extent assumed in the literature (our simple answer is no), and it signals several improvements that future research should incorporate to better understand if—and how—sanctions affect world trade.

Notes

The authors thank two anonymous referees, Dirk Akkermans, Stefan Goldbach, and participants at the 2016 CESifo Venice Summer Institute's Workshop on Disrupted Economic Relationships: Disasters, Sanctions, and Dissolutions, for helpful comments.

1. Throughout this chapter, we refer to economic sanctions, although we use the term interchangeably with "sanctions" for brevity.

2. Following convention, the sanctioning state is referred to as the "sender" and the sanctioned state as the "target."

3. For example, if Vietnam decides to place an import tariff on foreign computers to protect its domestic industry, this is not considered an economic sanction.

4. The formula used is [(natural number e to the power of the estimated coefficient)−1] multiplied by 100%.

References

Anderson, J. E., and E. van Wincoop. 2003. "Gravity with Gravitas: A Solution to the Border Puzzle." *American Economic Review* 93 (1): 170–192.

Baer, G. W. 1973. "Sanctions and Security: The League of Nations and the Italian–Ethiopian War, 1935–1936." *International Organization* 27 (2): 165–179.

Baier, S. L., and J. H. Bergstrand. 2007. "Do Free Trade Agreements Actually Increase Members' International Trade?" *Journal of International Economics* 71 (1): 72–95.

Baker, S. R., N. Bloom, and S. J. Davis. 2016. "Measuring Economic Policy Uncertainty." *Quarterly Journal of Economics* 131 (4): 1593–1636.

Baldwin, R., and D. Taglioni. 2007. "Trade Effects of the Euro: A Comparison of Estimators." *Journal of Economic Integration* 22 (4): 780–818.

Bapat, N. A., and T. Clifton Morgan. 2009. "Multilateral versus Unilateral Sanctions Reconsidered: A Test Using New Data." *International Studies Quarterly* 53 (4): 1075–1094.

Barber, J. 1979. "Economic Sanctions as a Policy Instrument." *International Affairs (Royal Institute of International Affairs)* 55 (3): 367–384.

Biglaiser, G., and D. Lektzian. 2011. "The Effect of Sanctions on US Foreign Direct Investment." *International Organization* 65 (3): 531–551.

Caruso, R. 2003. "The Impact of International Economic Sanctions on Trade: An Empirical Analysis." *Peace Economics, Peace Science and Public Policy* 9 (2): 1–29.

Correia, S. 2017. "Linear Models with High-Dimensional Fixed Effects: An Efficient and Feasible Estimator." Working paper. Durham, NC: Duke University. http://scorreia .com/research/hdfe.pdf.

Drezner, D. W. 2000. "Bargaining, Enforcement, and Multilateral Sanctions: When Is Cooperation Counterproductive?" *International Organization* 54 (1): 73–102.

Drury, A., and Y. Li. 2006. "US Economic Sanction Threats against China: Failing to Leverage Better Human Rights." *Foreign Policy Analysis* 2 (4): 307–324.

Early, B. R. 2009. "Sleeping with Your Friends' Enemies: An Explanation of Sanctions-Busting Trade." *International Studies Quarterly* 53 (1): 49–71.

Elliott, K. A., and G. C. Hufbauer. 1999. "Same Song, Same Refrain? Economic Sanctions in the 1990s." *American Economic Review* 89 (2): 403–408.

Elliott, K. A., G. C. Hufbauer, and B. Oegg. 2008. "Sanctions." In *The Concise Encyclopedia of Economics*. Library of Economics and Liberty. http://www.econlib.org/library/Enc /Sanctions.html.

European Union. 2015. "EU Sanctions against Russia over Ukraine Crisis." http:// europa.eu/newsroom/highlights/special-coverage/eu_sanctions/index_en.htm.

Feenstra, R. C. 2004. *Advanced International Trade: Theory and Evidence*. Princeton, NJ: Princeton University Press.

Galtung, J. 1967. "On the Effects of International Economic Sanctions, with Examples from the Case of Rhodesia." *World Politics* 19(3): 378–416.

Head, K., and T. Mayer. 2014. "Gravity Equations: Workhorse, Toolkit, and Cookbook." In *Handbook of International Economics*, vol. 4, edited by G. Gopinath, E. Helpman, and K. Rogoff, 131–195. Amsterdam: Elsevier.

Hoffmann, F. 1967. "The Functions of Economic Sanctions: A Comparative Analysis." *Journal of Peace Research* 4 (2): 140–159.

Hufbauer, G. C., K. A. Elliott, T. Cyrus, and E. Winston. 1997. *US Economic Sanctions: Their Impact on Trade, Jobs, and Wages*. Washington, DC: Peterson Institute for International Economics.

Hufbauer, G. C., J. J. Schott, and K. A. Elliott. 1990. *Economic Sanctions Reconsidered: History and Current Policy*. Washington, DC: Peterson Institute for International Economics.

International Monetary Fund (IMF). 2013. *Direction of Trade Statistics*. Washington, DC: International Monetary Fund.

Kaempfer, W. H., and A. D. Lowenberg. 1988. "The Theory of International Economic Sanctions: A Public Choice Approach." *American Economic Review* 78 (4): 786–793.

Kobayashi, Y. 2013. "Implementation of Economic Sanctions." PhD diss., Rice University. http://hdl.handle.net/1911/71975.

Kohl, T. 2014. "Do We Really Know That Trade Agreements Increase Trade?" *Review of World Economics* 150 (3): 1–27.

Lacy, D., and E. Niou. 2004. "A Theory of Economic Sanctions and Issue Linkage: The Roles of Preferences, Information, and Threats." *Journal of Politics* 66 (1): 25–42.

Larch, M., J. Wanner, Y. V. Yotov, and T. Zylkin. 2018. "Currency Unions and Trade: A PPML Re-assessment with High-dimensional Fixed Effects." *Oxford Bulletin of Economics and Statistics* (forthcoming). https://onlinelibrary.wiley.com/doi/abs/10.1111/obes.12283.

Li, Y., and A. C. Drury. 2004. "Threatening Sanctions When Engagement Would Be More Effective: Attaining Better Human Rights in China." *International Studies Perspectives* 5 (4): 378–394.

Mayer, T., and S. Zignago. 2011. "Notes on CEPII's Distance Measures (GeoDist)." CEPII Working Paper 2011-25. Paris: Centre d'Etudes Prospectives et d'Informations Internationales.

Morgan, T. C., N. Bapat, and Y. Kobayashi. 2014. "Threat and Imposition of Economic Sanctions 1945–2005: Updating the TIES Dataset." *Conflict Management and Peace Science* 31 (5): 541–558.

Morgan, T. C., N. Bapat, and V. Krustev. 2009. "The Threat and Imposition of Economic Sanctions, 1971–2000." *Conflict Management and Peace Science* 26 (1): 92–110.

Olson, R. S. 1979. "Economic Coercion in World Politics: With a Focus on North-South Relations." *World Politics* 31 (4): 471–494.

Pape, R. A. 1997. "Why Economic Sanctions Do Not Work." *International Security* 22 (2): 90–136.

Peksen, D. 2009. "Better or Worse? The Effect of Economic Sanctions on Human Rights." *Journal of Peace Research* 46 (1): 59–77.

Peksen, D., and A. C. Drury. 2010. "Coercive or Corrosive: The Negative Impact of Economic Sanctions on Democracy." *International Interactions* 36 (3): 240–264.

Santos Silva, J. M. C., and S. Tenreyro. 2006. "The Log of Gravity." *Review of Economics and Statistics* 88 (4): 641–658.

Schreiber, A. P. 1973. "Economic Coercion as an Instrument of Foreign Policy: US Economic Measures against Cuba and the Dominican Republic." *World Politics* 25 (3): 387–413.

Tinbergen, J. 1962. *Shaping the World Economy; Suggestions for an International Economic Policy Book*. New York: Twentieth Century Fund.

Van Bergeijk, P. A. G. 1989. "Success and Failure of Economic Sanctions." *Kyklos* 42 (3): 385–404.

Van Bergeijk, P. A. G. 2009. *Economic Diplomacy and the Geography of International Trade*. Cheltenham: Edward Elgar.

Von Amerongen, O. W. 1980. "Economic Sanctions as a Foreign Policy Tool?" *International Security* 5 (2): 159–167.

Wallensteen, P. 1983. "Economic Sanctions: Ten Modern Cases and Three Important Lessons." In *Dilemmas of Economic Coercion: Sanctions in World Politics*, edited by M. Nincic and P. Wallensteen, 87–129. New York: Praeger.

Wood, R. M. 2008. "'A Hand upon the Throat of the Nation': Economic Sanctions and State Repression, 1976–2001." *International Studies Quarterly* 52 (3): 489–513.

World Bank. 2013. *World Development Indicators*. http://data.worldbank.org/indicator.

Yang, J., H. Askari, J. Forrer, and H. Teegen. 2004. "US Economic Sanctions: An Empirical Study." *International Trade Journal* 18 (1): 23–62.

Yang, J., H. Askari, J. Forrer, and L. Zhu. 2009. "How Do US Economic Sanctions Affect EU's Trade with Target Countries?" *World Economy* 32 (8): 1223–1244.

5 Measuring Smartness: The Economic Impact of Targeted Sanctions against Russia

Daniel P. Ahn and Rodney D. Ludema

5.1 Introduction

While broad economic sanctions and trade embargoes have long been used as instruments of foreign policy, targeted sanctions focusing on specific individuals, entities, and transactions are relatively new. A prominent example of this new approach to sanction policy is the targeted sanction program of the United States and the European Union, imposed in response to Russia's annexation of Crimea and its alleged use of force in eastern Ukraine. The United States and European Union targeted a select list of Russian individuals and companies starting in March 2014. Over the next two years, the list of targets grew in scope and was met by Russian countersanctions on agricultural imports.

Understanding the impact of these targeted sanctions on Russia is essential to assessing their efficacy. Clouding the picture, however, is the fact that the conflict in 2014 roughly coincided with a series of powerful macroeconomic shocks, especially a dramatic decline in the price of oil (Russia's main export), which jolted both the Russian and world economies.

The difficulty inherent in attributing Russia's poor economic performance following sanctions to a single cause has allowed for a wide range of conflicting claims regarding the economic costs of the sanctions to Russia and to neighboring economies (principally members of the European Union). Opponents of sanctions, in particular, claim that sanctions have caused little pain to the specific targets while inflicting untold economic damage on the Russian people and on neighboring countries. Such assertions pose a challenge for the sanction policy, which was intended to be "smart" in the sense of hitting those responsible for the offending policy while inflicting minimal collateral damage.

The purpose of this chapter is to fill this information gap with empirical evidence. While several credible institutions provided model-based estimates of the potential impact of sanctions in the months after they went into effect, and others have chronicled the collapse of the Russian economy and its trade with the rest of the world, this chapter uses pre- and postsanction data to measure the actual effect of sanctions and countersanctions from the surrounding macroeconomic shocks.

To measure the "smartness" of the sanctions' impact, we proceed in two steps. First, we examine whether the sanctions hit the intended targets. We do this using data on individual firms from Bureau van Dijk's ORBIS database. To our knowledge, this chapter represents the only study that uses detailed firm-level data to understand the economic impacts on the targets themselves. Our main finding is that sanctioned companies are indeed harmed by sanctions relative to non-sanctioned peer companies. On average, a sanctioned company loses an estimated one-third of its operating revenue, over one-half of its asset value, and about one-third of its employees after being targeted compared to nonsanctioned companies. These estimates, which are large and appear highly robust statistically, suggest that targeted sanctions do have a powerful impact on the targets themselves.

Second, we examine the collateral damage. In particular, we consider the impact of the sanctions on Russia's GDP and on its imports from the European Union. In contrast to the firm-level approach, which fully controls for macroeconomic shocks with time-varying fixed effects, it is not possible to control for all conceivable confounders in the aggregate analysis. Instead, we dial back our ambition and consider only how much of the postsanction performance of the Russian economy can be explained either directly or indirectly by falling oil prices, with the residual capturing the combined effect of sanctions and any other exogenous factors. We find that oil price volatility explains the vast majority of the decline in Russia's GDP and import demand, with very little left to be explained by sanctions or other factors. Thus, either sanctions had only a small negative effect on these variables or other positive factors largely canceled out the effect of sanctions. The most plausible candidate factor would be the Russian policy response, which is probably not exogenous to sanctions.

Finally, we find that sanctions and countersanctions have had a small effect on the economies of most EU countries. Adding together the impacts of sanctions and countersanctions on exports—the main vulnerability—gives a median impact across EU countries of just –0.13 percent of GDP. The reasons for this are that (1) Russia generally accounts for a small share of total EU countries' exports and that (2) most of the decline in Russian imports is explained by lower oil prices and trend factors.

Economic sanctions are meant to signal international disapproval, deter further aggression, and create leverage in negotiations with the targeted country aimed at reversing the offending policies. Whether sanctions will ultimately accomplish these goals is a key question but is beyond the scope of this chapter.[1] If the success of the sanctions depends on delivering a focused impact with minimal collateral damage, our results suggest that the targeted sanctions are acting as advertised.

The remainder of the chapter proceeds as follows. Section 5.2 reviews the literature on the economic impact of sanctions against Russia. Section 5.3 provides a description of the targeted sanction program. Section 5.4 presents the empirical methodology and analysis and results of the firm-level approach, along with various robustness checks. Section 5.5 considers the collateral damage to the broader economic performance of the Russian and EU economies. Section 5.6 presents our conclusions.

5.2   Literature Review

The literature, both theoretical and empirical, on economic sanctions is vast. However, most empirical studies cover the period when policymakers invoked comprehensive sanctions involving broad countrywide trade embargoes rather than selective sanctions against specific targets.

The academic literature on these comprehensive sanctions, such as those against Iraq after the 1990–1991 Gulf War, has tended to give only mixed support for the effectiveness of sanctions. Many studies have focused on the secondary effects of sanctions on corruption and humanitarian consequences without matching political dividends. Recent surveys are provided in Hufbauer et al. (2007) and Drezner (2011).

Empirical studies of targeted sanctions are much fewer, partially because of the relatively short history of targeted sanction programs and the related paucity of examples involving sanction programs that are purely targeted instead of becoming part of a broader comprehensive sanction program. Indeed, US-EU targeted sanctions against Russia in the wake of the Ukraine crisis represent a fairly rare example of purely targeted sanctions against a middle-income economy fairly well integrated into the global economic and financial system.

Economists attempting to empirically estimate the impact of sanctions on Russia face the challenge of disentangling the impact of sanctions from the confounding effects of the broader political uncertainty stemming from the Ukraine crisis and the dramatic drop in oil prices discussed earlier. However, most studies conclude that oil prices were far more important in explaining Russia's post-2014 macroeconomic weakness, with a relatively small effect ascribed to sanctions.

A 2015 International Monetary Fund (IMF) report, using a generic macroeconomic model, forecasted that sanctions could reduce Russia's real output by about 1 to 1.5 percent of GDP via weaker investment and consumption. A World Bank (2015) study similarly argues that sanctions against Russia and its countersanctions in response may have affected investment and consumption, but it does not provide any specific numbers. Neither of these studies attempts to directly measure the economic impact of sanctions.

Dreger et al. (2015) used a VAR model featuring oil prices, the ruble exchange rate, and a sanction news index to argue that the oil price drop was the primary driver of the ruble's depreciation but that sanction news surprises may have had some impact on the ruble's conditional volatility. The study does not consider the effect on GDP growth or imports. Tuzova and Qayum (2016) present another reduced-form VAR model featuring a variety of Russian macroeconomic variables, including GDP, the real exchange rate, inflation, fiscal and consumption expenditures, and external trade, to argue that oil prices were the main cause of Russia's poor macroeconomic outlook. Moret et al. (2016) also looked at country-level trade data and compared trading volumes between Russia and the European Union pre- and postcrisis and concluded that the Baltic states suffered the greatest relative losses, similar to what we find in section 5.5 of this chapter.[2]

Lacking from all of this literature is the use of firm-level data to empirically estimate the impact on the economic performance of the targets themselves. The paper closest to our chapter is Stone (2016), which uses an event study methodology to study the impact of sanctions news events on the asset prices of sanctioned sectors and the 11 largest energy firms and banks. Stone finds a negative impact on the asset prices of targeted sectors compared to nontargeted sectors but no significant difference between targeted and nontargeted firms within a sector.

Compared to the previous literature, our chapter is unique in several respects. First, ours is the first to use detailed firm-level data to empirically estimate the impact on the real performance, such as operating revenue and employment, of targeted firms themselves. Second, we consider a comprehensive sample of firms, including all targeted firms (not only financial and energy firms) as well as firms associated with sanctioned individuals. Third, we find strong evidence that sanctioned firms are indeed harmed by sanctions relative to their nonsanctioned peers.

5.3   Description of Targeted Sanctions

5.3.1   Overview of US and EU Targeted Sanction Policy against Russia

On March 6, 2014, US president Barack Obama declared a national emergency and issued the first of four executive orders to deal with the threat posed by the situation in Ukraine, including the actions of the government of the Russian Federation. Issued in March and December of 2014, these executive orders provided the authority for various departments of the US government, including Treasury, State, Commerce, and others, to impose targeted sanctions, primarily on Russian entities.[3] The US Department of the Treasury's Office of Foreign Asset Control is the primary entity responsible for implementing targeted sanctions. The targets are determined by the secretary of the treasury, in consultation with the secretary of state, after a careful investigation and vetting process.

Targeted sanctions by the United States with respect to the Ukraine/ Russia crisis fall into two broad categories:

• SDN sanctions: blocking sanctions against individuals and entities on the List of Specially Designated Nationals and Blocked Persons (SDN).

• SSI sanctions: partial sanctions against entities operating in the financial, energy, and defense sectors of the Russian economy listed on the Sectoral Sanctions Identification (SSI) List.

Designated SDN entities and individuals face asset freezes and travel bans in the United States, and unless otherwise authorized or exempt, all trade and financial transactions and other activities by US persons (individuals or entities) with these designated SDN individuals and entities are prohibited.[4]

Meanwhile, the SSI entities represent those entities for which US persons are prohibited from engaging in certain transactions. Notably, US persons cannot transact in or issue debt with a maturity longer than 30 days or acquire new equity with targeted companies in the Russian financial sector or the Russian defense sector. Similar restrictions also apply to transactions in or issuance of debt with a maturity longer than 90 days with targeted companies in the Russian energy sector.

Furthermore, US persons are prohibited from transacting in certain technologies and services related to deepwater, Arctic offshore, or shale oil activity with the Russian energy sector.

The European Union also developed a targeted sanction policy in the form of EU Council Regulations starting in March 2014.[5] From these EU Council Regulations, the European Union maintains a categorization of targeted sanctions similar to that of the United States in response to the events in Ukraine and Russia in 2014:

• Restricted Measures List: Asset freezes and visa bans apply to entities and individuals designated on the EU Restricted Measures List.

• Sectoral Sanctions List: The EU also prohibits EU nationals and companies from transacting in equity or debt instruments having a maturity exceeding 30 days with entities on the EU Sectoral Sanctions List.

Similar to the United States with its sectoral sanctions, the European Union imposed an embargo on trade in arms and dual-use goods and technology with Russia, covering all items on the EU common military and dual-use lists, as well as an embargo on the export of certain energy-related equipment and technology for offshore deepwater, Arctic, or shale oil exploration and production.

5.3.2 Identifying US and EU Sanction Targets
This section discusses the number of targets selected by the United States and the European Union for targeted sanctions. Figure 5.1 shows,

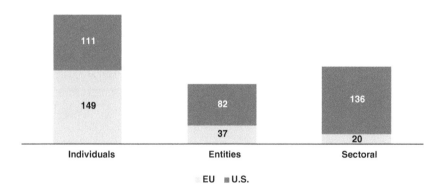

Figure 5.1
Overview of US and EU sanctions against Russia. *Sources:* US Treasury Office of Foreign Asset Control and Council of the European Union.

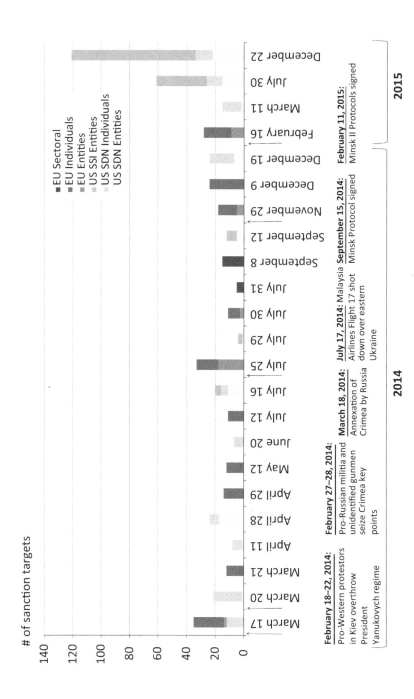

Figure 5.2
Timeline of US and EU targeted sanction designations. *Source:* US Treasury Office of Foreign Asset Control, Council of the European Union, and BBC.

as of July 1, 2016, the overview of entities or individuals explicitly sanctioned by US and EU authorities, beginning on March 17, 2014.

Altogether, the United States has designated 111 individuals and 82 entities on its SDN List as related to its Russia/Ukraine-related sanction program. Also, the United States has explicitly designated 136 entities on its SSI List as facing sectoral sanctions. Meanwhile, as of July 1, 2016, the European Union had placed 149 individuals and 37 entities on its EU Restricted Measures List and placed 20 entities on its EU Sectoral Sanctions List. Figure 5.2 shows the timeline of these sanctions.

We have classified sanctioned individuals into two categories: political and business figures. A political figure is an individual whose primary occupation appears to be political rather than commercial in nature, such as a legislator, a government official, or a military commander. However, a named individual would be classified as a business figure (even if he or she had worked in public service) if the individual could be identified as being "associated" with a company according to the Bureau van Dijk standardized positions database. These associations include being part of corporate management, on the board of directors, or a major shareholder.

According to this classification, of the 111 individuals on the US SDN List, 87 appear to be purely political figures, while 24 appear to have business associations. Hence, of the US SDN individuals, about one-fourth are business figures. Meanwhile, the EU sanctions against individuals are skewed more heavily toward political figures. Of the 149 individuals on the EU Restricted List, only 6 have business associations.

We subsequently identified 269 companies as being "associated," either in the past or present, with a US- or EU-sanctioned individual. Figures 5.3, 5.4, and 5.5 present Venn diagrams of the space of US- and EU-sanctioned entities by category, including associations with sanctioned individuals.

As discussed earlier, this tabulation captures those entities or individuals explicitly listed by the US and EU governments as facing sectoral restrictions. However, both the United States and European Union follow a 50 percent ownership rule whereby those subsidiaries 50 percent or more owned, directly or indirectly, by an explicitly sanctioned entity also face the same sanctions. The United States appears to be more forward-leaning in explicitly identifying subsidiaries that should also face sanctions according to this rule.[6]

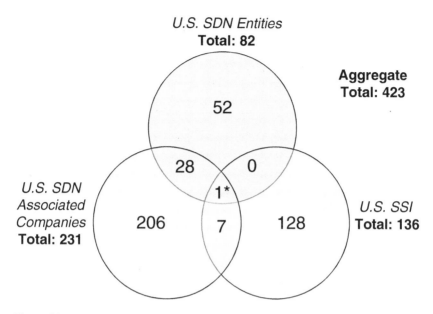

Figure 5.3
US sanctioned entities by type. *Source:* US Treasury Office of Foreign Asset Control.

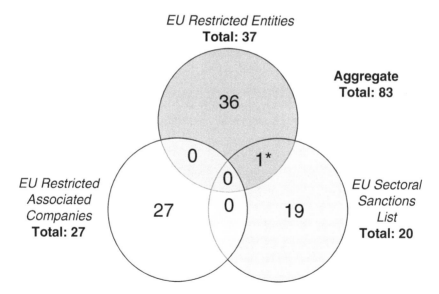

Figure 5.4
EU sanctioned entities by type. *Source:* Council of the European Union.

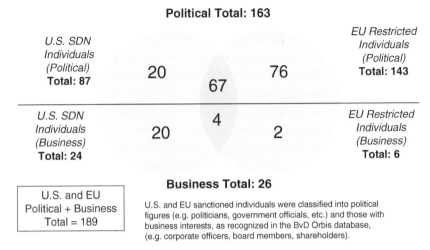

Figure 5.5
US SDN and EU restricted individuals, by type. *Sources:* US Treasury Office of Foreign Asset Control, Council of the European Union.

Having described the US and EU targeted sanctions policy against primarily Russian targets in response to the crisis, we turn next to estimating the economic impact of these sanctions on the targets themselves.

5.4 Firm-Level Economic Impact of Targeted Sanctions

In this section, we provide our methodological specification and the results of our empirical analysis of the effects of targeted sanctions.

5.4.1 Data

Our firm-level approach requires a careful examination of the sanctions lists of the United States and the European Union along with firm-level data covering sanctioned and nonsanctioned companies. Our firm-level data come from the Bureau van Dijk (BvD) ORBIS database,[7] and we track a universe of 78,381 companies. These include 433 specific companies identified as being sanctioned that are also present in the BvD database. The remainder is a control group of peer companies, constructed by collecting all companies that share the same home country and sector of business operation as the sanctioned companies in the global BvD database.[8]

Table 5.1
Cross-sectional regression results.

	(1)	(2)	(3)	(4)
Variables	d_Active	lOpRev	lAsset	lEmp
d_Sanc	−0.0229**	−0.3353***	−0.8052***	−0.3581***
	(0.009)	(0.130)	(0.091)	(0.062)
Observations	235,143	9,383	20,080	13,896
R^2	0.051	0.085	0.143	0.304
Number of id	78,381	5,872	9,602	6,871

Note: Robust standard errors in parentheses.
* $p < 0.1$; ** $p < 0.05$; *** $p < 0.01$.

For each company, we track its home country location, sector of business operation (according to the four-digit NAICS code specification), and total operating revenue, total assets, and number of employees for the years 2013, 2014, and 2015. We also track the status of the firm, whether it remains active or whether it has become bankrupt, liquidated or dissolved, or changed to some other inactive status.

5.4.2   Empirical Methodology

Our econometric specification is a standard difference-in-differences approach,

$$\ln y_{isct} = \alpha_i + \lambda_{st} + \theta_{ct} + \beta d_{it} + \varepsilon_{isct}, \tag{5.1}$$

where the subscript i denotes company identification, s denotes sector, c denotes country, and t denotes time period.

The dependent variable y_{isct} on the left-hand side tracks the particular firm's financial metrics of total operating revenue, total asset value, and number of employees. Also, we construct a dummy variable, which equals 1 if the firm is active in that year and 0 if the firm loses its active status because of bankruptcy, liquidation, or another reason. The variables α_i capture company fixed effects, λ_{st} capture sector-time fixed effects, θ_{ct} capture country-time fixed effects, and d_{it} are the sanction treatment dummies. Our sanction dummies d_{it} capture those periods when firm i faces any of our three categories of targeted sanctions by either US or EU authorities.

Table 5.1 displays our headline results, which show the coefficients from regressing the log operating revenue, log assets, and log employee

Table 5.2
Headline sanctions' impact on targeted companies.

	Estimated average impact on indicators of financial health			
	Higher probability of bankruptcy	Fall in operating revenue	Fall in total assets	Fall in number of employees
Sanctions on average target company	2.3%**	28.5%***	55.3%***	30.1%***

* $p<0.1$; ** $p<0.05$; *** $p<0.01$.

count on our sanction dummy d_Sanc. Only for d_Active, our dummy indicating firm active status, do we show the results of a probit regression. The number of observations can vary across regression variables as a result of missing or nonreported data for many companies.

We note that this result arises after controlling for both sector-time and country-time fixed effects, which should eliminate oil factors and other factors that may apply to companies in particular sectors or countries. The sectors are determined by the four-digit NAICS core code, providing a high degree of granularity. The robustness of our results to these controls lends confidence in our results.

Table 5.2 converts the log coefficients in table 5.1 into the estimated average impact on the firm performance metrics. We find that targeted sanctions do have a statistically significant negative impact on the firm's financial health relative to nonsanctioned peer companies. After facing targeted sanctions, a company on average faces a 2 percent increased likelihood of losing its active status. Also, its operating revenue falls by about 30 percent, total assets by 55 percent, and employee count by about 30 percent compared to nonsanctioned companies. These results are highly statistically significant. The significance is at the 1 percent confidence level for all of our financial health variables with the exception of the status dummy variable, which is significant at the 5 percent level.

Although the magnitudes of the estimated losses are large, these results should be interpreted with caution. In particular, one should not simply add the firm-level losses of all targeted companies together to arrive at a macro-level impact. The reasons are twofold. First, the effect does not necessarily apply uniformly to all targeted companies, and may be smaller in proportional magnitude for larger-sized targets. This is also in part because the largest companies tended to face only sectoral sanctions, which are deliberately designed not to have a large immediate impact but affect their long-term health via their access to credit and technology. This is one reason why the concentrated impact at the firm level does not necessarily translate into a large macroeconomic impact, despite the fact that the target list contains some of the largest Russian state-owned enterprises.

Second, the results capture the *differential* impact of sanctions on the performance of targeted companies compared to nontargeted companies. They do not measure factors that might equally affect all firms in a sector or a country. For example, if sanctions contributed to a depreciation in the ruble, and this depreciation improved the performance of all firms, whether specifically targeted or not, this impact of sanctions would not be reflected in the performance differential exploited by the regression. For this reason, a separate analysis needs to be done to capture macroeconomic impacts of the sanctions, as discussed in section 5.5.

5.4.3 Robustness Checks

An important assumption underlying our difference-in-differences methodology is the "parallel trends" assumption, that targeted firms would have experienced the same average change in performance as their nontargeted peers (in the same sector and country) had they not been targeted. This assumption could be violated if, for example, targeted companies tend to grow more slowly than nontargeted peers for reasons other than sanctions.

It seems unlikely that there is an inherent bias for slow-growing firms to be targeted. However, targeted firms were larger on average than their nontargeted peers in 2013. If hypothetically larger firms tend to grow more slowly than smaller firms, conditional on survival, then the parallel trends assumption may be violated, and our estimates could be biased.

To address this concern, we use a matching estimator. For each targeted firm, a matching algorithm is used to find the nontargeted firm that is most similar to the targeted firm in terms of industry, country, and size in 2013, measured by assets.[9] We then compare the average change in performance of all such matched pairs between the pre- and postsanction years. For robustness, we consider two different matching estimators: a nearest-neighbor matching estimator, which minimizes the Mahalanobis distance between matched pairs, and a propensity score matching estimator. The two estimators produce practically the same results.

Table 5.3
Matching estimation results.

	(1)	(2)	(3)
Variables	DlOpRev	DlAsset	DlEmp
	Propensity score matching		
ATE	−0.8816*	−1.7081***	−0.6123***
Standard error	(0.501)	(0.084)	(0.053)
	Nearest-neighbor matching		
ATE	−0.8503**	−1.5226***	−0.4455**
Standard error	(0.417)	(0.124)	(0.176)
Observations	2,817	6,950	6,408

*$p < 0.1$; **$p < 0.05$; ***$p < 0.01$.

One complication in implementing this approach is that targeted firms are sanctioned at different times, some in 2014 and some in 2015. Thus, we need to be careful that each matched pair is compared across the same years, depending on when the targeted firm was sanctioned. For firms sanctioned in 2014 and their matched peers, we compare the difference in performance between 2013 and the 2014–2015 average. For firms sanctioned in 2015 and their matched peers, we compare the difference in performance between the 2013–2014 average and 2015.

The results in table 5.3, which show the average treatment effect (ATE), are in line with our headline results reported in table 5.1. In each case, the impact of sanctions is to reduce the performance of targeted firms relative to their nontargeted peers. The results are statistically significant, and the magnitudes are consistently larger than in table 5.1. This indicates that our difference-in-differences estimates are not only robust but likely conservative.

5.5   Collateral Damage

In this section, we consider the impact of sanctions on Russian GDP and on its imports from the European Union, both of which declined substantially after the imposition of sanctions. We are interested in the contribution of sanctions to these declines, as opposed to contributions from other macroeconomic shocks, such as the major decline in oil prices. The answer is critical to the question of collateral damage, which is the second of the two criteria for "smartness."

In principle, sanctions can directly impact a country's aggregate supply by affecting firms' access to credit or technology or by creating uncertainty for investors (both domestic and foreign), leading to capital flight and the postponement of investments and purchases of durable goods. Sanctions may also impact aggregate demand, by increasing the cost of borrowing or increasing precautionary savings. However, these effects may have been mitigated in the short run by ruble depreciation and other government policies—such as expansionary fiscal policy and Russia's own embargo on agricultural imports—which passed the burden in the form of higher inflation and a larger budget deficit.

As discussed, the main empirical problem is that, while all of these macroeconomic consequences were present in the Russian economy in the immediate aftermath of sanctions, all of them could be explained by other factors. As seen in figure 5.6, the world oil price (Brent) fell from over $100 per barrel in the second quarter of 2014 to under $60 by the end of 2014, and declined further in the second half of 2015. A common rule of thumb for oil exporters suggests a $40 drop in the

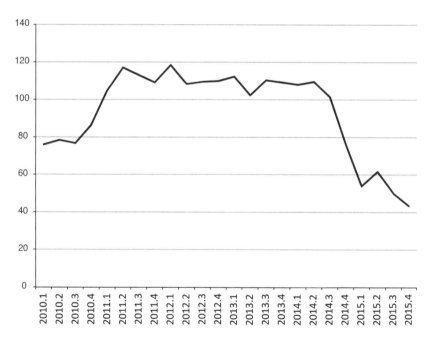

Figure 5.6
World oil price for Brent Crude, in US dollars, by quarter, 2010–2015.

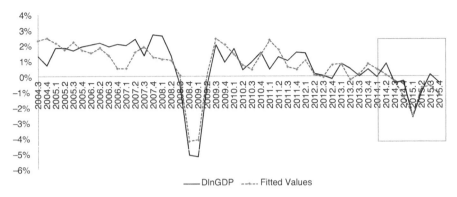

Figure 5.7
Actual versus predicted Russian real GDP growth.

world price of oil should shrink energy-dependent Russia's GDP by
4–5 percent.

But even before oil prices began falling, Russia's growth had been on
the decline in recent years (figure 5.7, black line), and growth projections
were downgraded beginning in late 2013, when the Russian regime's
weak commitment to structural reform became clear. For example, the
IMF nearly halved its forecast for Russia's 2014 growth rate between April
2013 and January 2014, well before the Crimea aggression. Real GDP
growth fell from 1.2 percent in 2013 to 0.7 percent in 2014 and –3.7 percent
in 2015 before recovering slightly. From peak to trough, real GDP fell
about 5 percent. Import demand in US dollars was about 37 percent lower.

5.5.1 Strategy for Estimating the Macroeconomic Impact of Sanctions

Many factors can determine Russian macroeconomic variables such as
GDP growth and import demand. These include oil prices, sanctions,
and other factors, such as consumer sentiment, investor expectations,
exchange rates, and so on.

Suppose we can approximate the relationship with a linear function
of the form $g = \beta_0 + \beta_1 e + \beta_2 s + \beta_3 X$, where g is the Russian macroeconomic variable of interest, such as real GDP growth or import
demand, e measures the change in oil price (possibly including lags),
s is a sanction policy indicator, X is a vector of other factors, and $\{\beta_i\}$ is
a set of parameters.

Oil prices and sanctions are exogenous to the Russian economy,
whereas X contains many elements that are potentially influenced by oil

prices and sanctions. Similarly, we can represent X as $X = \delta_0 + \delta_1 e + \delta_2 s + \delta_3 Z$, where Z is a set of exogenous factors uncorrelated with e or s.

Putting these equations together gives a reduced-form equation of $g = (\beta_0 + \beta_3 \delta_0) + (\beta_1 + \beta_3 \delta_1) \; e + (\beta_2 + \beta_3 \delta_2) \; s + \beta_3 \delta_3 Z$, which states that GDP growth is influenced both directly and indirectly by oil prices and sanctions and separately by exogenous factors Z. Assuming the parameters of this model are stable, we can estimate a regression, $g_t = \gamma_0 + \gamma_1 e_t + \varepsilon_t$, over the decade prior to the imposition of sanctions to obtain an unbiased estimate of the impact (direct and indirect) of oil prices on growth, where $\gamma_0 = (\beta_0 + \beta_3 \delta_0) + \beta_3 \delta_3 \overline{Z}$, $\gamma_1 = (\beta_1 + \beta_3 \delta_1)$, and ε_t is a mean-zero error.

Finally, letting T denote the sanction period, $\hat{g}_t = \hat{\gamma}_0 + \hat{\gamma}_1 e_T$ gives an unbiased out-of-sample estimate of the oil component of growth in period T. It follows that $E(g_T - \hat{g}_T) = \widehat{(\beta_2 + \beta_3 \delta_2)} s_T$. In other words, the difference between actual growth during the sanction period and our oil-based out-of-sample forecast gives an unbiased estimate of the direct and indirect effects of sanctions on growth. Of course, it is possible that regime shifts in the underlying coefficients may have occurred, or that there may have been deviations in other exogenous factors (i.e., deviations in Z) that have confounded the sanctions' impact at exactly the same time. While these are possibilities, they are unlikely.

5.5.2 Impact on GDP Growth

We begin with an extremely simple reduced-form model, which attempts to explain quarterly variation in Russia's real GDP growth between 2004 and 2014 as a function of the log change in world oil prices (both current and one period lagged), a linear time trend (to capture Russia's long-term slowdown), a season dummy (winter), and a global financial crisis dummy (2007-Q4 to 2009-Q2).[10] We then use this model to conduct an out-of-sample prediction of Russia's quarterly GDP growth in 2014 and 2015 and ask how well this prediction matches the actual growth, leaving the remainder as what is left to be explained by other factors such as sanctions.

The regression (table 5.4, column 1) explains about three-quarters of the historical variation in Russia's GDP, and all explanatory variables except the winter season dummy are statistically significant.[11] Figure 5.8 shows actual GDP growth compared to that predicted by the model. Most of the deviation occurs in the first half of the sample period. Indeed, if the model is estimated from 2007 onward, instead of from 2004, the overall model fit rises to over 85 percent. Of particular interest

Table 5.4
Reduced-form macro model.

	(1)	(2)
Variables	Dlngdp	Dlnimp
Dlnoil	0.051***	0.28
	−0.01	−0.036
Dlnoil_01	0.043***	0.304***
	−0.009	−0.059
Time	−0.0002*	−0.001*
	(−0.0001)	(−0.001)
Crisis	−0.013***	−0.038*
	−0.004	(−0.02)
Winter	0.004	0.056***
	−0.003	−0.015
Constant	0.021**	0.058
	−0.008	(−0.041)
Observations	40	40
R^2	0.77	0.77

Note: Robust standard errors in parentheses.
* $p<0.1$; ** $p<0.05$; *** $p<0.01$.

is the out-of-sample prediction in 2014 and 2015. The model fits almost exactly in 2014 and actually underpredicts GDP growth in late 2015.

Hence, we find that oil prices managed to drive the majority of Russian economic performance since 2004, with sanctions playing a secondary role compared to oil prices at the macroeconomic level. From peak to trough, Russia's real GDP declined by about 5 percent, and therefore at most 20 percent of that, or 1 percent of GDP, can potentially be explained by sanctions.[12]

Of course, this is not definitive proof. It could be that, absent sanctions, the model would have underpredicted postsanction GDP growth even more than it does. Yet, given its historical accuracy, we find it implausible that the statistical relationship between oil and Russian economic output would dramatically shift in the out-of-sample forecast.

5.5.3   Import Demand and EU Effects

The main economic vulnerability of EU countries to sanctions is their exports to Russia, which have declined sharply since mid-2014. However, as with its GDP, Russia's imports from the European Union could also be driven by oil prices and the deterioration in Russia's economic performance caused by domestic policies. One key determinant of a coun-

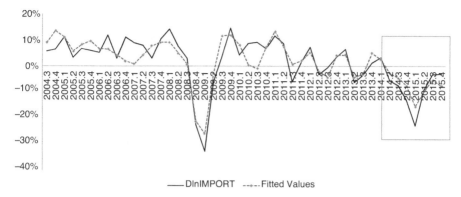

Figure 5.8
Actual versus predicted Russian import demand growth.

try's imports is its national income, which we have already seen is well explained by oil prices. Another is the relative price of imports, which is affected by exchange rates, which are in turn affected by oil prices. Given that energy exports account for the vast majority of Russia's total export revenue, it is reasonable to assume that the depreciation of the ruble in 2014 was largely driven by the oil price decline and therefore indirectly captured in our regression.

Note that Russia's recession and depreciation would likely affect its demand for imports in general, not exclusively from the European Union or other sanctioning countries. The ruble declined strongly against all major currencies. The only exceptions were countries of the Commonwealth of Independent States (CIS), which because of their dependence on exports to Russia devalued their own currencies to avoid losing ground. However, it is also possible that sanctions, and certainly Russia's countersanctions, had a discriminatory effect, reducing Russia's imports specifically from the European Union (and other sanctioning countries).

In what follows, we repeat the exercise of the previous subsection for Russia's total imports to get an estimate of how much of the decline needs explaining after oil prices are taken into account. From this we construct an estimate of the nondiscriminatory effect of sanctions. We then adjust our estimates to account for countersanctioned agricultural products, which are clearly subject to discrimination.[13]

The results are found in table 5.4, column 2, which is quite similar to the GDP model. Figure 5.8 shows the out-of-sample prediction. Here we find that in the first year of the sanction period, the model predicts a smaller decline in Russia's total imports than actually occurred.

Adding up the quarterly gaps between predicted and actual, we can say that 80 percent of the difference in total imports between 2015 and 2013 is explained by oil. This amounts to about $26 billion in imports. The rest is caused by other factors, one of which could be sanctions.

For countersanctioned agricultural products, we know that Russia's embargo directly suppresses imports specifically from the European Union (as well as the United States, Norway, and Australia). Nevertheless, our model is useful for determining how much of the decline can be attributed to the embargo and how much would have occurred anyway, as the result of lower oil prices. If we assume that agricultural imports from the European Union would have declined in proportion to all other imports absent the countersanctions, and that 80 percent of that decline was driven by oil, then the effect of countersanctions can be computed as a remainder.

As a final step, we distribute the decline in imports to each EU country according to its 2013 level of exports to Russia and express the declines as a percentage of each EU country's GDP. The results are reported in figures 5.9 and 5.10. The key result is that the impact of sanctions on the exports of most EU countries is quite small.

We find that sanctions and countersanctions have had a small effect on the economies of most EU countries. Adding together the impacts of sanctions and countersanctions on exports—the main vulnerability—gives a median impact across EU countries of just –0.13 percent of GDP (figure 5.9). The reasons for this are that (1) Russia generally accounts for a small share of total EU countries' exports and that (2) most of the decline in Russian imports is explained by lower oil prices and trend factors.

The countries that seem to be impacted the most by sanctions are the Baltic states. Lithuania has been hit the hardest, with a sanction-induced drop in exports of about 2.5 percent of GDP. The exports of Estonia and Latvia fell by around 1 percent. (Incidentally, these countries are also strong supporters of sanctions.) The hit on exports for all other EU countries ranges from –0.01 percent to –0.3 percent of GDP.

To summarize, at the macroeconomic level, given that oil price fluctuations alone can account for 80 percent or more of the drop in Russian economic output and import demand, sanctions appear to have had a second-order impact, translating into relatively small spillover effects on the economies of the European Union.

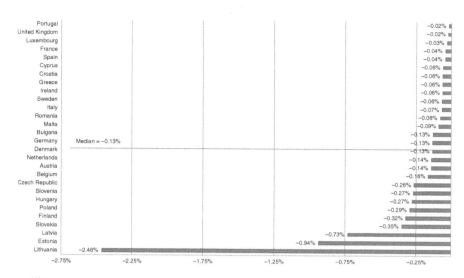

Figure 5.9
Estimated decline in EU exports to Russia from sanctions and countersanctions, as a percentage of GDP. *Source:* OCE estimates of export declines from sanctions and countersanctions, Global Trade Atlas, IMF World Economic Outlook 2015.
Note: Decline from 2013 to 2015.

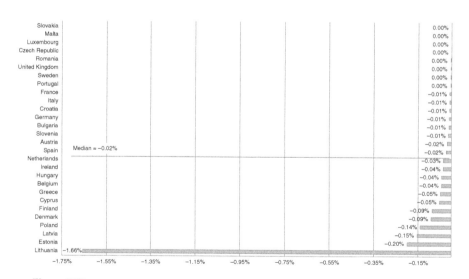

Figure 5.10
Estimated decline in EU exports to Russia from Countersanctions, as a percentage of GDP. *Source:* OCE estimates of export declines from countersanctions, Global Trade Atlas, IMF World Economic Outlook 2015.
Note: Decline from 2013 to 2015.

5.6   Conclusion

In 2014, the United States and the European Union deployed targeted sanctions against Russia in response to the crisis in Ukraine. However, at the same time, macroeconomic shocks, notably a fall in the price of oil, obscured the economic impact of sanctions. This allowed partisans to make conflicting claims on the economic efficacy of sanctions, with critics claiming a limited impact on the targets while inflicting large damage on collateral bystanders and neighboring economies.

Using firm-level empirical data, we find strong evidence that sanctions affected the financial health of the targeted firms. Targeted sanctions by the United States and European Union appear to be "smart" in the sense of hitting the intended targets with significant economic damage while causing minimal collateral damage.

Notes

1. See Harrell (2015) for further discussion on the policy implications drawn from the Russian sanction experience.

2. Crozet and Hinz (2016) use detailed monthly trade data at both the country level and firm level for France to estimate the impact of sanctions on trading activity. They find large impacts on trade (as much as $60 billion collectively) between Russia and many EU economies. The authors recognize that most of this effect is caused by oil prices, Russian economic underperformance, and political uncertainty. The effect from targeted sanctions appears to be at most $3 billion.

3. These are executvie orders 13660 (March 6, 2014), 13661 (March 16, 2014), 13662 (March 20, 2014), and 13685 (December 19, 2014).

4. 50% Rule: Transactions with an entity that is 50 percent or more owned, whether individually or in the aggregate, directly or indirectly, by an SDN designated entity or individual, is also blocked, regardless of whether the entity itself is listed.

5. EU Council Regulations 269/2014, 284/2014, 433/2014, 833/2014, and 960/2014.

6. In ongoing research, we are investigating how much overlap there would be if we could include those companies implicitly sanctioned via this ownership rule, and whether those companies that are implicitly sanctioned also face the same economic effects as those explicitly sanctioned.

7. More information about the database can be found on Bureau van Dijk's homepage at www.bvdinfo.com.

8. Bureau van Dijk assigns a unique identification number that tracks a company through name and ownership changes.

9. We use NAICS industries rather than four-digit NAICS sectors to guarantee that the matching estimation satisfies the common support assumption (i.e., that there are both sanctioned and nonsanctioned firms in each industry). For the same reason, we consider

only two countries, Russia and Ukraine, which together comprise 97 percent of the companies in our sample.

10. We attempted multiple specifications using the ruble-to-dollar exchange rate, Russian consumer sentiment, and other variables and found that the results are almost identical, with no additional explanatory power, likely for the reasons discussed earlier.

11. The insignificance of the winter dummy is not surprising, given that quarterly real GDP is already seasonally adjusted.

12. Interestingly, this impact of 1 percent of GDP is similar to the IMF's estimate of a 1–1.5 percent impact on GDP from a completely different methodology.

13. It is also possible that noncountersanctioned products are affected by sanctions in a discriminatory way beyond the scope of this study and that a more disaggregated approach, such as that of Crozet and Hinz (2016), is required.

References

Crozet, M., and J. Hinz. 2016. "Collateral Damage: The Impact of Russia Sanctions on Sanctioning Countries' Exports." CEPII Working Paper 2016-16. Paris: Centre d'Etudes Prospectives et d'Informations Internationales.

Dreger, C., J. Fidrmuc, K. Kholodilin, and D. Ulbricht. 2015. "The Ruble between the Hammer and the Anvil: Oil Prices and Economic Sanctions." DIW Berlin Discussion Paper 1488. Berlin: DIW Berlin, German Institute for Economic Research.

Drezner, D. 2011. "Sanctions Sometimes Smart: Targeted Sanctions in Theory and Practice." *International Studies Review* 13 (1):96–108.

Harrell, P. 2015. *Lessons from Russia for the Future of Sanctions*. Economic Statecraft Series. Washington, DC: Center for a New American Security.

Hufbauer, G., C. Jeffrey, J. Schott, K. A. Elliott, and B. Oegg. 2007. *Economic Sanctions Reconsidered*, 3rd ed. Washington, DC: Peterson Institute for International Economics.

International Monetary Fund. 2015. *Staff Report for the Article IV Consultation: Russian Federation*. Washington, DC: International Monetary Fund.

Moret, E., T. Biersteker, F. Giumelli, C. Portela, M. Veber, D. Jarosz, and C. Bobocea. 2016. *The New Deterrent: International Sanctions against Russia over the Ukraine Crisis*. Geneva: Institute of International and Development Studies in Geneva.

Stone, M. 2016. "The Response of Russian Security Prices to Economic Sanctions: Policy Effectiveness and Transmission." Working paper, US Department of State. https://2009 -2017.state.gov/e/oce/rls/papers/262748.htm.

Tuzova, Y., and F. Qayum. 2016. "Global Oil Glut and Sanctions: The Impact on Putin's Russia." *Energy Policy*, 90:140–151.

World Bank. 2015. *The Dawn of a New Economic Era?* Russia Economic Report 33. Washington, DC: World Bank.

6 Political Conflict and Service Trade

Kilian Heilmann

6.1 Introduction

Trade in services is as important as it is mysterious. Formerly believed by economists to be nontradable, the exchange of transportation, leisure travel, communication, financial, and other services has been on the rise in the last 30 years. Service trade now accounts for a large share of overall global trade. Hoekman (2006) estimates its share to be about 20–25 percent of all trade flows, with an outlook for continued increases in the future.

At the same time, service trade has been recognized by the trade and development community to be an integral factor for the growth strategy of the least developed and less developed countries. The World Bank has emphasized the contribution of the service sector (which is thought to be larger than that of the agriculture and manufacturing sectors) to poverty reduction and its role in providing education and health services as outlined in the Millennium Development Goals (World Bank 2010). Best practices in the development community now feature the strengthening of service trade in order to enhance developing countries' participation in international trade and their ability to reap the gains from it. Empirical studies such as that of Faber and Gaubert (2016), for example, have shown the positive impact on local development that service trade has had in the case of tourism in Mexico.

However, the trade community has just started to study the factors driving service trade. For example, little is known of the interplay between the political environment and the extent of service trade. While political and ethnic tensions have been shown to affect domestic marketplaces (Zussman 2016; Bar and Zussman 2017), the evidence for international trade is less strong. The literature has documented negative impacts of political tension of all kinds on overall trade (Chavis and Leslie 2009; Davis and Meunier 2011; Fuchs and Klann 2013; Heilmann 2016), but there is, to the best of my knowledge, no study on how service trade particularly reacts to conflict.

There is reason to believe that political conflict affects trade in services differently than it affects trade in goods. Hoekman and Primo Braga (1997) note that trade in services in general requires direct interaction between providers and consumers and that, unlike goods trade, there is usually no spatial separation between production and consumption. Therefore, political tension between trading partners that have to meet face-to-face to complete their transaction might be more salient than for anonymous goods exchange and thus might have a more negative effect on this type of international trade.

In this chapter, I look at the impact of political conflict on service trade in a natural experiment setting. In 2005, the publication of the so-called Muhammad cartoons in a Danish newspaper caused tension between Denmark and the Muslim world that eventually led to a consumer boycott of Danish brands. Exploiting variation in political sentiment plausibly unrelated to confounding factors of trade, I show that service trade was significantly disrupted after the boycott was announced. This effect was, however, short-lived and mainly concentrated in the recreational and travel service sectors.

The remainder of the study is organized as follows. Section 6.2 describes the background of the case study, section 6.3 explains the data source and empirical strategy to measure the effect of political conflict on service trade, section 6.4 presents the results, and section 6.5 offers conclusions.

6.2   Background

The Muhammad cartoon scandal lends itself well to the study of the relationship between conflict and service trade, because unlike other political conflicts it appeared suddenly and was unrelated to any other confounding factors. In September 2015, the Danish newspaper *Jyllands-Posten*, in an attempt to challenge the self-censorship of professional illustrators, called for caricatures of the Islamic prophet Muhammad and eventually published a series of Muhammad cartoons on September 30, 2005. The cartoons depicted the Islamic prophet in several derogatory circumstances, which included a picture of him with a bomb, thus drawing a connection between Islam and terrorism.

What followed was a public outcry by Muslims in Denmark, which later extended into the whole Muslim world after the cartoons were reprinted in several Arabic newspapers (Klausen 2009). Months of violent protests and burnings of the Danish flag in front of embassies were the consequence. After the Danish government refused the demand of an apology from several Muslim countries, boycott lists of Danish brands appeared online and an official boycott against these brands was called for by religious leaders in Saudi Arabia in early 2006. In the period that followed, many Danish firms reported drops in sales in the Muslim world, and several supermarkets preemptively cleared their shelves of Danish products (for a more detailed narration of the events leading up to the boycott, see Jensen 2008).

6.3   Methodology and Data

6.3.1   Empirical Setting
I estimate a standard "one-way" gravity model of Danish service exports within a difference-in-differences framework. I am interested in estimating the effect of the political conflict independent of changes in other factors that affect trade. The gravity specification controls for confounders like GDP and bilateral distance that explain a large share of the variation of bilateral trade and have been widely used in the literature to measure determinants of international trade volumes.

Since I am interested in the effect of political conflict, in an ideal world I would determine the treatment status of being in a conflict by using a direct measure of the sentiment of a country toward Denmark before and after the publication of the cartoons. However, this sentiment is not directly observed, and potential measurements in the form of sentiment polls are sparse and are not collected regularly for a multitude of countries. To solve this issue, I approximate the sentiment toward Denmark by the Muslim share of a country's population. Since Muhammad was the founder of Islam and all modern branches of this religion consider him to be the prophet sent by God, the insult of Muhammad carries over directly to all Muslims. The share of the population within a country that adheres to Islam approximates for the weight of Muslims within the political decision process and the consumer decisions for that country. Thus, countries with a large Muslim share will be more likely to follow a boycott call by religious leaders. In reality, Muslims differ across countries in their adherence to religious leaders and tolerance toward perceived blasphemy, so the treatment

Table 6.1
Variable description.

Name	Description
Y_{it}	Log exports from Denmark to country i in time t
GDP_{it}	Gross domestic product of country i
$Dist_i$	Great circle distance between country i and Denmark
$Muslim_i$	Muslim share as a percentage of the total population in country i
$Post_t$	Indicator for being in the treatment period (i.e., 2006 and on)

estimate should be interpreted as an average effect of the different Muslim communities.

In the following, I estimate difference-in-differences models of logged service exports from the boycotted country Denmark (Y_{it}) to its trading partners i at time t at yearly frequency. I include the typical gravity regressors GDP and distance and also control for year fixed effects. In particular, I use ordinary least squares (OLS) to estimate the following specification with the variable names explained in table 6.1:

$$Y_{it} = \alpha + \beta_1 \, Muslim_i + \beta_2 \, Post_t + \beta_3 \, Muslim_i \times Post_t \qquad (6.1)$$
$$+ \beta_4 \log GDP_{it} + \beta_5 \log Dist_i + Year_t + \varepsilon_{it}.$$

The parameter of interest is β_3 on the interaction term $Muslim_i \times Post_t$, which measures the differential change between exports to countries with a higher Muslim share before and after the outbreak of the conflict. The key identifying assumption in this setup is that there is no correlation between the interaction $Muslim_i \times Post_t$ and any confounding factors in the error term that also affect Danish exports. This would be violated if trade volumes had been timed in anticipation of the conflict or if the conflict was planned in response to current or future expected trade flows.

The natural experiment setting assures that this is not the case and that the treatment status and the timing are as good as randomly assigned. The outbreak of the political conflict was sudden and was caused by a single newspaper article; it was not an official act of the Danish government or any other. Potentially a concern, the timing of the boycott call by the Muslim world could be in response to future expected trade flows. Maybe the boycotting countries participated in the boycott only because they knew that imports from Denmark would have declined even in the absence of the boycott. In figure 6.1, I show that the pretrends do not indicate such a pattern and that this alterna-

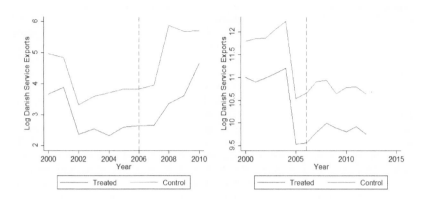

Figure 6.1
Time trends of Danish service exports by country group. Left panel: TradeMap data; right panel: Trade in Services Database (TSD) data. Treated: Countries with a Muslim majority of at least 70 percent. Control: Countries with a Muslim minority of less than 10 percent.

tive explanation is not plausible. While the two data sources do not give a uniform picture of the level trend in service trade flows from Denmark, neither graph suggests that there were pretreatment divergences between Muslim and non-Muslim countries that might confound the treatment effect of the boycott.[1]

6.3.2   Data

Data on international trade in services are notoriously sparse and of dubious quality. Unlike the transfer of goods, which is codified in bills of lading, service trade is particularly hard to measure, as it rarely appears in official accounts and its definition varies between countries.[2] In recent times, however, several organizations have made efforts to collect and organize trade volume in services.

The International Trade Centre has compiled bilateral service trade flows in its TradeMap database product. From this database, I collected Danish service imports and exports yearly for the years 2000 to 2013. The dataset features the statistics for trade with 238 partner countries and entities with varying data availability.[3] Additionally, I use the Trade in Services Database (TSD) from the World Bank. This dataset consolidates multiple data sources, such as the Organisation for Economic Cooperation and Development (OECD), United Nations, International Monetry Fund (IMF), and Eurostat, to create exporter-importer service trade volumes. The special feature of the TSD product is the

Table 6.2
Descriptive statistics.

Variable	Observations	Mean	Std. Dev.	Min	Max
TradeMap data					
Log exports	1,527	10.684	2.338	5.118	16.048
Log imports	1,512	10.676	2.332	5.118	15.933
Log GDP	1,512	24.599	2.200	18.740	30.384
Log distance	1,512	8.325	0.933	6.109	9.788
Share Muslim	1,512	0.230	0.355	0	0.999
Trade in Services Database					
Log exports	1,205	3.875	2.141	−2.539	9.198
Log imports	1,220	3.894	2.189	−0.511	9.330
Log GDP	1,220	24.519	2.222	18.740	30.300
Log distance	1,220	8.278	0.944	6.109	9.788
Share Muslim	1,220	0.236	0.355	0	0.999

fine classification of service trade that allows readers to distinguish the different services such as transportation, travel, and financial services. From this database, I collected service trade flows for the years 2000 to 2010.

To estimate the gravity equation outlined in subsection 6.3.1, I collected data on gross domestic product, bilateral distances, and the share of Muslim population from various sources. GDP data are taken from the World Bank's World Development Indicators where available. Bilateral distances are measured as the great circle distance as provided by the CEPII Gravity Dataset. The share of Muslim population is taken from the Pew Research Center's data website. Tables 6.1 and 6.2 provide detailed variable descriptions and report descriptive statistics for both datasets.

First, I compared the two data sources for consistency. Both datasets have a very similar coverage of partner countries, as witnessed by matching statistics in GDP and distance statistics. The differences in the service trade measure simply reflect different units, and the correlation between the two datasets is very high for both service exports ($\rho = 0.942$) and imports ($\rho = 0.944$).

6.4   Results

This section reports the empirical results for both TradeMap and TDS datasets and compares the two approaches.

6.4.1 TradeMap Data

Table 6.3 reports the results for Danish services exports from regression equation (6.1). Unsurprisingly, service trade exports in the cross section react strongly to the traditional gravity regressors of GDP and distance with estimated elasticities of .87 (GDP) and −.37 (distance). The level effect of being in the treatment group independent of the conflict is large but imprecisely measured. On average, a country with a 10 percent higher Muslim share imports 3.6 percent fewer exports from Denmark than a country that is comparable in the other predictors. The large standard error of this coefficient estimate suggests that there is high heterogeneity between the Muslim countries.

The average effect of the Muhammad cartoon conflict on Danish-Muslim trade relationships is indicated by the DID interaction term. The coefficient on $\text{Muslim}_i \times \text{Post}_t$ represents the treatment effect and is estimated to be −.41, statistically significant at the 10 percent level. This suggests that for each 10 percent higher Muslim share, a country imports 5.1 percent fewer services from Denmark after the publication of the comics. This effect is quite large and is stronger than the average effect on merchandise trade as reported in Heilmann (2016) but less

Table 6.3
Dependent variable: Value of service trade (TradeMap).

	(1)	(2)	(3)	(4)
	Log exports	Log exports	Log imports	Log imports
Log GDP	0.869***	0.319**	0.786***	0.0221
	(0.0402)	(0.157)	(0.0491)	(0.132)
Log distance	−0.374***		−0.435***	
	(0.0911)		(0.0922)	
Post	−0.0856		−0.190	
	(0.120)		(0.126)	
Muslim share	−0.368		−0.387*	
	(0.232)		(0.227)	
Post×Muslim	−0.425*	−0.254*	−0.578***	−0.0644
	(0.222)	(0.153)	(0.193)	(0.142)
Country fixed-effects	No	Yes	No	Yes
Observations	1527	1527	1512	1512
R^2	0.771	0.961	0.703	0.966

Source: TradeMap.
Note: Standard errors clustered at the country level in parentheses.
* $p<0.10$; ** $p<0.05$; *** $p<0.01$.

than the effect on consumer goods. When controlling for country fixed effects that might take up large parts of the variation from the cross-sectional regression, the coefficient drops to −.254.

When considering Danish service imports, the results are less robust. Again, the coefficients on GDP and distance in the cross-sectional regression in column 3 have the expected signs, and I initially estimate a strong decline in service imports from Muslim countries of 5.7 percent per every 10 percent higher Muslim share, which is statistically significant. However, this result vanishes completely after controlling for country fixed effects. The coefficient on $Muslim_i \times Post_t$ collapses to −.06 and is furthermore very imprecisely measured. The within-country time-series variation therefore cannot support evidence of an actual reduction of Danish service imports from Muslim countries after the boycott call.

The estimated treatment effects in the previous regressions are averages over all post-treatment periods. An interesting question is whether the treatment effect varies over time. It is quite plausible that political conflict affects international trade only in the short run. In another specification, I investigate this issue and allow the treatment effect to vary by year. Figure 6.2 plots the estimated coefficients for β_3 by year.

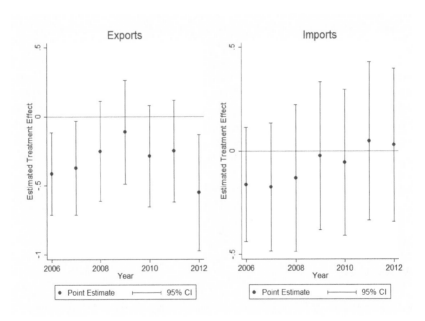

Figure 6.2
Estimated treatment effect coefficients over time.

Here we see an overall decaying structure of the impact. The treatment effect is strongly negative at first and then decays until 2009. Statistical significance vanishes after 2008, suggesting that service trade exports revert to normal levels after about two years. There is, however, a strong (negative) spike in 2012, which is surprising at first. This effect, however, might be connected to the release of the movie *Innocence of Muslims*, which again caused widespread tension between the Muslim world and the West.

For service imports, there is a similar pattern of an initially negative but then decaying treatment effect. Neither of the coefficients is significant at the 5 percent significance level, indicating that the treatment effect is imprecisely measured because of the higher variation of Danish service imports, which cannot be explained by the traditional gravity regressors. This result is not particularly surprising given the nonresult in the prior specification.

6.4.2 Trade in Services Database

In this subsection, I seek to confirm the results found using the Trade-Map data and make use of the Trade in Services Database (TSD). The TSD provides data for a shorter time span and only includes service trade volume up to 2010. I run the same regressions as earlier and report the results in table 6.4. Compared to the TradeMap data, the simple difference-in-differences model leads to very similar coefficients for the trade elasticity with respect to the GDP and bilateral distance. Unlike the earlier regression, the TSD data confirm statistically significant overall lower trade levels of Muslim countries (−.687 compared to −.368). Estimating a higher coefficient on Muslim, it is therefore not surprising that the treatment effect in column 1 is slightly smaller than in the TradeMap data, as the lower overall trade levels persist in the post-treatment period. However, the estimated treatment effect of −0.397 is still significant at the 5 percent significance level, and the two estimates are well within their confidence bands in both regressions. When adding country fixed effects in column 2, I again see a similar drop in the estimated effect of $Muslim_i \times Post_t$ (down to −.303). However, the difference-in-differences treatment effect is significant at the 10 percent significance level, indicating a sharp drop in Danish service exports to the Muslim world in response to the boycott call in 2006.

For imports, the two databases result in in slightly different conclusions. While the cross-sectional regression results for the treatment effect are reasonably close (−.578 compared to −.448), including fixed effects

Table 6.4
Regression results. Dependent variable: value of service trade (TSD).

	(1)	(2)	(3)	(4)
	Log exports	Log exports	Log imports	Log imports
Log GDP	0.741***	−0.0646	0.807***	0.249
	(0.0363)	(0.209)	(0.0309)	(0.213)
Log distance	−0.392***		−0.309***	
	(0.0883)		(0.0932)	
Post	0.148		0.393***	
	(0.115)		(0.106)	
Muslim share	−0.687***		−0.372**	
	(0.214)		(0.171)	
Post × Muslim	−0.397**	−0.303*	−0.448***	−0.370***
	(0.176)	(0.155)	(0.139)	(0.140)
Country fixed-effects	No	Yes	No	Yes
Observations	1,205	1,205	1,220	1,220
R^2	0.753	0.949	0.810	0.955

Source: Trade in Services Database.
Note: Standard errors clustered at the country level in parentheses.
* $p<0.10$; ** $p<0.05$; *** $p<0.01$.

in column 2 does not eradicate the result as in the TradeMap data. Instead, the coefficient is largely robust and changes only slightly to −.370, and it is still significantly different from zero. Therefore, the TSD suggests that there was indeed an effect of the boycott on Danish service imports that is in fact of the same magnitude as the effect on exports.

6.4.3   Results by Service Type
The Trade in Services Database records service trade flows by certain types. It features the ten categories transportation, personal and recreation, travel, communication, construction, insurance, finance, computer and information services, royalties, and government services, and a classification for other services. This distinction allows me to get at the mechanisms through which political conflict affects international trade. Table 6.5 reports the difference-in-differences result by service type, revealing strong heterogeneity in the estimated treatment effects.

Surprisingly, only one of the ten categories shows a negative and significant treatment effect. The disruption seems to be concentrated in personal, cultural, and recreational services and travel, where for the latter the coefficient is the only statistically significant one. While some of the other coefficients on $Muslim_i \times Post_t$ are negative, they are not

Table 6.5
Regression results by type. Dependent variable: value of service trade exports.

	(1) Transport	(2) Recreation	(3) Travel	(4) Communication	(5) Construction	(6) Insurance	(7) Financial	(8) Information	(9) Royalties	(10) Government
Log GDP	0.726***	0.718***	0.673***	0.711***	0.506***	0.654***	0.572***	0.821***	0.830***	0.457***
	(0.0699)	(0.142)	(0.0957)	(0.0756)	(0.0782)	(0.119)	(0.147)	(0.106)	(0.159)	(0.0901)
Log distance	-0.124	-0.980***	-0.727***	-0.968***	-0.932***	-0.716***	-0.811***	-0.934***	-0.858***	-0.0476
	(0.106)	(0.177)	(0.126)	(0.140)	(0.149)	(0.133)	(0.233)	(0.149)	(0.189)	(0.173)
Post	0.191	1.197*	0.317*	-0.211	-1.385**	-0.907	-0.584	0.415	-0.334	-0.381
	(0.122)	(0.642)	(0.174)	(0.296)	(0.630)	(0.884)	(0.512)	(0.579)	(0.414)	(0.483)
Muslim share	-0.364	-0.240	0.732*	-1.050***	-0.0527	-1.449***	0.130	-1.592***	-0.886*	0.223
	(0.323)	(0.639)	(0.425)	(0.388)	(0.583)	(0.403)	(0.628)	(0.439)	(0.464)	(0.632)
Post×Muslim	-0.145	-1.086	-0.936***	0.552	-0.559	0.130	-0.816	0.162	-0.283	-0.160
	(0.440)	(0.717)	(0.243)	(0.505)	(0.655)	(0.375)	(0.790)	(0.426)	(0.342)	(0.513)
Observations	646	385	619	423	313	383	307	393	362	412
Adjusted R^2	0.543	0.464	0.495	0.620	0.458	0.478	0.306	0.568	0.396	0.226

Source: Trade in Services Database.

Note: Standard errors clustered at the country level in parentheses.

* $p<0.10$; ** $p<0.05$; *** $p<0.01$.

statistically significant at any reasonable confidence level, and some coefficients are even estimated to be positive, for example communication, insurance, and information services. Although the sample size of some categories is quite small, this hints toward the explanation that most of the disruption in service trade exports is driven by services that are consumed by private consumers as compared to activities that are more business related. Recreational services and travel services are strongly interlinked, and it makes sense that they would see a very similar effect. It appears that Muslims around the world readily reacted to the political conflict by not making leisure trips to Denmark and reducing the consumption of cultural and recreational services.

These results are in line with previous findings for the effect of conflict on merchandise trade. Heilmann (2016) showed that the effect of the Muhammad cartoon conflict and other boycotts was concentrated in consumer goods. The rationale here was that the cost of boycotting goods that are deemed to be consumed is less than for intermediate and capital goods that are used in production. The results for service trade are in line with this view. Recreational services and travel are directed at consumers, while other service types, such as communication, construction, and financial services, often cater to business customers, who have little incentive to disrupt trade in response to political conflict.

6.5 Conclusion

This study has investigated the effect of political conflict on service trade in a natural experiment setting of the Muhammad cartoon crisis of 2005–2006 using new service trade datasets. Implementing a difference-in-differences research design and exploiting variation in the share of Muslim population between countries, I show that service trade exports from Denmark to the Muslim world were significantly disrupted in the aftermath of the crisis. Based on two independent data sources, I estimate negative treatment effects on the scale of 30–50 percent that are largely robust between different specifications.

These results are similar to the estimated effects on merchandise trade as explored by previous studies. At first, the negative effect on exports from the targeted country is large and statistically significant throughout different econometric specifications and different datasets. The effect, however, seems to be rather short lived and appears to be dying out after at most two years. A similar result has been noted for trade patterns during other conflicts. Furthermore, the negative effects appear to be concentrated in service types that cater directly to consumers, namely recreational and travel services, while the effect is not detectable in categories that primarily serve business customers. A similar effect has been shown for merchandise trade, where political conflict appeared to hurt consumer goods only. This reassures us that political conflict has only a limited and temporary effect on international trade patterns.

Notes

I would like to thank Gordon Hanson, Marc Muendler, Volker Nitsch, and Tibor Besedeš for helpful comments.

1. The sudden drop in the TSD data from 2005 is puzzling, but it does not necessarily indicate issues relevant for the estimation procedure. It is most likely the result of a change in the data collection process. I observe the same drop in the import data, suggesting that some service trade flows might have been taken out of the statistics. Since this issue does not appear to affect the treatment and control groups separately, the parallel trend assumption of the difference-in-differences estimator is not obviously violated.

2. A further issue complicating service trade measurement is the accounting of service flows within multinational enterprises solely for tax-saving purposes. Since these "pseudoflows" are controlled within a firm, they should not be affected by political conflict and are ignored in the remainder of this study.

3. Around two-thirds (2,249 out of 3,332) of the year-partner combinations contain non-missing export data.

References

Bar, R., and A. Zussman. 2017. "Customer Discrimination: Evidence from Israel." *Journal of Labor Economics* 35 (4): 1031–1059.

Chavis, L., and P. Leslie. 2009. "Consumer Boycotts: The Impact of the Iraq War on French Wine Sales in the U.S." *Quantitative Marketing and Economics* 7 (1): 37–67.

Davis, C. L., and S. Meunier. 2011. "Business as Usual? Economic Responses to Political Tensions." *American Journal of Political Science* 55 (3): 628–646.

Faber, B., and C. Gaubert. 2016. "Tourism and Economic Development: Evidence from Mexico's Coastline." Technical Report. Cambridge, MA: National Bureau of Economic Research.

Fuchs, A., and N. H. Klann. 2013. "Paying a Visit: The Dalai Lama Effect on International Trade." *Journal of International Economics* 91 (1): 164–177.

Heilmann, K. 2016. "Does Political Conflict Hurt Trade? Evidence from Consumer Boycotts." *Journal of International Economics* 99: 179–191.

Hoekman, B. 2006. "Liberalizing Trade in Services: A Survey." World Bank Policy Research Working Paper 4030. https://openknowledge.worldbank.org/handle/10986/9004.

Hoekman, B., and C. A. Primo Braga. 1997. "Protection and Trade in Services: A Survey." *Open Economies Review* 8 (3): 285–308.

Jensen, H. R. 2008. "The Mohammed Cartoons Controversy and the Boycott of Danish Products in the Middle East." *European Business Review* 20 (3): 275–289.

Klausen, J. 2009. *The Cartoons That Shook the World*. New Haven, CT: Yale University Press.

World Bank. 2010. "Role of Services in Economic Development." Policy Report.

Zussman, A. 2016. "Conflict and the Ethnic Structure of the Market Place: Evidence from Israel." *European Economic Review* 90: 134–145.

7 Do Natural Disasters Increase International Trade?

Chenmei Li and Peter A. G. van Bergeijk

7.1 Introduction

Disruption of international trade and investment flows is a topic of growing concern, both in science and in policy-making. The topic of trade disruptions has risen on the research agenda as a result of three factors. First, the 2008–2009 trade collapse (which reduced real global trade by about 20 percent in only a few months) has stimulated new research on trade uncertainty (Grossman and Meissner 2010; van Bergeijk 2010; Wagner and Gelübcke 2014; Bloom 2014; Novy and Taylor 2014). The trade collapse turned out to be a short- to medium-term phenomenon: by November 2010, real world imports had reached the April 2008 peak level again. The trade collapse is therefore best considered a one-time shock, although the growth of world trade appears to have slowed down (van Bergeijk, Brakman, and van Marrewijk 2017). Second, a substantial increase in implemented economic sanctions (boycotts and embargoes) and sanction threats can be observed. The increase in sanction frequency reflects geopolitical factors (such as the end of the superpower conflict in the 1990s), economic factors (globalization), and greater efficacy in implementation, especially regarding multilateral sanctions (Biersteker and van Bergeijk 2015). Third, economic security and economic vulnerability have become important issues for research and policy in particular, with a view toward resilience and preventing trade disruptions (van Bergeijk and Moons 2009; Lazzaroni and van Bergeijk 2014; van Bergeijk, Brakman, and van Marrewijk 2017).

So far, interest regarding trade disruption has been mainly focused on man-made shocks (including those resulting from malfunctioning of the economic system), where a rich and comprehensive body of literature has emerged. In this chapter, we will focus on natural disasters and their impact on trade (both imports and exports). We think

Table 7.1
Overview of empirical multicountry trade studies on the impact of disasters.

	Dependent variable	Political variable	Period	Country coverage	N
Heger, Julca, and Paddison (2008)	Import, export share in GDP	No	1970–2006	16 countries	363
Gassebner, Keck, and Teh (2010)	Real level of bilateral imports	Democracy	1962–2004	176 exporters 163 importers	281,762
Oh and Reuveny (2010)	Real bilateral imports	Political safety	1985–2003	116 countries	127,270
Pelli and Tschopp (2012)	Change in log export value	No	1995–2005	38 countries	679,056
Felbermayr and Gröschl (2013)	Nominal bilateral imports	No	1950–2008	94 or 164 countries	821,177
El Hadri, Mirza, and Rabaud (2017)	Nominal (agricultural) exports	No	1979–2000	109 (103) countries	71,764 (13,420)
Oh (2017)	Average of bilateral trade	Political stability	1982–1998	53 countries	17,828

that this is a topic worthy of investigation for four reasons: first because causality may be an issue in man-made shocks; second, because natural disasters typically have a shorter duration than man-made shocks such as recessions and sanction episodes; third, because natural disasters, unlike sanctions, for example, do not restrict trade per se; and fourth, because the empirical literature on this topic is scarce.[1] The review article on the climate change economics literature by Dell, Jones, and Olken (2014, 768), for example, points out that "the trade channel has been the subject of comparatively few studies exploiting weather shocks."[2]

Table 7.1 lists the available econometric multicountry studies. These studies provide econometric models of trade flows containing an indicator that specifies the occurrence (and sometimes severity) of a natural disaster. Five studies use models with a geographical dimension and include distance either between the trade partners (a gravity trade model is used by Gassebner, Keck, and Teh 2010; Oh and Reuveny 2010; Felbermayr and Gröschl 2013;[3] and Oh 2017) or between the trade partners and the center of the disaster (e.g., Pelli and Tschopp 2012). Major differences can be observed with respect to the period of the sample, the country coverage, and the inclusion or noninclusion of a political variable.

As with any emerging field in economic science, the findings are too heterogeneous to already arrive at a consensus, although this has hardly been noted, because of the unambiguous conclusions that the authors themselves draw from their findings. The seminal study by Gassebner, Keck, and Teh (2010, 351), for example, reports: "As a conservative estimate, an additional disaster reduces imports on average by 0.2% and exports by 0.1%." Likewise, Oh and Reuveny (2010, 251) conclude that "an increase in climatic disasters … for either the importer or exporter countries reduces their bilateral trade."

In our opinion, the empirical evidence does not support these conclusions, especially since the conclusions are based on an analysis of the importing country (the destination of the trade flow) and cannot be generalized to the exporting country (the origin of the trade flow). Moreover, the parameters reported in these two studies on balance show opposite signs for the origin and destination of the trade flows. Tables 7.2 and 7.3 summarize these parameter estimates for imports and exports, respectively.[4]

The papers in table 7.2 predominantly use a gravity approach, making it possible to distinguish between the impact of a disaster in the destination (the importing country) or in the origin (the exporting country) of a trade flow. For the *disaster-hits-destination* effect, the majority of the reported parameters (22) are positive (the average of the 34 coefficients in table 7.2 is 0.301), and 12 of these coefficients are significantly positive at the usual confidence levels, compared to only 2 significantly negative coefficients. Note that Heger, Julca, and Paddison (2008), using a different methodology without origin effects for a subsample of Caribbean countries, report positive impacts on imports in the first and second periods. All in all, the evidence in table 7.2 could be consistent with a positive impact of a disaster on a country's imports. For the *disaster-hits-origin* effect, the opposite occurs: only 3 significantly positive coefficients compared to 17 significantly negative coefficients (the average of the 25 coefficient in table 7.2 is −0.56). Importantly, it is not strictly logical to interpret the disaster-hits-origin effect in an import gravity model as showing that disasters reduce exports. Actually, this inference (which is generally made in the literature) can only be valid under three strict conditions: (a) the absence of zero trade flows, (b) fully symmetric trade matrices, and (c) symmetric trade costs of disasters. This apparently is not the case. All that has been demonstrated is that importers import less from exporters that have been hit by disasters. Only the parameters reported in table 7.3 can be interpreted as genuine estimates of a disaster's impact on exports, since the dependent variable is exports. The studies reported in table 7.3 use total exports as the

Table 7.2
Parameter estimates reported in empirical multicountry studies on the impact of disasters on imports.

	Disaster	Specification	Disaster in — Destination	Disaster in — Origin	Including political variable — Disaster in — Destination	Including political variable — Disaster in — Origin
Heger, Julca, and Paddison (2008)	Catastrophic	OLS — Direct	1.99***			
		OLS — Lag 1 period	1.14*			
		OLS — Lag 2 periods	-2.54***			
		OLS — Lag 3 periods	-0.49			
		GMM — Direct	5.08*			
		GMM — Lag 1 period	0.64			
		GMM — Lag 2 periods	-2.78**			
		GMM — Lag 3 periods	-0.71			
		"Most precise estimate"	0.023***			
Gassebner, Keck, and Teh (2010)	Natural and technological	Country-specific	0.006	-0.001	0.024**	-0.019*
		Pair-specific	-0.004	-0.006	0.011	-0.018**
		Country-specific — Country size correction	0.43	-1.983***	1.499*	-2.655***
		Pair-specific	0.208	-2.052***	2.052***	-2.79***
	Devastating	Country-specific	0.011	-0.006	0.023***	-0.023***
		Pair-specific	0.002	-0.008	0.012	-0.017**
		Country-specific — Country size correction	0.627*	-0.955*	0.877**	-0.884**
		Pair-specific	0.399	-0.884**	0.935***	-0.965***
Oh and Reuveny (2010)	Geophysical and climatic	Isolated — Geophysical	0.034	0.0199**	0.0053	0.0216***
		Combined — Geophysical	-0.0273***	-0.0062**	-0.0268***	-0.0059**
		Combined — Climatic			0.0059	0.0223***
Felbermayr and Gröschl (2013)	Total of "large" earthquakes, volcanic eruptions, tsunamis, storms, storm floods, and droughts	Gravity, FE, PPML (94 countries) — Models' interaction with financial remoteness	0.02*	-0.009		
		Full model	0.255**	-0.218*		
		Full model	0.329***	-0.250**		
		Full sample (162 countries)	0.187***	-0.297***		

* 90% confid... ** 95% confid... *** 99% confid...

Table 7.3
Parameter estimates reported in empirical multicountry studies on the impact of disasters on exports.

	Disaster	Specification		Impact
Heger, Julca,	Catastrophic	OLS	Direct	1.07**
and Paddison		OLS	Lag 1 period	−1.04*
(2008)		OLS	Lag 2 periods	−0.16
		GMM	Direct	1.88
		GMM	Lag 1 period	−1.10*
		GMM	Lag 2 periods	−0.19
		"Most precise estimate"		0.01
Pelli and	Hurricanes	Static baseline	Developing	−1.116
Tschopp (2012)			countries	
		Static baseline	All countries	−0.587
		Dynamic	Baseline	−1.116
		Dynamic	Convergence	−1.023***
		Dynamic	Convergence 3 periods	−2.075***

	Disaster	Specification	Income	Population
El Hadri,			Income	Population
Mirza, and	Flood	Above median	0.013	1.002
Rabaud (2017)		Below median	0.435	−2.528*
	Storm	Above median	2.292***	0.630
		Below median	−4.583***	2.099**
	Earthquake	Above median	−4.530***	−3.641
		Below median	3.413	0.201
	Temperature	Above median	0.145	0.204
		Below median	−2.175	−1.341
	All goods,	Above median	1.493***	
	all disasters	Below median	−2.551***	

* 90% confidence; ** 95% confidence; *** 99% confidence.

dependent variable arguing, among other things, that natural disasters are supply shocks that a priori affect bilateral export flows in the same way (e.g., El Hadri, Mirza, and Rabaud 2017, 3). The evidence in table 7.3 is clearly mixed: 60 percent of results are insignificant, and 53 percent of the coefficients are negative (eight coefficients are statistically significant), almost balancing the 47 percent of coefficients that are positive (four are significantly positive).

Tables 7.2 and 7.3 demonstrate that the existing empirical evidence for a negative relationship between disasters and exports is less convincing than often claimed and is even contradictory for imports.[5] The conclusions of the studies by Oh and Reuveny (2010) and Gassebner, Keck, and Teh (2010) are, however, widely cited in the literature. The dominant view of the profession seems to be that disasters in general tend to be negative for trade. This chapter adds to the existing empirical literature both by providing an analysis of disasters for a comprehensive country sample (we started data collection with 197 countries and have all necessary data available for 63 countries) and a longer and more recent period (1970 to 2014 inclusive), and in our exploratory analysis we increase the number of explanatory variables, which enables us to investigate factors that have been suggested in the literature as issues for further research and/or potentially relevant determinants of resilience regarding trade shocks. It should be noted from the start that our analysis is exploratory in nature and aims at distilling some stylized facts and especially at identifying research puzzles for further research.

The remainder of this chapter is structured as follows. Section 7.2 reviews the literature dealing with mechanisms that create positive and/or negative impacts of natural disasters on exports and imports. Section 7.3 introduces and discusses our data sources. Section 7.4 introduces a set of quasi-reduced form equations based on the seminal study by Jones and Olken (2010) and presents and discusses our empirical findings. Section 7.5 suggests avenues for further research.

7.2   Literature Review

7.2.1   Impact on Trade

Typically, disasters are seen as disruptions of normal economic activity as a result of loss of production, human and physical capital, and/or infrastructure. Geophysical disasters (earthquakes, volcanic eruptions, etc.) and floods destroy or limit the use of roads, bridges, airspace, telecommunications, and harbors, increasing the logistical costs, and thus may have a negative impact on both imports and exports (Gassebner, Keck, and Teh 2010; Oh and Reuveny 2010; Martincus and Blyde 2013; Hayakawa, Matsuura, and Okubo 2015). A meta-analysis of 64 empirical studies on the impact of natural disasters established a significant direct impact of natural disasters on gross domestic product (Lazzaroni and van Bergeijk 2014), reflecting both loss of life and capital goods and the disturbance of daily life.[6] Assuming that the ensuing reduction of GDP (per capita) results in lower effective demand (for consumption, investment, and public expenditures, because of lower tax receipts), Oh and Reuveny (2010) and Gassebner, Keck, and Teh (2010) expect that disasters will have a negative impact on import demand. Moreover, Oh and Reuveny (2010) point out that disasters may lead to collapsing markets (because of the demoralizing effect of disasters), and the disappearance of markets adds to increased trade uncertainty, which is already higher because of the occurrence of the disaster. This leads to higher risk premiums and trading costs and thus to lower exports and imports.

Adam (2013), Oh and Reuveny (2010), and Gassebner, Keck, and Teh (2010), however, recognize that a disaster will also shift the import demand function upward in order to replace lost production and production capacity. Reconstruction that requires imports and foreign firms may fill in the gap that domestic firms cannot fill. Natural disasters may thus offer opportunities for foreign exporting firms to enter the market, also because domestic competitive pressures will be reduced. More counterintuitive is that disasters may also have positive effects on the supply side of the economy and thereby on exports. Pelli and Tschopp (2012) point out the creative destruction aspect of natural disasters: replacing old capital goods by new capital goods, incorporating recent technology, may increase productivity (see also chapter 5 of Brata 2017, which provides a firm-level analysis of productivity in the case of Indonesian geophysical disasters). Natural disasters may thus shake up the production structure, force low-level firms out of the market, and increase the competitive position of exporting firms. Pelling, Özerdem, and Barakat (2002) argue that policymakers will give priority to export sectors, and a similar policy preference for intermediate imports can be expected. Finally, with domestic markets under pressure, firms may allocate output to foreign markets that was previously destined for domestic markets.[7]

7.2.2 Vulnerabilities and Resilience Factors

The literature has identified many factors that increase or mitigate the impact of disasters, suggesting three sets of factors that may influence the effects of natural disasters on trade: the level of economic development, the availability and level of foreign direct investment (FDI), and the condition of political institutions. We will review the three factors from the perspective of the country that is hit by a natural disaster.

7.2.2.1 Level of development (GDPpc, OECD dummy, and LDC dummy) The influence of the level of (economic) development on the economic impact of external shocks (natural disasters) is complex. A higher level of development is associated with better and well-established warning and reaction systems (Elliott 2012). Moreover, it is

often assumed that OECD countries typically are more diversified and have sounder macroeconomic structures, markets that function better, and more scope for macroeconomic management (for a relevant ranking of 86 countries in the early twenty-first century that substantiates this hypothesis, see Briguglio et al. 2009). All these factors are assumed to increase trade resilience and reduce the impact of disasters. Similarly, a lower level of development is often associated with a stronger impact from disasters. This also is noted in the literature on climate change (e.g., Jones and Olken 2010).[8]

The empirical evidence, however, is again mixed. According to Noy (2009), "A disaster of similar magnitude affects a developing country more significantly than a developed one." Noy's study indicates that higher per capita income is "important in preventing negative impacts of natural disasters." In contrast, for Asia over the years 1970 to 2005, Padli and Habibullah (2009) find "an inverse proportion between economic development and disaster resistance." In other words, a lower level of development appears to be associated with higher disaster resilience. According to Kellenberg and Mobarak (2008), the relationship is nonlinear. We will take this empirical ambiguity on board by including per capita GDP simultaneously linearly and squared. This is an improvement relative to Jones and Olken (2010) and El Hadri, Mirza, and Rabaud (2017), who use binary dummies to test for above and below median per capita income levels in a linear manner. Additionally, we use dummy variables for OECD membership and LDC status to test for well-defined country groupings at the tails of the distribution. OECD membership requires better macroeconomic and structural conditions (such as flexible product and labor markets), which would seem to be conducive to mitigating disasters. LDC status is associated with low levels of per capita income but also indicates better access to foreign aid.[9] In view of these factors, we will investigate nonlinear relationships between disaster impact and the level of GDP per capita, which we include both linearly and squared and also to test for OECD and LDC status.

7.2.2.2 Foreign Direct Investment (FDI)

The literature on FDI and natural disasters typically focuses on how natural disasters influence FDI. The general finding is that disaster occurrence and higher disaster frequency reduce FDI inflows for the country hit by a disaster. We depart from this literature and focus on how existing FDI levels *before* the disaster may influence disaster impact.[10] This change in perspective may be highly relevant for FDI, which is important not only as a financial flow but also because it brings market access and commitment by private partners, potentially ensuring continuation of investment and risk-sharing (in a low-profit or loss situation, the level of repayment of profits will be adjusted downward). Long-run relationships—emerging in international value chains—may indeed help reduce the cost of a disaster for the country that is hit by the disaster and speed up economic recovery and reconstruction by bringing in new technology and encouraging new industries.[11] FDI, however, also creates vulnerabilities and may actually dry up in the wake of a disaster. In this respect, it is important to distinguish between the *pre-crisis* stock of FDI and the pre-disaster change in that stock (the flow of FDI).[12]

7.2.2.3 Political institutions and trade uncertainty as a result of disasters The literature on the impact of disasters often considers political institutions. The seminal study is by Kahn (2005), who finds that countries that are more democratic experience lower death counts. Accounting for democracy, Gehlbach and Keefer (2011), Escaleras, Anbarci, and Register (2007), Raschky (2008), and Dell, Jones, and Olken (2012) find similar results. In contrast, Yamamura (2011a, 2011b) finds a negative and significant effect for democracy per se but also that law and order and quality of government reduce disaster impact. As already discussed in the introduction, recent literature that links trade collapses in general to an underlying increase in trade uncertainty finds that trade shocks have a stronger impact in democracies (for a discussion, see van Bergeijk 2018).

In conclusion:

• The empirical literature on the level of development is inconclusive, suggesting a nonlinear relationship.

• The existing empirical literature on FDI and natural disasters agrees on a negative association (based on the assumption that natural disasters influence FDI decisions), but the impact of pre-disaster FDI is underresearched and not unambiguous.

• Political factors suggest that the impact of trade shocks may be larger the more democratic the country that is hit by the disaster.

7.3 Data Description

Our sample is restricted by data availability because multiple data sources were used. We have complete data for 63 countries (see the appendix). Exclusions from the dataset mainly result from missing or incomplete data in the World Development Indicators. The excluded countries are either very small countries with small populations and little international economic activity or countries that ceased to exist during the research period, such as the Union of Soviet Socialist Republics, Czechoslovakia, Yugoslavia, and East Germany.

Table 7.4 describes our variables and sources. The dependent variable, total imports or total exports, is measured in constant US$. The value represents all goods and services received from or sold to the rest of the world. Using total trade rather than data disaggregated by country destination or product group has the benefit of avoiding measurement errors related to misclassification, which may create serious problems, especially for developing countries. We expect total trade data also to be more accurately measured because these data can be and are checked using national income identities in the process of producing national accounts.

The natural disaster dataset EM-DAT is the most comprehensive dataset and the most commonly used data source in the relevant litera-

Table 7.4
Variables—descriptions and sources (data for 1970–2014 inclusive).

Variable	Description	Source
IMPORT	Import annual growth rate (constant prices)	WDI
EXPORT	Export annual growth rate (constant prices)	WDI
GDPpc	One-year lag of GDP per capita (10,000 dollars, constant prices)	WDI
Poor	Dummy = 1 if the country's GDPpc is lower than the median level	WDI
OECD	Dummy = 1 if the country is an OECD member in a specific year, otherwise 0	OECD
LDC	Dummy = 1 if the country is an LDC in a specific year, otherwise 0	UN
FDI FLOW	One-year lag of FDI net inflow in % of GDP	UNCTAD STAT
FDI STOCK	One-year lag of FDI stock in % of GDP	UNCTAD STAT
polity2	One-year lag of institutional indicator (10 is most democratic level, −10 is most autocratic)	Center for Systemic Peace
DISASTER	Annual disaster frequency	EM-DAT

ture (for a discussion, see Lazzaroni and van Bergeijk 2014). EM-DAT provides country data for various indicators of natural disasters, distinguished by 11 types. It also provides detailed information on total killed and injured, total affected, total damage, and other data. We, however, will be interested in how the total occurrence of a natural disaster impacts trade flows. Therefore we created the variable DISASTER as the total number of natural disasters happening to a country within one year.[13]

For the economic variables, we use the World Development Indicators, with the exception of the FDI stock as a percentage of GDP, which is taken from the United Nations Conference on Trade and Development and has slightly better coverage. We use *polity2* as a measure for the political-institutional framework derived from the institutional dataset of the Center for Systemic Peace.

We started collecting data for 197 countries for the years 1970–2014 inclusive and ended with 63 countries for which we have sufficient data. Data for lagged variables were collected also for 1969 so that the starting point of the analysis is 1970. A general point to note is that we are missing many small island economies that tend to have more disasters (particularly storms and floods). Note that because of the varying availability of data for specific variables, the number of observations included can change for different specifications of our regression models.

7.4 Empirical Findings

Our core model is based on Jones and Olken (2010), with $\log(Trade_{it})-\log(Trade_{it-1})$ as the left-hand-side variable. In their empirical research, *Trade* is defined as exports distinguished by product groups, but in this chapter we investigate both exports and imports at the aggregate level.[14] Jones and Olken use temperature and precipitation as measures of climate shock as explanatory variables, and a slope dummy variable *Poor*, which assumes the value 1 if a country's GDP per capita is below the median value. Our model differs in two respects: (a) rather than using a dummy variable (which actually reduces the available information into a binary variable), we use per capita GDP, and (b) as discussed, we use a count variable that measures the actual occurrence of a natural disaster of any type instead of the temperature and precipitation data. So our core model becomes

$$\log(Trade_{it})-\log(Trade_{it-1})=\alpha+\beta \cdot DISASTER_t+\gamma \cdot DISASTER_t \cdot GDPpc_{t-1} \quad (7.1)$$
$$+\lambda_c+\lambda_t+\varepsilon,$$

Table 7.5
Panel estimate core model for annual real exports and imports (FGLS).

	(1)	(2)	(3)	(4)	(5)	(6)	(7)	(8)	(9)
	1979–2000	1970–2014				1970–2008		1990–2014	
	Import	Export	Export	Import	Import	Export	Import	Export	Import
DISASTER	1.49***	0.303***	0.38***	0.36***	0.31***	0.29***	0.32***	0.29***	0.40***
	(3.2)	(4.0)	(4.2)	(4.6)	(3.4)	(3.6)	(3.9)	(3.4)	(4.6)
DISASTER*Poor	−2.55**								
	(−2.3)								
DISASTER*GDPpc		−0.83***	−1.8***	−0.90***	−0.34	−0.80***	−0.75***	−0.82***	−1.02***
		(−4.5)	(−2.8)	(−4.78)	(−0.5)	(−4.1)	(−3.7)	(−4.0)	(−4.9)
DISASTER*GDPpc2			0.00		0.00				
			(1.6)		(−0.9)				
FEE	Yes	Yes	Yes	Yes	Yes	Yes	Yes	Yes	Yes
N	71,764	5,260	5,260	5,260	4,356	4,356	4,356	3,511	3,511
R^2	0.36	0.16	0.16	0.16		0.19	0.19	0.17	0.18

Notes: Column 1 reports the findings of El Hadri, Mirza, and Rabaud (2017). t statistics in parentheses.
** $p < 0.05$; *** $p < 0.01$.

where λ_c and λ_t are fixed country and time effects, respectively, and ε is the error term. Like Jones and Olken (2010) and El Hadri, Mirza, and Rabaud (2017), we estimate equation (7.1) by Feasible Generalized Least Squares (FGLS), in view of the substantial heteroskedasticity in export and import growth rates. We estimate this model (and its extensions) for three periods: the full sample 1970–2014 and, to check for robustness, two subperiods, 1970–2008 (our motivation is to exclude the exceptional trade collapse in 2008–2009 and the ensuing trade slowdown) and 1990–2014 (our motivation is to exclude the pre-1990 period of the Cold War). We always add fixed time and country effects in the estimated equations.

Table 7.5 reports the results. Column 1, for purposes of comparison, reports the findings by El Hadri, Mirza, and Rabaud (2017), which replicate Jones and Olken (2010) with a disaster variable instead of temperature and precipitation shocks but like Jones and Olken (2010) use the dummy variable *Poor*, which indicates below median per capita income. Column 4 replicates their findings for a longer time period and using actual observations on country *GDPpc* with qualitatively similar results in terms of sign and significance for *DISASTER*.[15] In contrast with these studies, but in line with Padli and Habibullah (2009), we find that a lower level of development is associated with higher disaster resilience. This result is confirmed in columns 7 and 9 for the subperiods 1970–2008 and 1990–2014, respectively. Columns 2, 6, and 8 report our findings for exports, and again we find a positive and significant coefficient for *DISASTER* and a negative coefficient when we interact *DISASTER* and *GDPpc*. Next, we test for possible nonlinearity regarding the impact of the level of development by estimating

$$\log(Trade_{it}) - \log(Trade_{it-1}) = \alpha + \beta \cdot DISASTER_t$$
$$+ \gamma DISASTER_t \cdot GDPpc_{t-1} \qquad (7.2)$$
$$+ \delta \cdot DISASTER \cdot GDPpc_{t-1}{}^2 + \lambda_c + \lambda_t + \varepsilon.$$

Columns 3 and 5 of table 7.5 report the empirical findings for exports and imports, respectively, for the years 1970–2014. Regressions for the subperiods (not reported) show similar findings: the estimations of equation (7.2) do not provide evidence that the disaster impact on trade and the level of development have a (inverted) u-shaped pattern. In conclusion, we use equation (7.1) as the core model for further research. To this core, we add resilience and vulnerability factors (*RESVUL*) as identified in subsection 7.2.2:

$$\log(Trade_{it}) - \log(Trade_{it-1}) = \alpha + \beta \cdot DISASTER_t$$
$$+ \gamma DISASTER_t \cdot GDPpc_{t-1} \qquad (7.3)$$
$$+ \delta \cdot DISASTER \cdot RESVUL_{t-1} + \lambda_c + \lambda_t + \varepsilon.$$

Tables 7.6 and 7.7 report exploratory findings for 1970–2014 for exports and imports, respectively, when we separately add FDI flows, FDI stocks, *polity2* (our measure of democracy), and dummy variables for LDCs and OECD membership to the core model.[16] The dummy variables for OECD membership and LDC status offer an additional test for nonlinearities or effects that are not related to variation in income level or other (institutional) characteristics. OECD membership is never significant. LDC status gives mixed results, depending on the time period under investigation, but in general LDC status is associated with larger trade resilience, possibly because of better access to aid and greater awareness of the aid community. The political variable *polity2* is only marginally significant in the export equations (and not for the 1970–2008 subperiod) and never in the import equations. Our conclusion from this finding is that our research does not offer support for the view that the political system is an important determinant of trade resilience. The exploratory estimates provide preliminary evidence that

Table 7.6
Panel estimates for annual real export (FGLS, 1970–2014).

	(1)	(2)	(3)	(4)	(5)	(6)
DISASTER	0.33***	0.26***	0.34***	0.38***	0.27***	0.33***
	(4.74)	(3.25)	(4.31)	(4.32)	(4.57)	(4.55)
*DISASTER*GDPpc*	−0.94***	−0.89***	−0.97***	−0.59***	−0.77***	−1.24**
	(−5.09)	(−4.53)	(−4.61)	(−2.70)	(−4.65)	(−2.74)
*DISASTER*FDIflow*		0.05***				
		(2.04)				
*DISASTER*FDIstock*			0.00			
			(0.09)			
*DISASTER*polity2*				−0.02*		
				(−1.80)		
*DISASTER*LDC*					1.03**	
					(2.84)	
*DISASTER*OECD*						0.11
						(0.64)
N	5,253	4,753	4,216	4,782	5,253	5,253
R^2	0.158	0.163	0.158	0.161	0.161	0.160

Note: t statistics in parentheses.
* $p<0.1$; ** $p<0.05$; *** $p<0.01$.

Table 7.7
Panel estimates for annual real import (FGLS, 1970–2014).

	(1)	(2)	(3)	(4)	(5)	(6)
DISASTER	0.39***	0.40***	0.43***	0.32***	0.32***	0.34***
	(4.9)	(4.6)	(5.2)	(3.5)	(4.3)	(4.0)
DISASTER*GDPpc	−1.01***	−1.08***	−1.35***	−1.09***	−0.84***	−1.34***
	(−5.24)	(−5.39)	(−6.24)	(−4.64)	(−4.49)	(−3.28)
DISASTER*FDIflow		0.01				
		(0.58)				
DISASTER*FDIstock			0.01**			
			(2.46)			
DISASTER*polity2				0.01		
				(0.88)		
DISASTER*LDC					0.61*	
					(1.81)	
DISASTER*OECD						0.17
						(1.01)
N	5,253	4,753	4,216	4,782	5,253	5,253
R^2	0.153	0.155	0.158	0.162	0.153	0.149

Note: t statistics in parentheses.
* $p<0.1$; ** $p<0.05$; *** $p<0.01$.

FDI enhances trade resilience but also that the mechanism by which this takes place differs for exports and imports: for exports, the effect appears to be associated with the flow of FDI, and for imports the association is with stocks (thus the long-run accumulation of flows).

It is noteworthy that this section reported on different specifications and period subsamples. Because of variations in data availability regarding some of the resilience factors, the number of observations varies. The regressions on different subsamples offer some additional indication for the robustness of the consistent findings for DISASTER.

7.5   Conclusions, Caveats, and Issues for Further Research

The empirical findings of this chapter offer an alternative perspective on the emerging literature on trade and natural disasters. In particular, using the seminal framework developed by Jones and Olken (2010), we offer a different perspective on the question of the impact of disasters on trade flows. In the early phase of research in this field, this issue was predominantly studied using gravity models, but methodological heterogeneity is developing. That alternatives for gravity models are being developed and applied is also good because the supply-side and demand-side shocks of natural disasters a priori would impact trade in general rather than the bilateral trade flows that are the focus of gravity models. The findings of the emerging literature, as demonstrated in tables 7.2 and 7.3, are less convincing than often assumed by those who adhere to the emerging consensus view that disasters are bad for trade.

This chapter adds our exploratory empirical findings to the emerging literature on natural disasters and trade: disasters in our sample are associated with higher import growth and higher export growth. This finding looks completely different from the results reported in the early literature only because the earliest researchers themselves have erroneously drawn the conclusion that disasters reduce trade, despite empirical findings that actually are more in line with our findings and interpretation (as we discussed earlier when we presented this literature in tables 7.2 and 7.3). Regarding imports, our findings reflect that disasters imply the need for reconstruction and imports to replace domestic production that is destroyed by the disaster. In our opinion, this finding for imports is supported by the underlying evidence of the available studies and could form the basis for a new consensus in the field. For exports, our results are in line with the Schumpeterian destructive creation hypothesis and also reflect that firms that are confronted with a reduction of domestic demand may seek international markets. It is important to point out that the early literature on the export effect of disasters is less convincing than often assumed but also more convincing than the early findings on import effects. Clearly, our findings do not tip the balance. Much more research is necessary to arrive at a consensus.

We argue not that our findings show that disasters are always good for trade but rather that economic mechanisms are operating that are not yet well understood. In this context, country case studies that investigate these mechanisms both at the macro level and micro level will be very useful. Indeed, research on this topic could be furthered not only by multicountry studies but also by single-country studies that could allow the use of better and/or more detailed data (including microdata or country-specific sets) that may enable researchers to focus more directly on the underlying mechanisms in the trade-disaster nexus.

From the perspective of this book, such research could help strengthen our understanding of the productivity impact of trade shocks. Moreover, such studies will be important to strengthen the basis for research synthesis by means of a meta-analysis. Given the developments in the field, we expect that a useful meta-analysis will be possible in the years to come.

Our econometric analysis offers no empirical support for the importance of democracy as a trade resilience factor or for nonlinearities between the impact of disasters on exports (imports) and level of development. When we include potential factors of trade resilience, particularly pre-disaster FDI stocks and flows, we find different impacts in export and import equations. An important issue for future research is to recognize these differences (which are also identified in country-specific studies). Conclusions about the impact of natural disasters need to be differentiated with respect to the trade flow and need to be based on analyses that deal with exports and imports specifically.

We are well aware of the limitations of the estimated small quasi-reduced form equations that we have used, and we acknowledge that their explanatory power is on the low side. For testing hypotheses regarding the sign of the impact of disasters on trade flows, the approach pioneered by Jones and Olken (2010) is informative and acceptable, but clearly more research is needed on the underlying mechanisms and in particular could reflect on several underlying heterogeneities. El Hadri, Mirza, and Rabaud (2017), for example, investigate different forms of disasters and report different and sometimes contradictory impacts in their analysis of agricultural imports. If anything, more research for different countries and periods is necessary in view of the still limited amount of studies on this important topic.

Appendix: List of Countries Included in Dataset

Afghanistan, Albania, Algeria, Angola, Argentina, Armenia, Australia, Austria, Azerbaijan, The Bahamas, Bahrain, Bangladesh, Barbados, Belarus, Belgium, Belize, Benin, Bhutan, Bolivia, Bosnia and Herze-govina, Botswana, Brazil, Brunei Darussalam, Bulgaria, Burkina Faso, Burundi, Cabo Verde, Cambodia, Cameroon, Canada, Central African Republic, Chad, Chile, China, Colombia, Comoros, Costa Rica, Côte d'Ivoire, Croatia, Cuba, Cyprus, Czech Republic, Democratic Republic of the Congo, Democratic Republic of Korea, Denmark, Djibouti, Dominican Republic, Ecuador, Egypt, El Salvador, Equatorial Guinea, Eritrea, Estonia, Ethiopia, Fiji, Finland, France, Gabon, The Gambia, Georgia, Germany, Ghana, Greece, Guatemala, Guinea, Guinea-Bissau, Haiti, Honduras, Hong Kong SAR (China), Hungary, Iceland, India, Indonesia, Iran, Ireland, Israel, Italy, Jamaica, Japan, Jordan,

Kazakhstan, Kenya, Kosovo, Kuwait, Kyrgyz Republic, Lao PDR, Latvia, Lebanon, Lesotho, Liberia, Libya, Lithuania, Luxembourg, Macao SAR (China), Macedonia (FYR), Madagascar, Malawi, Malaysia, Maldives, Mali, Malta, Martinique, Mauritania, Mauritius, Mexico, Moldova, Mongolia, Montenegro, Morocco, Mozambique, Myanmar, Namibia, Nepal, Netherlands, New Zealand, Nicaragua, Niger, Nigeria, Norway, Oman, Pakistan, Panama, Papua New Guinea, Paraguay, Peru, Philippines, Poland, Portugal, Puerto Rico, Qatar, Republic of the Congo, Republic of Korea, Romania, Russian Federation, Rwanda, Samoa, Saudi Arabia, Senegal, Serbia, Seychelles, Sierra Leone, Singapore, Slovak Republic, Slovakia, Slovenia, Somalia, South Africa, South Sudan, Spain, Sudan, Swaziland, Sweden, Switzerland, Syrian Arab Republic, Tajikistan, Tanzania, Thailand, Timor-Leste, Togo, Trinidad and Tobago, Tunisia, Turkey, Turkmenistan, Uganda, Ukraine, United Arab Emirates, United Kingdom, United States, Uruguay, Uzbekistan, Vanuatu, Venezuela (RB), Vietnam, Zambia, Zimbabwe.

Notes

1. It is increasingly being recognized that individual natural disasters provide natural experiments that can be used to test trade and trade-related theories because infrastructure and trading routes are (temporarily) distorted. For examples, see Martincus and Blyde (2013) and Besedes and Murshid (2014).

2. Related literature on climate change and trade is better developed. While relevant, these contributions deal not so much with trade shocks (the topic of this chapter) but rather with more or less structural changes in temperature and humidity as well as the potential role of trade (openness) in mitigating the impact of such changes. For examples, see Burgess and Donaldson (2010), Jones and Olken (2010), Tekce and Deniz (2016), and Costinot, Donaldson, and Smith (2016).

3. Note that the results reported by Felbermayr and Gröschl were produced in an investigation into the question of whether openness affects per capita GDP, in which natural disasters are an instrument variable. Their research design and thus the definition of natural disasters and the sample are driven by a different research question, but their findings regarding standard gravity are still very informative.

4. Oh (2017) investigates the average of bilateral exports and imports with statistically negative coefficients for the occurrence of one disaster (either in the origin or destination) and two disasters (in both origin and destination). This result is driven by the trade between developed and developing nations, as it is not significant in North-North and South-South trade.

5. Individual country studies also point out different and asymmetric impacts of disasters on imports and exports. See, for example, Abe (2017), Li, Xiang, and Gu (2015), and Meng et al. (2015).

6. This meta-analysis, moreover, offers additional support for the view that the trade-disaster nexus is underdeveloped in the literature, as only 9 percent (direct costs) and 40

percent (indirect costs) of the 64 primary studies consider openness as an explanatory variable. See van Bergeijk, Brakman, and van Marrewijk (2017, 2).

7. Note that natural disasters may thus stimulate the export decisions of individual firms, a mechanism that is less likely or unlikely to occur in certain man-made trade shocks, such as economic sanctions.

8. It is worth noting that the underlying assumption that lower levels of development lead to higher impact is often based on the observation that countries with a higher temperature are less developed on average (Dell, Jones, and Olken 2012). This is a well-established stylized fact, but the assumption (Jones and Olken 2010; El Hadri, Mirza, and Rabaud 2017) that this is also true for disasters (especially those not related to temperature) suffers from the Fallacy of Hasty Generalization.

9. Note, however, that the impact of aid and preferential treatment may be ambiguous—see, for example, Rajan and Subramanian (2008)—and that developing country classification and access to financial instruments are complicated by overlap and multistatus countries. See, for example, Fialho and van Bergeijk (2016).

10. Raschky and Schwindt (2009) investigated a similar change in perspective from the foreign post-disaster aid analyzed in the mainstream literature as they studied the impact of foreign pre-disaster development aid on disaster outcome. See also Andergassen and Sereno (2014) for an analysis of private-firm decision-making on mitigation investment in the context of different forms of financial support by donors. Oh (2017) develops a multinational's perspective on different forms of man-made and natural disasters but leaves FDI for future research.

11. See van Bergeijk (2013) for an analysis that shows the dampening effect of international value chains in the downturn of the 2008–2009 world trade collapse. See Korniyenko, Pinat, and Dew (2017) for an analysis that focuses on transmission of trade shocks via international value chains.

12. An additional argument to focus on in the empirical investigation on stocks could be that FDI stocks are measured more accurately than FDI flows (see van Bergeijk 1995).

13. We decided to drop two types of disasters: "animal accident" (Niger, 2014, total deaths 12, *DISASTER* 1) and "impact" (Russia, 2013, total deaths 0, *DISASTER* 1, affected 300,000). These disaster types have only one observation each in EM-DAT.

14. The Jones-Olken approach appears to be recognized as a standard approach by policymakers. See, for example, International Monetary Fund (2017), chap. 3.

15. The difference in size of the estimated coefficient reflects both the different level of aggregation of the trade variable and the transformation by El Hadri, Mirza, and Rabaud (2017) of the *DISASTER* variable as a log (which requires the addition of an arbitrary constant to deal with zero-disaster cases).

16. The nonreported findings for subperiods are qualitatively comparable.

References

Abe, S. 2017. "Impact of the Great Thai Floods on the International Supply Chain." *Malaysian Journal of Economic Studies* 51:147–155.

Adam, C. 2013. "Coping with Adversity: The Macroeconomic Management of Natural Disasters." *Environmental Science and Policy* 27:S99–S111.

Andergassen, R., and L. Sereno. 2014. "Natural Disasters, Mitigation Investment and Financial Aid." *Environment and Development Economics*1 (5): 1–23.

Besedes, T., and A. P. Murshid. 2014. "The Effects of Airspace Closures on Trade in the Aftermath of Eyjafjallajökull." Georgia Institute of Technology. Mimeo.

Biersteker, T., and P. A. G. van Bergeijk. 2015. "How and When Do Sanctions Work? The Evidence." In *EU Sanctions as Security Policy Tools*, edited by I. Dreyer and J. Luengo-Cabrera, 17–27. Paris: European Union Institute for Security Studies.

Bloom, N. 2014. "Fluctuations in Uncertainty." *Journal of Economic Perspectives* 28 (2): 153–175.

Brata, A. G. 2017. "The Socio-economic Impacts of Natural Disasters." PhD thesis, Vrije Universiteit, Amsterdam.

Briguglio, L., G. Cordina, N. Farrugia, and S. Vella. 2009. "Conceptualizing and Measuring Economic Resilience." *Oxford Development Studies* 37 (3): 229–247.

Burgess, R., and D. Donaldson. 2010. "Can Openness Mitigate the Effects of Weather Shocks? Evidence from India's Famine Era." *American Economic Review* 100 (2): 449–453.

Costinot, A., D. Donaldson, and C. Smith. 2016. "Evolving Comparative Advantage and the Impact of Climate Change in Agricultural Markets: Evidence from 1.7 Million Fields around the World." *Journal of Political Economy* 124 (1): 205–248.

Dell, M., B. F. Jones, and B. A. Olken. 2012. "Temperature Shocks and Economic Growth: Evidence from the Last Half Century." *American Economic Journal: Macroeconomics* 4 (3): 66–95.

Dell, M., B. F. Jones, and B. A. Olken. 2014. "What Do We Learn from the Weather? The New Climate-Economy Literature." *Journal of Economic Literature* 52 (3): 740–798.

El Hadri, H., D. Mirza, and I. Rabaud. 2017. "Natural Disasters and Countries' Exports: New Insights from a New (and an Old) Database." Orleans Economics Laboratory Working Paper LEO 2503. Orleans: University of Orleans. http://data.leo-univ-orleans.fr/media/search-works/2503/dr201710.pdf.

Elliott, J. 2012. "Earthquake Disasters and Resilience in the Global North: Lessons from New Zealand and Japan." *Geographical Journal* 178 (3): 208–215.

Escaleras, M., N. Anbarci, and C. A. Register. 2007. "Public Sector Corruption and Major Earthquakes: A Potentially Deadly Interaction." *Public Choice* 132 (1–2): 209–230.

Felbermayr, G., and J. Gröschl. 2013. "Natural Disasters and the Effect of Trade on Income: A New Panel IV Approach." *European Economic Review* 58 (1): 18–30.

Fialho, D., and P. A. G. van Bergeijk. 2016. "The Proliferation of Developing Country Classifications." *Journal of Development Studies* 53 (1): 99–115.

Gassebner, M., A. Keck, and R. Teh. 2010. "Shaken, Not Stirred: The Impact of Disasters on International Trade." *Review of International Economics* 18 (2): 351–368.

Gehlbach, S., and P. Keefer. 2011. "Investment without Democracy: Ruling-Party Institutionalization and Credible Commitment in Autocracies." *Journal of Comparative Economics* 39 (2): 123–139.

Grossman, R. S., and C. M. Meissner. 2010. "International Aspects of the Great Depression and the Crisis of 2007: Similarities, Differences, and Lessons." *Oxford Review of Economic Policy* 26 (3): 318–338.

Hayakawa, K., T. Matsuura, and F. Okubo. 2015. "Firm-Level Impacts of Natural Disasters on Production Networks: Evidence from a Flood in Thailand." *Journal of the Japanese and International Economies* 38: 244–259.

Heger, M., A. Julca, and O. Paddison. 2008. "Analysing the Impact of Natural Hazards in Small Economies: The Caribbean Case." UN-WIDER Research Paper 2008/25. Helsinki: World Institute for Development Economics Research, United Nations University.

International Monetary Fund (IMF). 2017. *World Economic Outlook*, October. Washington DC: International Monetary Fund.

Jones, B. F., and B. A. Olken. 2010. "Climate Shocks and Exports." *American Economic Review* 100 (2): 454–459.

Kahn, M. E. 2005. "The Death Toll from Natural Disasters: The Role of Income, Geography, and Institutions." *Review of Economics and Statistics* 87 (2): 271–284.

Kellenberg, D. K., and A. M. Mobarak. 2008. "Does Rising Income Increase or Decrease Damage Risk from Natural Disasters?" *Journal of Urban Economics* 63 (3): 788–802.

Korniyenko, Y., M. Pinat, and B. Dew. 2017. "Assessing the Fragility of Global Trade: The Impact of Localized Supply Shocks Using Network Analysis." IMF Working Paper 17/30. Washington, DC: International Monetary Fund.

Lazzaroni, S., and P. A. G. van Bergeijk. 2014. "Natural Disasters' Impact, Factors of Resilience and Development: A Meta-analysis of the Macroeconomic Literature." *Ecological Economics* 107: 333–346.

Li, C., X. Xiang, and H. Gu. 2015. "Climate Shocks and International Trade: Evidence from China." *Economics Letters* 135: 55–57.

Martincus, C. V., and J. Blyde. 2013. "Shaky Roads and Trembling Exports: Assessing the Trade Effects of Domestic Infrastructure Using a Natural Experiment." *Journal of International Economics* 90 (1): 148–161.

Meng, Y., S. Yang, P. Shi, and C. C. Jeager. 2015. "The Asymmetric Impact of Natural Disasters on China's Bilateral Trade." *Natural Hazards and Earth System Sciences* 15 (10): 2273–2281.

Novy, D., and A. M. Taylor. 2014. "Trade and Uncertainty." NBER Working Paper 19941. Cambridge, MA: National Bureau of Economic Research.

Noy, I. 2009. "The Macroeconomic Consequences of Disasters." *Journal of Development Economics* 88 (2): 221–231.

Oh, C. H. 2017. "How Do Natural and Man-Made Disasters Affect International Trade? A Country-Level and Industry-Level Analysis." *Journal of Risk Research* 20 (2): 195–217.

Oh, C. H., and R. Reuveny. 2010. "Climatic Natural Disasters, Political Risk, and International Trade." *Global Environmental Change* 20 (2): 243–254.

Padli, J., and M. S. Habibullah. 2009. "Natural Disaster Death and Socio-economic Factors in Selected Asian Countries: A Panel Analysis." *Asian Social Science* 5 (4): 65–71.

Pelli, M., and J. Tschopp. 2012. "The Creative Destruction of Hurricanes." http://www.freit.org/RMET/2012/SubmittedPapers/Martino_Pelli03.pdf.

Pelling, M., A. Özerdem, and S. Barakat. 2002. "The Macro-economic Impact of Disasters." *Progress in Development Studies* 2 (4): 283–305.

Rajan, R. G., and A. Subramanian. 2008. "Aid and Growth: What Does the Cross-Country Evidence Really Show?" *Review of Economics and Statistics* 90 (4): 643–665.

Raschky, P. A. 2008. "Institutions and the Losses from Natural Disasters." *Natural Hazards and Earth System Sciences* 8 (4): 627–634.

Raschky, P. A., and M. Schwindt. 2009. "Aid, Natural Disasters and the Samaritan's Dilemma." World Bank Policy Research Working Paper Series 4952. Washington, DC: World Bank.

Tekce, M., and P. Deniz. 2016. "The Impacts of Climate Change on Agricultural Trade in the MENA Region." *Research in World Economy* 7 (2): 1–14.

Van Bergeijk, P. A. G. 1995. "The Accuracy of International Economic Observations." *Bulletin of Economic Research* 47 (1): 1–20.

Van Bergeijk, P. A. G. 2010. *On the Brink of Deglobalization: An Alternative Perspective on the World Trade Collapse.* Cheltenham: Edward Elgar.

Van Bergeijk, P. A. G. 2013. "The World Trade Collapse and International Value Chains: A Cross-Country Perspective." *International Economic Journal* 27 (1): 41–53.

Van Bergeijk, P. A. G. 2018. "On the Brink of Deglobalization … Again." *Cambridge Journal of Regions, Economy and Society* 11 (1): 59–72.

Van Bergeijk, P. A. G., S. Brakman, and C. Marrewijk. 2017. "Heterogeneous Economic Resilience and the Great Recession's World Trade Collapse." *Papers in Regional Science* 96 (1): 3–12.

Van Bergeijk, P. A. G., and S. Moons. 2009. "Economic Diplomacy and Economic Security." In *New Frontiers for Economic Diplomacy*, edited by C. Costa, 37–54. Lisbon: CAPP.

Wagner, J., and J. P. W. Gelübcke. 2014. "Risk or Resilience? The Role of Trade Integration and Foreign Ownership for the Survival of German Enterprises during the Crisis 2008–2010." *Jahrbücher für Nationalökonomie und Statistik* 234 (6): 757–774.

Yamamura, E. 2011a. "Death Caused by Natural Disasters: The Role of Ethnic Heterogeneity." EERI Research Paper Series 10/2011. Brussels: Economics and Econometrics Research Institute.

Yamamura, E. 2011b. "Institution, Economic Development, and Impact of Natural Disasters." Munich: Munich Personal RePec Archive.

8 Exploring the Long-Term Evolution of Trade Survival

Wolfgang Hess and Maria Persson

8.1 Introduction

Starting with the seminal contributions by Besedeš and Prusa (2006a, 2006b), research on international trade has had to take into account the fact that trade flows are not at all as stable and long lived as previously thought. Focusing on the number of years that a single bilateral trade flow survives from the first year of trade until the value of trade is again zero for this particular product, the literature on the *duration of trade* attempts to explain what determines the survival of international trade flows. This is an important question to answer, not least from a development perspective. As shown empirically by Besedeš and Prusa (2011), high death rates among new trade flows can, for instance, prevent badly needed long-term export growth. In other words, understanding why and how trade relationships are disrupted is a central part of the larger theme of disrupted economic relationships.

We hope to make two contributions in this chapter. First, we offer an extensive literature review of the existing research on trade durations. Importantly, we cover both the literature that—similar to Besedeš and Prusa (2006a, 2006b)—uses data at the country-product level as the basis for analysis *and* the somewhat separate literature that investigates firms' trading behavior. Based on this survey, we will discuss a set of general conclusions about what we have learned on this issue so far, including identifying a list of explanatory variables that have been shown to matter for explaining trade survival patterns. Second, as a complement to this literature review, we offer new empirical evidence that the explanatory factors that have previously been identified as relevant are not enough to explain the variation in trade survival over time. To do so, our empirical strategy takes as its starting point the striking result in Hess and Persson (2011) that short duration is actually a very persistent characteristic of trade throughout time, and in fact trade relationships in the 1960s died as early as they do today.[1] Using the same data, and including as many of the variables as possible that have been identified as relevant by the previous literature,[2] we show that this stability is the result of two trends in opposite directions. On the one hand, positive trends in several of the *observed* explanatory variables—which in turn influence the hazard of trade flows dying in a negative direction— imply that the hazard tends to decrease over calendar time. In fact, if we only take these effects into account, the estimated first-year hazard would go from 34 percent in the early 1960s to a level of only 3 percent in 2006. On the other hand, there is also a positive trend in the hazard resulting from *unobserved* factors, which are captured by the calendar year dummies. In other words, when disregarding the observed explanatory variables, there is an upward trend in the hazard, implying that trade flows, ceteris paribus, are more likely to die quickly at the end of the time period under study. Holding all other determinants constant, the hazard of a trade flow dying in its first year increases from 34 percent at the beginning of the period to 90 percent at the end. How should these results be interpreted? Our interpretation is that if only the explanatory variables that have so far been identified as important mattered, trade would be quite long lived today. Since it is not, this is clear empirical evidence that more research is needed to identify additional variables that can help us understand what drives trade survival.

The remainder of the chapter is organized as follows. In section 8.2, we present our survey of the existing relevant research studies and discuss the conclusions that can be drawn from the overall research field. We then turn to our empirical investigation. In section 8.3, the data used are briefly presented. Section 8.4 then discusses the empirical strategy and presents the regression results. In section 8.5, we illustrate that the regression results can be used to draw conclusions about how much of the change in the duration of trade over time is explained by factors commonly used as explanatory variables and how much is explained by factors not yet identified. Lastly, section 8.6 summarizes the main findings and conclusions.

8.2   Survey of the Literature on Trade Duration

In this section, we will present and discuss our survey of the existing research studies in the field of trade duration. It should be noted that any attempt to summarize a research field will inevitably be somewhat

Table 8.1
Overview of studies using country-level data.

Study	Data/Sample	Methodology	Question/Findings
Besedeš (2008)	US imports of differentiated products. Exporter- and product-specific. 1972–1988: 7-digit US Tariffs Schedule (TS); 1989–2001: 10-digit Harmonized System (HS).	Stratified Cox	Shows that the incidence and duration of imports are consistent with a search model of international trade. Larger initial purchases result in longer durations. Higher reliability and lower search costs lead to larger initial purchases and longer duration.
Besedeš (2011)	Exports from transition economies, 1996–2006. Exporter-, importer-, and product-specific (6-digit HS).	Probit	Focuses on differences across homogeneous goods, reference-priced goods, and differentiated products. Finds significant differences in the hazard across both countries and time.
Besedeš (2013)	Exports from Canada, Mexico, and United States, 1990–2007. Exporter-, importer-, and product-specific (6-digit HS).	RE Probit	Exports within NAFTA face lower hazard, but the creation of NAFTA increased the hazard for Mexican and US intra-NAFTA exports.
Besedeš, Moreno-Cruz, and Nitsch (2015)	Imports to 180 countries, 1962–2005. Exporter-, importer-, and product-specific (5-digit SITC).	RE Probit	Economic integration (covering many different types of agreements) increases the duration of trade relationships that started before the agreement but reduces the duration of trade relationships that started after the agreement.
Besedeš and Prusa (2006a)	US imports. Exporter- and product-specific. 1972–1988: 7-digit TS and 160 trading partners; 1989–2001: 10-digit HS and 180 trading partners.	Kaplan-Meier	Initial paper outlining the short duration of trade. Broad descriptive analysis.
Besedeš and Prusa (2006b)	US imports. Exporter- and product-specific. 1972–1988: 7-digit TS and 160 trading partners; 1989–2001: 10-digit HS and 180 trading partners.	Cox	Product characteristics matter. Higher hazard for homogeneous goods than for differentiated goods.
Besedeš and Prusa (2013)	Quarterly US imports, 1990–2006. Exporter- and product-specific (10-digit HS).	RE Probit	Antidumping action increases the hazard rate by more than 50%. Investigation effects larger than during the final duty phase.
Brenton, Saborowski, and von Uexküll (2010)	Exports from 82 exporters to 53 importers, 1985–2005. Exporter-, importer-, and product-specific (5-digit SITC).	Cloglog	Discusses the appropriateness of using Cox models to estimate the duration of trade and proposes the use of a cloglog model. Empirical analysis shows that experience with exporting the same product before or the same product to other markets decreases the hazard.

(continued)

Table 8.1 (continued)

Study	Data/Sample	Methodology	Question/Findings
Carrère and Strauss-Kahn (2014)	114 developing countries' exports to OECD countries, 1962–2009. Exporter-, importer-, and product-specific (5-digit SITC).	Cox, probit, linear probability model	Prior experience in non-OECD market decreases the hazard of exports to OECD markets dying, but the effect of experience depreciates rapidly.
Chen (2012)	Data as in Besedeš and Prusa (2006a), but sample reduced to 12 manufacturing industries' imports from 105 countries.	Stratified Cox	Innovation (captured by number of patents) has a positive effect on survival.
Jaud, Kukenova, and Strieborny (2012)	Exports to the United States from 143 countries, 1995–2005. Exporter- and product-specific (6-digit HS).	Stratified Cox	Shorter export duration if the export product does not represent a comparative advantage (in the Heckscher-Ohlin sense). That pattern is intensified if the exporting country has a well-developed banking system.
Hess and Persson (2011)	Imports to EU15 countries from 140 exporters, 1962–2006. Importer-, exporter-, and product-specific (4-digit SITC).	Various discrete-time duration models	Gravity variables matter for the duration of trade. Export diversification in terms of products and markets lowers the hazard of trade flows dying.
Hess and Persson (2012)	Replication of Besedeš and Prusa (2006b), so same data.	Compares Cox with probit, logit, and cloglog	Argues that estimating the duration of trade with Cox models leads to several econometric problems, some of which also apply to its discrete-time equivalent, the cloglog model. Proposes the use of probit or logit models (with proper controls for unobserved heterogeneity). Replicates Besedeš and Prusa (2006b) with new econometric methods to show that the theoretical problems do influence the results.
Nitsch (2009)	German imports, 1995–2005. Exporter- and product-specific (8-digit CN).	Stratified Cox	Gravity variables matter for the duration of trade.
Obashi (2010)	Trade among nine East Asian countries, 1993–2006. Importer-, exporter-, and product-specific (6-digit HS).	Cox	Trade in machinery parts and components has longer duration than trade in machinery finished products.

Table 8.2
Overview of studies using firm-level data.

Study	Data/Sample	Methodology	Question/Findings
Esteve-Pérez, Requena-Silvente, and Pallardó-Lopez (2013)	Spanish firm- and destination-specific exports (but not product), 1997–2006. Median duration is two years for a firm's export to a destination (any product).	Cloglog	Country (political) risk influences the effect of firm, product, and other destination characteristics on the duration of trade.
Fugazza and McLaren (2014)	Peruvian firm exports, 2002–2008. Firm-, destination-, and product-specific (2-digit HS2).	Various discrete-time duration models	Market access (summary of tariffs faced by exporters or bilateral measure of preferential margin) relative to those faced by competitors matters for duration.
Görg, Kneller, and Muraközy (2012)	Hungarian firm exports, 1992–2003. Firm- and product-specific (6-digit HS) but not destination-specific.	Cloglog	Firm productivity, product scale, and product tenure are associated with higher survival rates.
Gullstrand and Persson (2015)	Swedish firm agrifood exports, 1997–2007. Firm-, destination-, and product-specific (8-digit CN).	Various discrete-time duration models	The duration of exports is longer for firms' core markets, whereas export decisions for peripheral markets are of much shorter term. Explains apparent discrepancy between the literature on sunk costs and on trade duration.
Ilmakunnas and Nurmi (2010)	Finnish manufacturing firm exports, 1980–2005. Firm-specific.	Cloglog	Firm characteristics matter for duration. More productive firms with high capital intensity survive longer as exporters, as do foreign-owned firms (if large and productive).
Jaud and Kukenova (2011)	Firm exports from Ghana, Mali, Malawi, Senegal, and Tanzania, at most 2000–2008 (varies across countries). Exports to 254 countries. Firm-, destination-, and product-specific (8-digit HS).	Stratified Cox	Tests whether the effect of financial development on the survival of exports varies based on products' need of external financing. Findings suggest that agrifood products that require greater external financing have a longer export duration if the exporting country is more financially developed.

(continued)

Table 8.2 (continued)

Study	Data/Sample	Methodology	Question/Findings
Lejour (2015)	Dutch firm exports, 2002–2008. Firm, destination-, and product-specific ("5-digit product level"?).	Various discrete-time duration models	Hazard is lower if the destination country belongs to the European Union. New trade relations with new exporting firms or new destinations have lower hazard rates than those with new products.
Martuscelli and Varela (2015)	Georgian firm exports, 2006–2012. Firm-, destination-, and product-specific (6-digit HS).	Various discrete-time duration models	It matters how firms diversify. Many products increase survival, whereas firms with many destinations have lower survival rates. Production efficiency rather than size lowers the hazard. Evidence of network effects: hazard decreases with the number of firms that export the same product to the same destination. FTAs lower the hazard.
Sabuhoro, Larue, and Gervais (2006)	Canadian firm exports, 1993–2000. Firm-, destination-, and product-specific (?).	Cox	Early illustration of the fact that firm characteristics, such as size, matter for the duration of trade. The hazard is negatively affected by the number of export products and destinations.
Stirbat, Record, and Nghardsaysone (2015)	Laos firm exports, 2005–2010. Firm-, destination-, and product-specific (6-digit HS).	Various discrete-time duration models, plus competing risks model (allowing not only for "death" but also upgrades to superior products)	Having prior experience with the export product and destination decreases the hazard. Strong networks of similar firms also decrease the hazard.
Volpe-Martincus and Carballo (2008)	Peruvian firm exports, 2000–2006. Firm-, destination-, and product-specific (10-digit HS).	Cox	Geographic diversification and product diversification increase survival, and the former more than the latter.

selective. In our case, we specifically want to point out that we have chosen to focus on the *empirical* research contributions. There are also a number of very interesting papers offering *theoretical* frameworks for analyzing the duration of trade, but these will have to be discussed elsewhere. Also, we want to emphasize that we have concentrated on the studies that explicitly estimate the duration of trade. There is also a related set of papers that indirectly answer similar questions, for instance by dividing trade flows into "permanent" or "temporary," such as Békés and Murakózy (2012), or by analyzing the binary outcome of surviving the first year of trade or not, such as Cadot et al. (2013).[3] While indeed interesting, such papers have not been included in our survey since we want to focus on papers that analyze the same type of question.

Table 8.1 summarizes the empirical contributions using country-product trade data, while table 8.2 gives a corresponding overview for the papers analyzing firms' trading behavior. We will now discuss some overall conclusions that can be drawn from this field.

8.2.1 Trade Duration Really *Is* Very Short

While the idea of international trade being short lived and character-ized by a lot of movements in and out of the international market was initially surprising, there is now overwhelming empirical support for this result. We will use the surveyed literature to draw some more detailed conclusions about just how robust a result this is.

The first important conclusion that can be drawn from our literature survey is that the result that trade is short lived *holds for firms' trade as well as country-level trade*. Across the papers surveyed in table 8.1, focus-ing on country-level data, and table 8.2, focusing on firm-level data, all studies on trade duration tend to draw the same conclusion: trade dura-tions are short. To give some idea of the level of survival that the litera-ture tends to find, Hess and Persson (2011), studying imports to EU15 countries from 140 exporters during the period 1962–2006, find that almost 60 percent of all observed export spells cease during the first year of service. Furthermore, approximately 75 percent of all trade flows terminate within the first two years, and more than four in five trade relationships only last a maximum of three years. Gullstrand and Persson (2015) find similar results for Swedish firms: 69 percent of all firm-, prod-uct-, and destination-specific export spells last at most one year, and only 15 percent of new trade flows survive for more than two years.

Second, the result *holds for many different samples*. In the literature using country-level data, the various samples include trade for the United

States (see, e.g., Besedeš and Prusa 2006a, 2006b), NAFTA (Besedeš 2013), EU15 (Hess and Persson 2011), Germany (Nitsch 2009), East Asian countries (Obashi 2010), transition economies (Besedeš 2011), developing countries' exports to the OECD (Carrère and Strauss-Kahn 2014), and more. The literature focusing on firms' trade data also covers an impressive range of countries: Canada (Sabuhoro, Larue, and Gervais 2006), Peru (Volpe-Martincus and Carballo 2008; Fugazza and McLaren 2014), Finland (Ilmakunnas and Nurmi 2010), Ghana, Mali, Malawi, Senegal, and Tanzania (Jaud and Kukenova 2011), Hungary (Görg, Kneller, and Muraközy 2012), Spain (Esteve-Perez, Requena-Silvente, and Pallardó-Lopez 2013), Sweden (Gullstrand and Persson 2015), the Netherlands (Lejour 2015), Georgia (Martuscelli and Varela 2015), and Laos (Stirbat, Record, and Nghardsaysone 2015).

Third, the result holds up surprisingly well *over calendar time*. Since that is the topic of the empirical part of this chapter, we will refrain from discussing it further here.

Fourth, the result that trade durations are very short *does not depend on issues of aggregation*. This rather surprising finding was first reported by Besedeš and Prusa (2006a) for US imports. Studying EU imports, Hess and Persson (2011) illustrate that aggregating the data from the baseline four-digit SITC level to the three-, two-, or even one-digit levels has very small effects on the observed trade durations. In fact, even at the one-digit level, where only ten product categories exist, the median duration of imports is only two years, which can be compared with the one-year median duration at the four-digit level of aggregation. Similar conclusions are drawn by Gullstrand and Persson (2015) for the exports of Swedish firms: aggregating the data does not destroy the result that trade durations are very short.

Fifth, the result also *does not depend on how spells of trade are defined*. As discussed at length, for example, by Hess and Persson (2011), including only single spells (i.e., observations where a specific exporter-importer-product combination has only a single coherent period of trade) does not drastically alter the duration of trade. The same is true if only the first spells of trade are included or when analyzing spells where any one-year or two-year exits from the market are disregarded.

To summarize, the result that trade is very short lived is a remarkably robust empirical result, which holds for countries' trade as well as firms' trade, over a wide range of samples and across time, and using different levels of aggregation or ways to define trade spells. Trade duration really *is* very short.

8.2.2 What Explains Trade Duration?

Having concluded that there is strong empirical support for the notion that trade is short lived, we will now briefly discuss which explanatory variables have been identified as important determinants by the empirical literature.

Not surprisingly, the literature has shown that *gravity variables* matter when it comes to explaining the duration of trade. Empirical evidence of this is found in many papers, but early examples include Besedeš (2008), Nitsch (2009), and Hess and Persson (2011). For instance, if the importer or exporter is a large economy, this tends to lower the hazard rate. Furthermore, longer bilateral distances tend to increase the likelihood of failure, while sharing the same language or a joint colonial history tends to lower the hazard.

As shown by Besedeš and Prusa (2006b), Besedeš (2008), and others, the *size of the initial trade flow* is also an important determinant for the duration of the subsequent trade relationship. When a new trade relationship starts with a large initial transaction, the trade relationship will tend to last longer.

Diversification—defined in various ways—seems to matter quite a lot for the duration of trade. For instance, Volpe-Martincus and Carballo (2008) show that the hazard for exports from Peruvian firms is lower if the firm serves many export markets or exports a broad range of products. Hess and Persson (2011) confirm that the same finding holds for country-level trade and also find evidence that import diversification is less important than export diversification. Interestingly, Martuscelli and Varela (2015) find partly contradictory results, showing that Georgian firms with many export destinations experience lower survival rates.

There is evidence that *experience* matters for the survival of trade flows. For instance, Brenton, Saborowski, and von Uexküll (2010) find that prior experience with exporting the same product or exporting the same product to other markets decreases the hazard. Hess and Persson (2011) show that the longer the duration of a previous trade spell for the same trading relationship, the lower the hazard that the current spell will die. Carrère and Strauss-Kahn (2014) find that prior experience in a non-OECD market decreases the hazard for developing-country exports to OECD markets, even though the effect of experience depreciates rapidly. Studying exports from firms in Laos, Stirbat, Record, and Nghardsaysone (2015) conclude that having prior experience with the export product and destination decreases the hazard. There are also signs that *networks* matter. For firm exports from Laos, Stirbat, Record, and Nghardsaysone (2015) show that the higher the number of firms in the same Laotian province selling the same product to the same destination country in the same month, the lower the hazard. Martuscelli and Varela (2015) find similar evidence for Georgian firm exports.

A number of studies have looked at the effects of *market access* and *economic integration*. Focusing on the North American Free Trade Agreement (NAFTA), Besedeš (2013) finds that exports within NAFTA face a lower hazard, while the creation of NAFTA itself increased the hazard for Mexican and US intra-NAFTA exports. Studying Peruvian firm exports, Fugazza and McLaren (2014) show that market access relative to that faced by competitors matters for trade survival. More generally, Besedeš, Moreno-Cruz, and Nitsch (2015) find that economic integration—very widely defined—increases the duration of trade relationships that started before the agreement but reduces the duration of trade relationships that started after the agreement. Lejour (2015) shows that the hazard for Dutch firm exports is lower if the destination country belongs to the European Union. Lastly, focusing on antidumping, Besedeš and Prusa (2013) conclude that antidumping action increases the hazard rate by more than 50 percent. Interestingly, the authors also find that the effects of antidumping investigations are larger than the effects during the final phase when antidumping duties are charged.

Various *product characteristics* matter for the survival of trade flows. For instance, starting with Besedeš and Prusa (2006b), many studies have found that differentiated goods tend to have a lower hazard than homogeneous goods. Furthermore, Obashi (2010) has shown that trade in parts and components has longer duration than trade in finished products.

Many studies also find empirical evidence that *firm characteristics* are important for explaining variation in trade survival—examples include Sabuhoro, Larue, and Gervais (2006), Ilmakunnas and Nurmi (2010), Görg, Kneller, and Muraközy (2012), Gullstrand and Persson (2015), and Martuscelli and Varela (2015). For instance, larger firms have lower hazard rates (see, e.g., Gullstrand and Persson 2015), as do firms that are more productive (see, e.g., Ilmakunnas and Nurmi 2010; Görg, Kneller, and Muraközy 2012; Gullstrand and Persson 2015).

There is evidence that access to and need for *external financing* matters for trade duration. For instance, Jaud and Kukenova (2011) find that agrifood products that require greater external financing have higher export survival rates if the exporting country is more financially developed. Somewhat related to this, Jaud, Kukenova, and Strieborny (2012) show that export products that do not represent a *comparative advantage* tend to have shorter durations, and this relationship is intensified if the exporting country has a well-developed banking system. Other explanatory variables identified by the research literature include *risk*, for which Esteve-Perez, Requena-Silvente, and Pallardó-Lopez (2013) find that country political risk influences the effect of firm, product, and other destination characteristics on the duration of trade, and *innovation*, for which Chen (2012) concludes that the innovation—captured by the number of patents—has a positive effect on trade survival.

8.2.3 How Should Trade Duration Be Estimated?

Many of the papers in the literature follow Besedeš and Prusa (2006b) and estimate versions of a Cox proportional hazards model (see tables 8.1 and 8.2 for the estimation choices for each study). However, as argued by Hess and Persson (2012), this is a problematic choice. Quoting at length from Hess and Persson (2012), there are three main reasons why it is inappropriate to apply the Cox model when analyzing the duration of trade:

1. The Cox model is a continuous-time specification, whereas the duration of trade relationships is observed in discrete units of yearly length. As a consequence, many trade relations are observed to be of equal length, and no "natural way" exists to treat such tied duration times within the partial likelihood framework of the Cox model. The presence of ties causes asymptotic bias in both the estimation of the regression coefficients and in the estimation of the corresponding covariance matrix.

2. Unobserved heterogeneity cannot be included without the presence of multiple integrals, which makes estimation difficult, if not impossible. Ignoring unobserved heterogeneity causes—if it is indeed important—parameter bias and bias in the estimated survivor function.

3. The Cox model imposes the rather restrictive assumption of proportional hazards. In other words, the effects of explanatory variables on the hazard rate are assumed to be constant across duration time. This is unlikely to hold for the regressors typically employed to analyze the duration of trade relationships. Incorrectly imposing proportionality will produce misleading estimates of covariate effects.

Hess and Persson (2012) recommend that researchers instead use discrete-time versions of duration models, such as logit or probit models.[4] Replicating the results in Besedeš and Prusa (2006b) using discrete-time duration models, they illustrate that the choice of estimation method actually makes a difference for the predicted survivor functions and the estimated effects of explanatory variables on the hazard. In other words, it affects the economic conclusions drawn.[5]

Lastly, while the literature is increasingly using discrete-time duration models, another innovation can be found in Stirbat, Record, and Nghardsaysone (2015). These authors use competing risk models, allowing not only for trade death but also upgrades to superior products.

8.3 Data and Descriptive Statistics

We now turn to our empirical analysis.[6] We use data from the UN Comtrade Database on imports to EU15 countries from 1962 to 2006.[7] These data are at the four-digit level, classified according to the Standard International Trade Classification (SITC), Revision 1. Using these relatively aggregated four-digit data has two advantages. First, unlike customs product codes, according to which data that are more disaggregated are usually classified, products in the SITC are not reclassified from year to year, which strongly reduces problems with censoring. Second, data at a relatively high level of aggregation yield estimates that are more conservative, because if we do find short trade spells using relatively aggregated data, we can be more confident that this mirrors an economically significant phenomenon. Besedeš and Prusa (2011) use the same type of data in their analysis.

The sample of exporters consists of all countries that at some point during the observation period exported to any of the EU15 countries. Two groups of countries have been excluded from the sample, however. First, we exclude all EU27 countries as exporters, since we focus on studying the duration of the European Union's trade with the rest of the world. From a practical standpoint, it is a convenient choice to exclude intra-EU trade since that trade is to a large extent driven by a complex integration process that is difficult to properly control for. Second, we also exclude former Soviet republics and Southeast European transition economies, because trade in these centrally planned economies was arguably driven by political rather than economic factors. Following this, we obtain data on EU imports from 140 exporters, covering a broad range of income levels. The sample of exporting countries is shown in the appendix.

The estimation strategy is to study the duration of *bilateral* trade relationships. As importing countries, we consider all individual EU15 countries during the whole observation period from 1962 to 2006.[8] For each calendar year, we observe the value of any individual EU country's imports from a given country at the four-digit product level. For every combination of importing country, exporting country, and traded product (referred to as a *trade relationship*), we calculate the duration of trade as the number of consecutive years with nonzero imports. These different *spells* of trade constitute the core units of analysis in our empirical study. The number of spells differs from the number of trade relationships, since any of the trading parties may choose to terminate the trade relationship and revive it at a later date. Such reoccurring trade relationships are referred to as *multiple spells of service*. The conclusion that EU import flows are very short lived is robust to changes in the way spells are defined, the measurement of trade flows, and, remarkably, even the level of aggregation.[9]

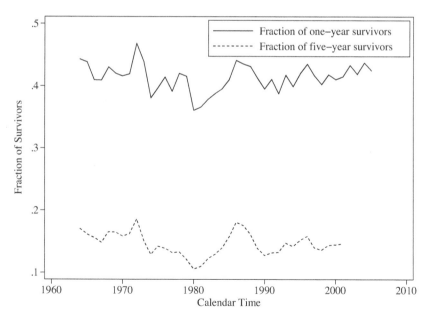

Figure 8.1
Fraction of surviving spells over calendar time. *Source:* Hess and Persson (2011).

As noted, one of the most intriguing results in Hess and Persson (2011) was that short duration is a persistent characteristic of trade throughout the observed time period. This point is illustrated in figure 8.1, which shows that the fraction of spells that survive the first and fifth years of service does not really change over calendar time but fluctuates around roughly 40 percent and 15 percent, respectively. There are certainly many short-term fluctuations from one year to another, but the overall conclusion drawn in Hess and Persson (2011) was nevertheless that short duration is a persistent characteristic of trade throughout the observed time period. In other words, despite all changes that have taken place in the world economy over this period, in the 1960s trade relationships died very early to the same extent as they do today. What lies behind this result? We will use the results of a regression analysis to shed some light on this issue.

8.4 Regression Analysis

As shown by Hess and Persson (2012), there are several reasons why it is inappropriate to apply the Cox model, despite its popularity in this literature, when analyzing determinants of trade duration. We therefore use discrete-time duration models that are more appropriate, with proper controls for unobserved heterogeneity. We estimate the baseline specification using discrete-time probit, logit, and cloglog models. All left-censored observations, which, if included, could lead to bias in the estimated hazard rate, are excluded. In all models, we include random effects for every exporter-product combination.[10] We estimate our main model for four different time periods: the full period from 1962 to 2006 and then three shorter periods starting in 1970, 1980, and 1990. Since Hess and Persson (2011) found that a probit model had the best fit for the data at hand, we only present results from that model.

The results from the estimations can be found in table 8.3. Table 8.A.1 in the appendix provides an overview of all variables and data sources. Note that, in addition to the explanatory variables whose parameters we will discuss shortly, the model also includes a large set of dummy variables aimed at controlling for unobserved heterogeneity. Our random effects control for all unobserved heterogeneity that is constant within exporter-product combinations. In addition, we include *importer dummies* to capture structural differences between importing countries and dummy variables capturing the *number of previous spells* for any

Table 8.3
Estimation results.

	Full period	1970–2006	1980–2006	1990–2006
Log distance	0.0396	0.0609	0.0607	0.0493
	(0.000)	(0.000)	(0.000)	(0.000)
Common language	−0.189	−0.1701	−0.1813	−0.1924
	(0.000)	(0.000)	(0.000)	(0.000)
Colonial history	−0.1032	−0.1241	−0.1222	−0.0991
	(0.000)	(0.000)	(0.000)	(0.000)
Log GDP (importer)	−0.2858	−0.2833	−0.336	−0.4202
	(0.000)	(0.000)	(0.000)	(0.000)
Log GDP (exporter)	0.0085	−0.0179	−0.0347	−0.0672
	(0.000)	(0.000)	(0.000)	(0.000)
Exporter LDC	−0.0572	−0.09	−0.0909	−0.0875
	(0.000)	(0.000)	(0.000)	(0.000)
Log number of export products	−0.2294	−0.2845	−0.2906	−0.2269
	(0.000)	(0.000)	(0.000)	(0.000)
Number of export markets	−0.0885	−0.0772	−0.0679	−0.0511
	(0.000)	(0.000)	(0.000)	(0.000)
Lagged duration	−0.0188	−0.0251	−0.0328	−0.0521
	(0.000)	(0.000)	(0.000)	(0.000)
Log initial import value	−0.076	−0.0755	−0.0763	−0.0765
	(0.000)	(0.000)	(0.000)	(0.000)
Differentiated product	−0.1095	−0.1311	−0.1516	−0.1579
	(0.000)	(0.000)	(0.000)	(0.000)
Log total import value	−0.0198	−0.0376	−0.0415	−0.0393
	(0.000)	(0.000)	(0.000)	(0.000)
EU member	−0.0427	−0.0436	−0.0741	−0.1387
	(0.000)	(0.000)	(0.000)	(0.000)
Δ log relative real exchange rate	0.0675	0.0736	0.1143	0.1192
	(0.000)	(0.000)	(0.000)	(0.000)
Duration dummies	Yes	Yes	Yes	Yes
Year dummies	Yes	Yes	Yes	Yes
Importer dummies	Yes	Yes	Yes	Yes
Spell number dummies	Yes	Yes	Yes	Yes
ρ	0.0561	0.0856	0.1052	0.1147
	(0.000)	(0.000)	(0.000)	(0.000)
Observations	2,220,871	1,887,638	1,432,718	895,433
Spells	692,148	640,848	531,054	381,658
Trade relations	265,396	256,058	236,630	202,567
Log likelihood	−895,709	−813,386	−651,646	−444,489

Note: P-values in parentheses. In all columns, a probit model with exporter-product random effects has been estimated, but on samples that cover various time periods. ρ denotes the fraction of the error variance that is caused by variation in the unobserved individual factors. A trade relation is defined as an importer-exporter-product combination. The number of observations is given by the total number of years with positive trade for all trade relationships.

given trade relationship (technically speaking, the latter are needed because our estimation methods assume that all spells are independent conditional on the covariates). We also model the baseline hazard in the most flexible fashion possible by using dummy variables that enable the estimation of period-specific intercepts. This, in turn, allows for unrestricted period-specific changes in the estimated hazard rates. Lastly, and most importantly, we include *calendar year dummies* to control for all such latent factors that are common to all country pairs and products in a given year but vary over time. We will return to the interpretation of these dummies in section 8.5.

Given our previous survey of the empirical literature, it is important to note that our set of included covariates resembles those found in comparable studies. One should, however, keep in mind that because of the very long time period under study, data limitations are fairly restrictive when it comes to our choice of potential explanatory variables.

To summarize the results, all covariates included have highly significant coefficients. Distance increases the hazard that trade relationships will die, whereas having a common language or a joint colonial history decreases the hazard. Economically large importers experience a lower hazard of having trade flows die, while the opposite is found for economically large exporters. The least developed countries will, everything else being equal, tend to have more long-lived export spells. Countries with a diversified export structure—either in terms of exporting many products or exporting the product in question to many destination countries—will have lower hazards than countries that trade few products and/or have few trading partners. If two countries have previously traded a particular product for an extended period of time, this will lower the hazard that the current trade flow will die. If the trade flow has a large initial value, if a differentiated product is involved, or if the total EU market for the product is large, the hazard is decreased. Countries that have already joined the European Union will also face a lower risk that bilateral import flows will die. Lastly, just as one would expect, an appreciation of the exporter's (relative) real exchange rate increases the risk that the trade flow will die.[11] Interestingly, as can be seen in table 8.3, using alternative time periods in our regressions does not lead to large changes in the results. The only exception is that the unexpected positive coefficient for the size of the exporter's GDP is turned into a negative coefficient as soon as we drop data from the

1960s. Apart from this, the similarity of the results regardless of time period is consistent with the finding that trade flows' survival does not change much over calendar time.

8.5   Exploring the Evolution of Trade Duration over Calendar Time

One of the most striking findings in Hess and Persson (2011) was that short duration is a persistent characteristic of trade throughout the very long time period under study. Specifically, the first- and fifth-year survival rates were found to fluctuate around a fairly constant level from as early as the 1960s until the 2000s. Since this is a new finding that has not previously been analyzed in the literature, in this section we will attempt to shed some further light on the issue. Specifically, we will use the results from the regression analysis to investigate why the duration of trade does not change much over calendar time.

In the regression analysis, we found several independent variables having a statistically significant effect on the hazard that trade flows will die. Most of these variables have negative coefficients, implying that the more they increase, the lower the hazard will be. In turn, this implies that if these variables exhibit any long-term upward or downward trend over the time period under study, this should have a long-term effect on the duration of trade. To investigate this issue, we begin, in figure 8.2, by plotting the yearly unweighted averages of all the time-varying explanatory variables.[12]

Figure 8.2 shows that five of the variables—GDP for the importers and exporters, the number of exported products, the value of EU imports, and EU membership—exhibit a clear long-term upward trend. For the remaining three, there is not as clear a long-term trend in either direction. Since the upward-trending variables all have negative coefficients,[13] this suggests that there should be a long-term downward trend in the hazard. In other words, since several of the variables that, according to our model, have significantly negative effects on the hazard exhibit positive trends over time, this should result in the hazard of trade flows dying becoming smaller and smaller throughout the time period under study.

To identify these effects, in figure 8.3 (the graph called "Hazard 1"), we have plotted the estimated first-year hazard over calendar time for period-specific means of covariates, holding the calendar year dummies fixed at their 1963 value. This allows us to single out the effects of the

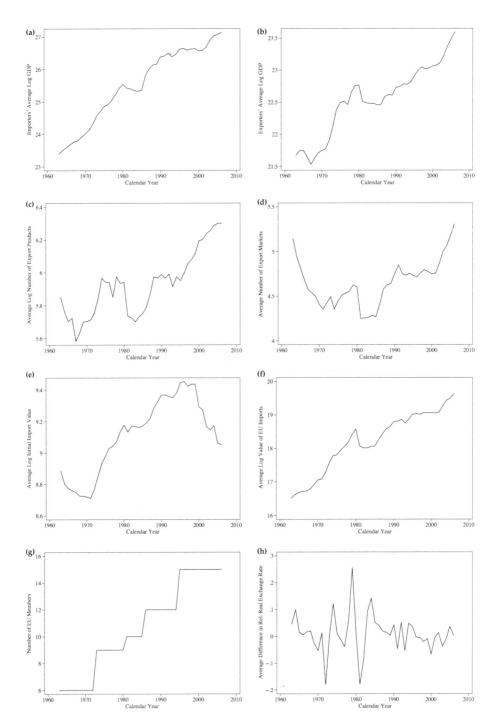

Figure 8.2
(a–h) Explanatory variables' trends over calendar time.

observed explanatory variables on the hazard while disregarding any changes in the hazard (specific to the calendar year) caused by other factors. The graph confirms what one would expect: the long-term trends in the model's explanatory variables, such as the trading countries' GDP or the level of export diversification, have contributed to *lowering* the hazard that trade flows will die. The effect is quite large indeed, with the estimated first-year hazard going from a level of 34 percent at the beginning of the period to a level of 3 percent at the end.

The calendar year dummies included in the estimated model capture all effects on the hazard that are common for all trade relationships in a given year but differ over calendar time. As illustrated in figure 8.4, the dummies' coefficients exhibit a positive upward trend. To see how this affects the estimated first-year hazards, in the second graph ("Hazard 2") of figure 8.3, the estimated first-year hazard is plotted, holding all other covariates at their 1963 value so that changes over time on the first-year hazard stem solely from the calendar year effects. As

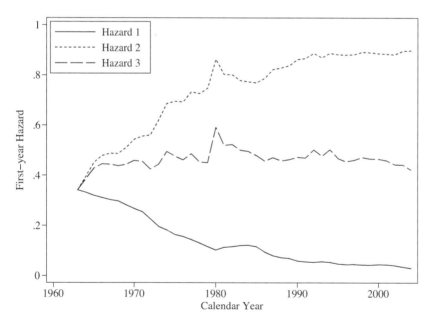

Figure 8.3
First-year hazards over calendar time. "Hazard 1" is the estimated first-year hazard over calendar time when changes in the estimated calendar year dummies do not contribute to the hazard, so that changes in the hazard are solely driven by changes in the observed covariates. "Hazard 2" is the corresponding graph when all observed covariates are held at their 1963 value, so only changes in the estimated calendar year effects contribute to the hazard. "Hazard 3" is the same graph at period-specific means of all covariates.

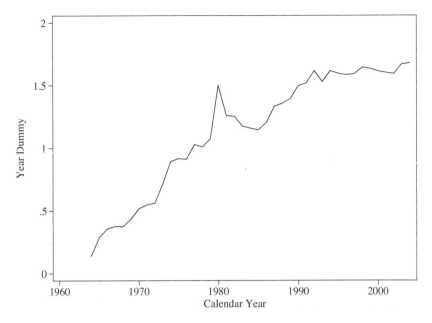

Figure 8.4
Estimated coefficients for calendar year dummy variables.

expected, given the positive trend in the estimated coefficients for the
calendar year dummies, the first-year hazard now exhibits an upward
trend, so the hazard that a trade relationship will die is much greater at
the end of the period. The change is even more substantial than the one
found when focusing on the observed explanatory variables: the hazard
increases from 34 percent to 90 percent over the time period under study.

In the last graph of figure 8.3 ("Hazard 3"), the estimated first-year
hazard is plotted, using period-specific averages of all covariates. In
other words, both the downward trend in hazard caused by changes
in the observed explanatory variables and the upward trend in hazard
resulting from the calendar year effects are taken into account here.
Evidently, this results in the same type of pattern that was found for
the empirical fraction of first-year survivors in figure 8.1: the estimated
first-year hazard and the observed fraction of first-year survivors both
fluctuate around a fairly constant level throughout the long time period.

To summarize, while short duration is a persistent characteristic of
trade over the long time period that we study, this constancy is the
result of two trends that work in opposite directions. On the one hand,
positive trends in several of the *observed* explanatory variables—which

in turn influence the hazard in a negative direction—imply that the hazard tends to decrease over calendar time. On the other hand, there is also a positive trend in the hazard because of *unobserved* factors specific to the calendar year. In other words, when disregarding the effects of the observed explanatory variables, there is an upward trend in the hazard, implying that trade flows, ceteris paribus, are more likely to die quickly at the end of the time period under study. Thus, if the observed determinants of trade duration, such as GDP or level of export diversification, had not changed since the beginning of the 1960s, the probability that a given trade flow would die in the first year of service would be almost three times higher at the end of the observation period.

What is the explanation behind this upward trend in the hazard? Which unobserved factors influence the hazard to increase over calendar time? While we do not have any definitive answers, one area where we believe future researchis particularly beneficial is the varying importance of trade costs. A large body of literature within international economics has discussed the fact that trade costs—for instance, captured by distance—may not be equally important at different points in time.[14] While it was anticipated that costs associated with distance would become less important because of, for example, falling transportation costs, empirical studies have tended to draw the opposite conclusion. As noted by Brun et al. (2005), for example, gravity studies have tended to find increasing effects of distance over time, and the conclusion that distance is of increasing importance as an impediment to trade is corroborated by papers such as Berthelon and Freund (2008), Carrère and Schiff (2005), and Disdier and Head (2008). The latter paper, for instance, performs an ambitious metastudy of 1,467 estimated distance effects from gravity studies and finds that the elasticity of trade with respect to distance does not decline over the years but instead increases. Of course, as noted by Carrère and Schiff (2005), there are two issues at stake here: even though trade costs themselves—such as transportation costs—fall, trade flows' sensitivity to a given level of trade costs could still increase. Reasons for an increased sensitivity could, for example, include a changing composition of trade, where distance could become more and more important as an impediment to trade because of the larger degree of time sensitivity among traded goods in later years.

Relating this to our empirical study, we note that distance is restricted to having an effect that does not vary over calendar time in the baseline regression. If distance is becoming more and more important as a trade impediment over calendar time, this could perhaps explain the upward trend in the hazard as captured by the calendar year dummies. While we cannot completely rule out this type of explanation, we note that we do not find any support for it in our empirical results. As described, part of our robustness analysis consisted of running the baseline regression on samples where observations from the 1960s, 1970s, and 1980s were progressively removed. The consequence of this is effectively to allow all variables, including distance, to have an effect that varies over calendar time. While there are indeed some small differences between the estimated coefficients, when we compare survivor functions between the samples for different given values of distance, the differences are not particularly striking.[15] This suggests that there must be other factors that have not been observed but that exhibit strong enough trends over time to induce the hazard to increase. While further investigations of this issue are beyond the scope of this chapter, it is indeed a promising area for future research.

8.6 Summary and Conclusions

Noting that the literature on trade duration has grown substantially over the last ten years or so, this chapter focuses on taking stock of this research field and trying to offer a sense of what we know and what we don't know. We approach this question from two perspectives. First, we perform an extensive survey of the existing research studies. This survey illustrates that short trade durations are a very robust empirical finding, and it further identifies a fairly large set of explanatory variables that have been found by the existing studies. It also offers a brief overview of methodological issues in this literature.

   In addition to the literature survey, we also offer new empirical results that suggest that the factors that have previously been identified as influencing the duration of trade—the explanatory variables discussed in our literature review—are not enough to explain the variation in trade survival over time. By estimating discrete-time duration models with a rich set of controls for unobserved heterogeneity, we show that there are some interesting patterns hiding behind the previously found result that trade survival does not change much over calendar time. On the one hand, positive trends in several of the *observed* explanatory variables—which in turn influence the hazard of trade flows dying in a negative direction—imply that the hazard tends to decrease over calendar time. In fact, if we took only these effects into account, the estimated first-year hazard would have gone from 34 percent in the early 1960s to a level of only 3 percent in 2006. On the other hand, there is also a positive trend in the hazard caused by *unobserved* factors, which are captured by the calendar year dummies. In other words, when disregarding the observed explanatory variables, there is an upward trend in the hazard, implying that trade flows, ceteris paribus, are more likely to die quickly at the end of the time period under study. Holding all other determinants constant, the hazard of a trade flow dying in its first year increases from 34 percent at the beginning of the period to 90 percent at the end. Our interpretation of this result is that if only the explanatory variables that have already been identified by the research literature mattered, trade flows would be very long lived today. Since they are not, we argue that this is clear empirical evidence that more research is needed to identify additional explanatory variables that can account for the increasing tendency for trade flows to die quickly.

Thus, to summarize, we hope to make two contributions in this chapter. First, we offer a substantive literature review of the existing research on trade duration. Second, as a complement to this literature review, we offer new empirical evidence that the explanatory factors that have previously been identified as relevant are not enough to explain the variation in trade survival over time. In other words, more research is needed to explain what drives the duration of trade. We hope this chapter can serve as a useful starting point for such future research.

Appendix: Overview of Exporting Countries

Afghanistan, Algeria, Angola, Antigua and Barbuda, Argentina, Australia, Bahamas, Bahrain, Bangladesh, Barbados, Belize, Benin, Bermuda, Bhutan, Bolivia, Brazil, Brunei, Burkina Faso, Burundi, Cambodia, Cameroon, Canada, Cape Verde, Central African Republic, Chad, Chile, China, Colombia, Comoros, Costa Rica, Côte d'Ivoire, Democratic Republic of the Congo, Djibouti, Dominica, Dominican Republic, Ecuador, Egypt, El Salvador, Equatorial Guinea, Eritrea, Ethiopia, Fiji, French Polynesia, Gabon, Gambia, Ghana, Greenland, Grenada, Guatemala, Guinea, Guinea-Bissau, Guyana, Haiti, Honduras, Iceland, India, Indonesia, Iran, Iraq, Israel, Jamaica, Japan, Jordan, Hong Kong, Kenya, Kiribati, Kuwait, Lao PDR, Lebanon, Libya, Liberia, Madagascar, Malawi, Malaysia, Maldives, Mali, Mauritania, Mauritius, Mexico, Mongolia, Morocco, Mozambique, Nepal, New Caledonia, New Zealand, Nicaragua, Niger, Nigeria, Norway, Oman, Pakistan, Panama, Papua New Guinea, Paraguay, Peru, Philippines, Qatar, Republic of the Congo, Republic of Korea, Rwanda, Samoa, San Marino, São Tomé and Principe, Saudi Arabia, Senegal,

Seychelles, Sierra Leone, Singapore, Somalia, Southern African Customs Union (Botswana, Lesotho, Namibia, South Africa, Swaziland), Sri Lanka, St. Kitts and Nevis, St. Lucia, St. Vincent and the Grenadines, Sudan, Suriname, Switzerland, Syria, Tanzania, Thailand, Togo, Tonga, Tunisia, Trinidad and Tobago, Turkey, Uganda, United Arab Emirates, United States, Uruguay, Vanuatu, Venezuela, Vietnam, Yemen, Zambia, Zimbabwe.

Table 8.A.1
Overview of variables and data sources.

Variable	Definition and data source
Trade duration	Length of trade spell in years. Constructed using four-digit SITC (Rev. 1) EU15 imports from the United Nations' Comtrade (henceforth referred to as the UN Comtrade data).
Log distance	Log of distance in kilometers between the trading countries' capitals. Data from Centre d'Études Prospectives et d'Informations Internationales (CEPII), http://www.cepii.fr.
Common language	Takes the value 1 if the trading countries share the same language. Data from CEPII, http://www.cepii.fr.
Colonial history	Takes the value 1 if the trading countries have a common colonial history. Data from CEPII, http://www.cepii.fr.
Log GDP	Log of importer's or exporter's GDP. Data from the World Bank's *World Development Indicators* (*WDI*) online.
Exporter LDC	Takes the value 1 if the exporter is classified as a least-developed country by the United Nations at the end of the time period studied.
Log number of export products	Log of the number of products shipped to any market by the exporter for every year of the spell. Constructed using the UN Comtrade data.
Number of export markets	Number of markets (not logged) to which the exporter ships the given product for every year of the spell. Constructed using the UN Comtrade data.
Lagged duration	Number of years that a previous spell of the same trade relationship lasted. Constructed using the UN Comtrade data.
Log initial import value	Log of the value of imports at the beginning of the spell. Constructed using the UN Comtrade data.
Differentiated product	Takes the value 1 if the product is classified as differentiated product according to Rauch (1999). Data from Jon Haveman's International Trade Data, http://www.macalester.edu/research/economics/page/haveman/trade.resources/tradedata.html. Concordance used to translate the Rauch classification from SITC (Rev. 2) to SITC (Rev. 1) from Feenstra (1997), http://cid.econ.ucdavis.edu/usixd/wp5990d.html.
Log total import value	Log of the total value of imports by all EU15 countries for the given product and every year of the spell. Constructed using the UN Comtrade data.

Variable	Definition and data source
EU member	Binary variable indicating for every year of a spell whether the respective importing country has—in the given calendar year—already joined the European Union or not.
Δ log relative real exchange rate	Yearly difference in log relative real exchange rate, where the relative real exchange rate is defined as nominal exchange rate (importer currency/exporter currency) adjusted by the respective consumer price indices and normalized by the average real exchange rate of all exporting countries against the importing country. Bilateral real exchange rates have been constructed using US exchange rates and national consumer price indices from the World Bank's *WDI*.

Notes

The authors are grateful for valuable comments from Mélise Jaud, two anonymous referees, and participants at the CESIfo Workshop on "Disrupted Economic Relationships: Disasters, Sanctions, and Dissolutions" in Venice, Italy, 2016. Maria Persson gratefully acknowledges financial support from the Swedish Research Council, grant number 384-2014-3987.

1. This is rather remarkable, considering how much more integrated the world economy has become over the same period. Since the 1960s, for instance, there have been several rounds of multilateral trade negotiations, a large number of new preferential trade agreements, closer links between economies as a result of foreign direct investment, modernized means of transportation, financial liberalization, and other advances, yet the survival of new trade relationships has remained pretty much constant throughout this period.

2. Please note that because of the long time period under study, unfortunately it isn't possible to include all the variables that have previously been identified as relevant—in many cases the data were simply not available until quite recently.

3. In addition to Békés and Muraközy (2012) and Cadot et al. (2013), other papers with analysis that is indirectly relevant include Lederman, Olarreaga, and Zavala (2015), Albornoz, Fanelli, and Hallak (2016), Araujo, Mion, and Ornelas (2016), and Fernandes, Freund, and Pierola (2016).

4. They note, however, that the cloglog model is less appropriate, since it also makes the assumption of proportional hazards.

5. It is worth noting that Brenton, Saborowski, and von Uexküll (2010) also argue against the Cox proportional hazards model. Their argument is that if there is unobserved heterogeneity that is not properly controlled for, the proportional hazards assumption that is implicitly made in a Cox model will not hold. They therefore suggest using the discrete-time equivalent of a Cox model, a cloglog model, where unobserved heterogeneity can much more easily be controlled for. However, as discussed by Hess and Persson (2012), this is a risky choice, because a cloglog model also assumes proportional hazards. Therefore, if that assumption is intrinsically invalid, the cloglog model will also be an inappropriate choice. In fact, Hess and Persson (2012) show empirically that with the data used by Besedeš and Prusa (2006b), the assumption of proportional hazards does not hold empirically, implying that, at least for those data, a cloglog model would not be a good choice.

6. Our empirical analysis closely follows Hess and Persson (2011).

7. For simplicity, we will refer to the "European Union," though, of course, this term will not be formally correct in some instances.

8. Since many EU15 countries joined the European Union after 1962, we include a dummy variable in our regressions that indicates for every year of a spell whether the respective importing country had already joined the European Union or not. It should be noted that, since Belgium and Luxembourg are treated as one trading block in the statistics, we have data for 14 importers in practice.

9. For a detailed descriptive analysis of the data, we refer to Hess and Persson (2011). They find that only considering the first spells that occurred for a given trade relationship in the period or only considering spells where there was no recurring trade for that trade relationship does not change the conclusions. Furthermore, ignoring one-, two-, or even three-year gaps with no trade does not change the results much, and using higher cutoff levels below which trade is not counted also has only minor effects. Lastly, aggregating the data all the way up to the one-digit level where there are only ten remaining categories of products results in a median duration of imports of two years.

10. It may be noted that likelihood-ratio tests strongly reject the null hypothesis of no latent heterogeneity for all model specifications, implying that unobserved heterogeneity plays a significant role in all model specifications and should not be ignored.

11. Hess and Persson (2011) show that using alternative ways of defining a spell, controlling for unobserved heterogeneity by means of fixed rather than random effects, or aggregating the trade data produces only marginal changes in the results.

12. Regarding the dummy for EU membership, we have—for ease of interpretation—simply plotted the actual number of EU members rather than an average of the dummy variable. Note that in this illustration we separate Luxembourg and Belgium even though they are actually treated as one entity in the trade statistics. It should further be noted that while the only remaining time-varying variable, the lagged duration, potentially could have a long-term trend, we have not included that variable here, as it was demonstrated earlier that the duration of trade does not exhibit any long-term trend.

13. The only exception being the Exporter's GDP, for which, however, as discussed in Hess and Persson (2011), the unexpected positive sign in the baseline regression is turned into a negative sign in several of the robustness analyses.

14. For an overview of the literature on trade costs, see, for example, Anderson and van Wincoop (2004).

15. Results are available upon request.

References

Albornoz, F., S. Fanelli, and J. C. Hallak. 2016. "Survival in Export Markets." *Journal of International Economics* 102:262–281.

Anderson, J. E., and E. van Wincoop. 2004. "Trade Costs." *Journal of Economic Literature* 42 (3): 691–751.

Araujo, L., G. Mion, and E. Ornelas. 2016. "Institutions and Export Dynamics." *Journal of International Economics* 98 (C): 2–20.

Békés, G., and B. Muraközy. 2012. "Temporary Trade and Heterogeneous Firms." *Journal of International Economics* 87 (2): 232–246.

Berthelon, M., and C. Freund. 2008. "On the Conservation of Distance in International Trade." *Journal of International Economics* 75 (2): 310–320.

Besedeš, T. 2008. "A Search Cost Perspective on Formation and Duration of Trade." *Review of International Economics* 16 (5): 835–849.

Besedeš, T. 2011. "Export Differentiation in Transition Economies." *Economic Systems* 35 (1): 25–44.

Besedeš, T. 2013. "The Role of NAFTA and Returns to Scale in Export Duration." *CESifo Economic Studies* 59 (2): 306–336.

Besedeš, T., J. Moreno-Cruz, and V. Nitsch. 2015. "Trade Integration and the Fragility of Trade Relationships: Theory and Empirics." Mimeo.

Besedeš, T., and T. Prusa. 2006a. "Ins, Outs and the Duration of Trade." *Canadian Journal of Economics* 39 (1): 266–295.

Besedeš, T., and T. Prusa. 2006b. "Product Differentiation and Duration of US Import Trade." *Journal of International Economics* 70 (2): 339–358.

Besedeš, T., and T. Prusa. 2011. "The Role of Extensive and Intensive Margins and Export Growth." *Journal of Development Economics* 96 (2): 371–379.

Besedeš, T., and T. Prusa. 2013. "Antidumping and the Death of Trade." NBER Working Paper 19555. Cambridge, MA: National Bureau of Economic Research.

Brenton, P., C. Saborowski, and E. von Uexküll. 2010. "What Explains the Low Survival Rate of Developing Country Export Flows?" *World Bank Economic Review* 24 (3): 474–499.

Brun, J. F., C. Carrère, P. Guillaumont, and J. De Melo. 2005. "Has Distance Died? Evidence from a Panel Gravity Model." *World Bank Economic Review* 19 (1): 99–120.

Cadot, O., L. Iacovone, M. D. Pierola, and F. Rauch. 2013. "Success and Failure of African Exporters." *Journal of Development Economics* 101:284–296.

Carrère, C., and M. Schiff. 2005. "On the Geography of Trade: Distance Is Alive and Well." *Revue Economique* 56 (6): 1249–1274.

Carrère, C., and V. Strauss-Kahn. 2014. "Developing Countries Exports Survival in the OECD: Does Experience Matter?" CEPR Discussion Paper 10059. Washington, DC: Center for Economic and Policy Research.

Chen, W.-C. 2012. "Innovation and Duration of Exports." *Economics Letters* 115 (2): 305–308.

Disdier, A.-C., and K. Head. 2008. "The Puzzling Persistence of the Distance Effect on Bilateral Trade." *Review of Economics and Statistics* 90 (1): 37–48.

Esteve-Perez, S., F. Requena-Silvente, and V. J. Pallardó-Lopez. 2013. "The Duration of Firm-Destination Export Relationships: Evidence from Spain, 1997–2006." *Economic Inquiry* 51 (1): 159–180.

Feenstra, R. C. 1997. "U.S. Exports, 1972–1994: With State Exports and other U.S. Data." NBER Working Paper 5990. Cambridge, MA: National Bureau of Economic Research.

Fernandes, A. M., C. Freund, and M. D. Pierola. 2016. "Exporter Behavior, Country Size and Stage of Development: Evidence from the Exporter Dynamics Database." *Journal of Development Economics* 119 (C): 121–137.

Fugazza, M., and A. McLaren. 2014. "Market Access, Export Performance and Survival: Evidence from Peruvian Firms." *Review of International Economics* 22 (3): 599–624.

Görg, H., R. Kneller, and B. Muraközy. 2012. "What Makes a Successful Export? Evidence from Firm-Product-Level Data." *Canadian Journal of Economics* 45 (4): 1332–1368.

Gullstrand, J., and M. Persson. 2015. "How to Combine High Sunk Costs of Exporting and Low Export Survival." *Review of World Economics* 151 (1): 23–51.

Hess, W., and M. Persson. 2011. "Exploring the Duration of EU Imports." *Review of World Economics* 147 (4): 665–692.

Hess, W., and M. Persson. 2012. "The Duration of Trade Revisited: Continuous-Time vs. Discrete-Time Hazards." *Empirical Economics* 43 (3): 1083–1107.

Ilmakunnas, P., and S. Nurmi. 2010. "Dynamics of Export Market Entry and Exit." *Scandinavian Journal of Economics* 112 (1): 101–126.

Jaud, M., and M. Kukenova. 2011. "Financial Development and Survival of African Agri-Food Exports." World Bank Policy Research Working Paper 5649. Washington, DC: World Bank.

Jaud, M., M. Kukenova, and M. Strieborny. 2012. "Finance, Comparative Advantage and Resource Allocation." World Bank Policy Research Working Paper 6111. Washington, DC: World Bank.

Lederman, D., M. Olarreaga, and L. Zavala. 2015. "Export Promotion and Firm Entry into and Survival in Export Markets." World Bank Policy Research Working Paper 7400. Washington, DC: World Bank.

Lejour, A. 2015. "The Duration of Dutch Export Relations: Decomposing Firm, Country and Product Characteristics." *De Economist* 163 (2): 155–176.

Martuscelli, A., and G. Varela. 2015. "Survival Is for the Fittest: Export Survival Patterns in Georgia." World Bank Policy Research Working Paper 7161. Washington, DC: World Bank.

Nitsch, V. 2009. "Die Another Day: Duration in German Import Trade." *Review of World Economics* 145 (1): 133–154.

Obashi, A. 2010. "Stability of Production Networks in East Asia: Duration and Survival of Trade." *Japan and the World Economy* 22 (1): 21–30.

Rauch, J. E. 1999. "Networks versus Markets in International Trade." *Journal of International Economics* 48 (1): 7–35.

Sabuhoro, J. B., B. Larue, and Y. Gervais. 2006. "Factors Determining the Success or Failure of Canadian Establishments on Foreign Markets: A Survival Analysis Approach." *International Trade Journal* 20 (1): 33–73.

Stirbat, L., R. Record, and K. Nghardsaysone. 2015. "The Experience of Survival: Determinants of Export Survival in Lao PDR." *World Development* 76 (C): 82–94.

Volpe-Martincus, C., and J. Carballo. 2008. "Survival of New Exporters in Developing Countries: Does It Matter How They Diversify?" *Globalization, Competitiveness and Governability* 2 (3): 30–49.

9 Finance and Export Survival: The Case of the MENA Region and Sub-Saharan Africa

Melise Jaud, Madina Kukenova,
and Martin Strieborny

9.1 Introduction

One way to examine disrupted economic relationships is to look at them in the context of the growing literature on the effects of financial factors on international trade. This literature has shown the beneficial impact of a well-functioning financial system on international trade flows, in particular for industries and firms that face credit constraints and/or require a high level of external financing for their operations (e.g., Beck 2002, 2003, Svaleryd and Vlachos 2005; Greenaway, Guariglia, and Kneller 2007; Manova 2008, 2013; Berman and Héricourt 2010; Bugamelli, Schivardi, and Zizza 2010; Minetti and Zhu 2011; Besedes, Kim, and Lugovskyy 2014; Fan, Lai, and Li 2015; Manova, Wei, and Zhang 2015; Muûls 2015; Chaney 2016; Crinò and Ogliari 2017). A related strand of scholarly work has explored how disturbances in a financial system spread into the real economy by adversely affecting international trade, especially in the context of the recent global financial crisis (e.g., Amiti and Weinstein 2011; Chor and Manova 2012; Paravisini et al. 2015; however, see Levchenko, Lewis, and Tesar 2011 for a skeptical look at this channel).

This chapter examines whether financial development can help prevent disruptions in existing trade relationships by examining its impact on the long-term survival of exports from developing countries. It does so using a large sample that includes four countries in the Middle East and North Africa (MENA) (Jordan, Kuwait, Morocco, and Yemen) as well as six countries in sub-Saharan Africa (SSA) (Ghana, Mali, Malawi, Senegal, Tanzania, and Uganda). We use unique data collected by local customs authorities that cover the universe of exports from these countries and contain information on firms' exports at the detailed product-destination level. Pooling together such data from several developing countries at the firm, product, and destination levels lends itself to a more robust and systematic exploration of the impact of financial development on export performance. The high dimensionality of the data enables us to go beyond existing work in accounting for unobserved heterogeneity at the product, firm, and destination market levels.

In our empirical strategy, we focus on agricultural exports, which constitute an important source of export revenues for many developing countries. In particular, we use the fact that a significant portion of the financial costs related to exports of agricultural goods emerges from required compliance with Sanitary and Phytosanitary Standards (SPS). These standards are particularly strict—and therefore compliance with them is particularly costly—in the case of exports to highly developed countries. The idea, following previous work by Jaud, Cadot, and Suwa-Eisenmann (2009) and Jaud, Kukenova, and Strieborny (2015), is thus to identify variations in SPS compliance costs at the level of individual products and use this variation as a proxy for financial needs associated with exports of agricultural products. Combining this measure with our firm, product, and destination data allows us to measure whether financial development particularly promotes exports characterized by high costs of SPS compliance. This would suggest that finance is important for long-term export survival—a higher level of financial development especially benefits exports that are costly and thus more reliant on a well-functioning financial environment in the exporting country.

We find that a higher level of financial development in the exporting developing country indeed promotes particularly those exports that face high costs of SPS compliance. The result remains robust when controlling for heterogeneity at the firm, product, and destination market levels. The finding also survives controlling for alternative economic channels that could link financial development to export performance.

This chapter complements the existing literature in three ways. First, we examine the impact of financial development on long-term export survival rather than on export entry or export volume, which are the focus of the bulk of the existing finance-trade literature. This is not only in accordance with the emphasis of this volume on disrupted economic relationships but also has an important policy dimension. It is well known that developing countries face particular difficulties when it comes to establishing a long-term sustainable presence for their products in foreign markets. When it comes to export performance, what distinguishes successful developing countries from unsuccessful ones is not the ability to enter foreign markets but rather the ability to establish a long-term presence and avoid disruptions to existing trade relationships (Besedes and Prusa 2011). Other papers specifically looking at the impact of financial factors on long-term export survival include Jaud, Kukenova, and Strieborny (2015, 2018), while Besedes and Prusa (2006a, 2006b, 2011), Nitsch (2009), Brenton, Saborowski, and von Uexkull (2010), Wei-Chih (2012), Besedes (2013), Cadot et al. (2013), and others examine trade survival in general. Görg and Spaliara (2014) investigate the impact of export status on the link between financial factors and firm survival but do not look at the link between finance and trade. The paper closest to this chapter is Jaud, Kukenova, and Strieborny (2015), which also relies on detailed data from customs authorities and a measure of SPS-related exporting costs to examine the impact of financial development on long-term export survival. The main difference between these two papers is in terms of data coverage. Jaud, Kukenova, and Strieborny (2015) use data from five sub-Saharan countries: Ghana, Mali, Malawi, Senegal, and Tanzania. This chapter adds another sub-Saharan country: Uganda. More importantly, the sample also includes four countries from a different developing region—the Middle East and North Africa (MENA): Jordan, Kuwait, Morocco, and Yemen. This is important in the context of the external validity and applicability of our results to developing countries in general. The MENA countries included are not only from a different geographical region but are also on average richer than the countries from sub-Saharan Africa. The extended sample also means that its firm dimension becomes more important than its product dimension, which leads to a slightly different empirical model, discussed in section 9.2. On the downside, the extended dataset in this chapter does not include the names of exporting firms, only their identification number. This prevents us from a closer examination of some aspects of firm heterogeneity—such as looking at the particular role of multinational corporations and trading companies in our sample.

Second, the existing finance-trade literature usually either attempts to identify financial constraints at the firm level or looks at the effect of financial development on industries dependent on external financing, following the idea from a seminal finance-growth paper by Rajan and Zingales (1998). In contrast, the measure used in Jaud, Kukenova, and Strieborny (2015) and in this chapter identifies financial needs at the product level.

Third, this chapter examines the specific issue of agricultural exports. This topic is rather underresearched, especially when compared to the extensive body of work examining international trade in manufactured goods. However, especially for developing countries, agricultural exports can play an important role. For example, Jaud, Cadot, and Suwa-Eisenmann (2009) cite Eurostat data documenting that the share of developing countries in the overall agricultural imports of the European Union increased from the already high level of 66 percent in 1988 to 75 percent in 2005. Trying to understand what factors may help agricultural exports from these countries survive competition in tough destination markets is thus especially important.

The remainder of the chapter is organized as follows. Sections 9.2 and 9.3 introduce the empirical strategy and data. Section 9.4 describes the main empirical results, while section 9.5 reports the results of several robustness checks. Section 9.6 offers our conclusions.

9.2   Empirical Strategy

Papers examining the impact of financial factors on international trade flows usually focus on the entry into exporting and somewhat neglect long-term export survival. Some papers look into the short-term year-to-year changes in the export status of products or firms (Manova 2008; Berman and Héricourt 2010). Our focus is instead on the long-run survival of products in foreign markets. In our opinion, survival analysis is probably the most suitable tool for studying the impact of financial development on longer-term export performance (see also Jaud, Kukenova, and Strieborny 2015, 2018).

In our dataset, we observe the exporting firm, exported product, destination market, and the year when the export takes place. We reduce the panel dimensions to three and study the length of trade relationships. A trade relationship is thus defined as a firm-product-destination triplet, and the duration of a trade relationship is defined as the time (in years) a triplet has been in existence without interruption.

We model the survival of trade relationships using a Cox proportional hazards model (Cox PH model, or CPHM). We assume that the duration of exports of product k by firm f from country c to destination country d depends on a set of explanatory variables X_{kfcd}. In the CPHM, the hazard function of a trade relationship is a multiplicative function between an unspecified time-dependent baseline hazard function and an exponential function of these explanatory variables. Jaud, Kukenova, and Strieborny (2015, 2018) provide further technical details about the Cox PH model.

In our case, the set of explanatory variables X_{kfcd} includes an interaction term between our measure of financial needs and the level of financial development, a set of controls, a set of fixed effects, and unobserved effects (error term). We further allow the shape of the baseline hazard function $h(t)$ to vary across exporting firms by fitting a stratified Cox PH model. Stratification according to the firm indicator variable η_f goes beyond the traditional use of firm fixed effects by allowing a different underlying hazard rate for each firm in our sample. This presents a modification from Jaud, Kukenova, and Strieborny (2015), who stratified the Cox PH at the product level and used fixed effects to control for firm heterogeneity. Here we use fixed effects to control for product heterogeneity and rely on the more sophisticated stratification approach to control for firm heterogeneity. The reason is the significantly increased size of the sample compared to Jaud, Kukenova, and Strieborny (2015), making the firm dimension (number of firms) more important than the product dimension in this chapter. The use of strata effects at the level of exporting firms also alleviates the need for using the exporting country fixed effects, as the latter are fully absorbed by the former.

Thus, we estimate the empirical model

$$h(t|X_{kfcd}, \eta_f = f) = h_f(t) \exp[\alpha FD_c \times sanitary\_risk_k \\ + \gamma\beta \, Controls_{kfcdt_0} + \Delta + \varepsilon_{kfcdt_0}], \tag{9.1}$$

where FD_c is the level of financial development in the exporting country c, $sanitary\_risk_k$ is the measure of export-related financial needs for product k, t_0 is the year when a given export spell was initiated, and ε_{kfcdt_0} is an unobserved effect. Δ is a set of fixed effects that varies across specifications. In our most stringent specifications, we control for fixed effects at the product, (destination country)*(year of the export spell initiation), and (exporting country)*industry levels, with industry and product being defined at the HS-2 and HS-8 levels of disaggregation, respectively.

To capture the differential effect of financial development across products, we interact the financial development at the country level with the financing needs at the product level ($FD_c \times sanitary\ risk_k$), while at the same time we control via stratification and fixed effects Δ for heterogeneity at the firm, product, (exporting country)*industry, and (destination country)*(year of the export spell initiation) levels. Our vector of controls includes various product and firm characteristics as well as traditional bilateral gravity variables. The firm-level variables take value at the initiation of the trade relationship. To reduce clutter in the notation, in the remainder of the text we omit the corresponding subscript for the year of the export spell initiation t_0.

Because of possible endogeneity issues, we measure financial development at the beginning of the sample period. Consequently, the direct effect of FD_c is absorbed by the exporting firm strata effects in most of our estimations. In one of the robustness tests, we also measure financial development in the year when a given export spell was initiated (t_0), so that its direct effect becomes time-varying and can be estimated.

Besides endogeneity, financial development in the exporting country or some other variable correlated with it might affect selection into export spells, raising the possibility of an omitted variable bias. However, such bias would mostly affect the direct effect of financial development on export survival, which is not the focus of our study and in most regressions is actually captured by exporting firm strata effects. The identification of our channel occurs instead within a difference-in-differences framework, with our main variable being an interaction term of financial development and a product-level measure of export-related financing needs (sanitary_risk$_k$). By its very construction, our measure of financing needs is independent of financial development or any other country-specific factors (see also section 9.3 and Jaud, Kukenova, and Strieborny 2015). This, together with measuring financial development at the beginning of our sample and an extensive use of strata and fixed effects, means that any kind of omitted variable bias would need to work in a rather complicated way in order to affect the estimated coefficient of our main interaction term. Besides, better financial development leading firms to enter foreign markets particularly with products with higher export-related financing needs would actually reinforce our results in the sense that financial development promotes both export entry and export survival of financially vulnerable products.

9.3   Data

Our analysis relies on a novel dataset collected within the framework of the Export Survival Project, implemented by the International Trade Department of the World Bank.[1] The dataset combines export data at the firm, product, and destination levels that were collected by customs authorities in four countries of the Middle East and North Africa (MENA) region (Jordan, Kuwait, Morocco, and Yemen) as well as in six countries from sub-Saharan Africa (SSA) (Ghana, Mali, Malawi, Senegal, Tanzania, and Uganda). Table 9.1 provides detailed summary statistics of the data coverage for the individual countries. The earliest year in our sample is 2000 and the latest year is 2012.

For the purposes of this chapter, we consider only exports of agrifood products, excluding beverages, animal feed, and tobacco. This corresponds to chapters 1 to 21 of the HS classification and restricts our sample to 845 product lines at the HS-8 level of disaggregation. Export flows are reported annually in values (US dollars) and quantities (tons).

As our measure of financial development (FD_c) in exporting countries, we use the ratio of private credit (i.e., bank credit extended to the private sector in a given country) to GDP. The data come from the database by Beck, Demirguc-Kunt, and Levine (2006). As an alternative measure of financial development, we also use the Ease of Getting Credit Index (EGC_c) from the World Bank Doing Business Survey (WBDBS). We also control for other country characteristics that might be correlated with the level of financial development in the exporting country: GDP per capita ($GDPpc_c$); Ease of Doing Business index (EDB_c), which measures the quality of the business environment; and Logistics Performance Index (LPI_c), which controls for a country's capacity to efficiently move goods and connect with international markets. The data come from WBDBS and from the World Bank Logistic Performance Indicator database.

To measure export-related financing needs of agricultural products, we rely on the variable Sanitary Risk Index ($sanitary\_risk_k$) introduced by Jaud, Cadot, and Suwa-Eisenmann (2009). This index is computed using data from the EU Rapid Alert System for Food and Feed (RASFF). The RASFF database reports all agrifood shipments to the European Union between 2001 and 2008 that have suffered rejection for food safety reasons, meaning they were rejected because of violations of the Sanitary and Phytosanitary Standards (SPS). Intuitively, the index captures the share of these rejections that arise as a result of technological product characteristics after controlling for economic and political variables that might affect the probability of agricultural exports being rejected at the EU border. The appendix provides more details about the construction of the index. As compliance with the SPS (necessary to avoid rejection at the border) is a costly process, the index captures

Table 9.1
Sample characteristics.

Country	Period	Number of observations	Observations per year	Number of firms	Number of destinations	Number of products (HS-6)	Destinations per firm	Products per firm
Ghana	2004–2008	21,374	6,804	2,595	72	280	6.7	10.6
Jordan	2003–2011	2,706	416	501	49	110	2.8	1.9
Kuwait	2008–2010	1,386	463	422	38	178	2.7	3.0
Morocco	2002–2010	23,173	2,527	3,290	76	253	3.0	3.0
Mali	2005–2008	195	56	64	26	33	1.9	2.2
Malawi	2004–2008	838	222	141	47	91	4.2	2.6
Senegal	2000–2008	1,894	261	296	40	213	2.4	3.0
Tanzania	2003–2009	6,641	1,099	759	67	299	4.3	3.3
Uganda	2004–2012	7,584	966	1,177	68	278	3.6	2.7
Yemen	2006–2010	7,388	1,541	985	65	235	6.1	7.0

Note: Although all our estimations are done at the more detailed eight-digit level of the Harmonized System (HS-8), the products in this table are defined at the HS-6 level. This is done for better comparability across countries, as HS-6 is an international classification while HS-8 is not.

the relative need for financial resources required for successful export of a given agricultural product. To our knowledge, there is no other measure of financing needs associated with exporting at the product level.[2] Arguably, the best proxy for export-related financing needs for agricultural products would be the cost of compliance with the SPS. Unfortunately, we do not directly observe these financial costs. The proxy used in this chapter might be the next best thing, measuring how SPS standards translate into inspections and rejections of noncompliant exports and thus how costly the compliance with the SPS might be for a given product.

To account for the possibility that our measure of export-related financing needs might be picking up other product characteristics, we control for the perishability index (perishability$_k$). The index takes value 1 if the product cannot be stored without refrigerator facilities and 0 otherwise. Perishable products typically include meat, fishery products, and fresh fruits and vegetables.

We include several other firm- and product-related control variables in our estimations. The value of exports in US dollars in the initial year of the trade relationship (initial_export$_{kfcd}$) reflects the level of confidence that importers have in the profitability of their trading partner (Rauch and Watson 2003; Albornoz et al. 2010). We also include the total number of destination markets served by firm f from exporting country c in the initial year of the trade relationship in log terms (NDestinations$_{fc}$) and the total value of exports of product k by a firm f from country c to the world market (total_export$_{kfc}$). These two variables allow us to control for the experience the firm has in exporting both in general and with a given product in particular. We control for the degree of export diversification of a given firm, incorporating the number of products exported by firm f from country c to the world market in the initial year of the trade relationship (NProducts$_{fc}$). We also include a dummy variable that is equal to 1 if a given export spell is part of a multiple spell. Multiple spells occur when a firm f from country c exits a given destination market d with a given product k and later reenters the same destination with the same product (multiple$_{kfcd}$). As there is a possibility of positive externalities and network effects among exporters, we also control for the number of firms from the same country c that export the same product k to the same destination d (NSuppliers$_{kcd}$).

Finally, data for the bilateral country-level gravity variables come from the CEPII database. These include measures of physical distance

Table 9.2
Descriptive statistics.

Variable	Obs.	Mean	Std. Dev.	Q1	Median	Q3
Sanitary risk (sanitary_risk$_k$)	73,179	3.4	4.5	0.0	2.3	4.9
Private credit to GDP (FD$_c$)	73,179	0.2	0.2	0.1	0.1	0.5
Ease of Getting Credit (EGC$_c$)	73,179	0.5	0.5	0.0	1.0	1.0
Perishability (perishability$_k$)	65,791	115.1	16.3	109.0	109.0	131.0
Logistics Performance Index (LPI$_c$)	73,179	3.0	0.0	3.0	3.0	3.0
GDPpc (constant 2000 USD) (GDPpc$_c$)	73,179	1185.6	3363.8	276.4	332.4	1351.3
Initial Export in logs (initial_export$_{kfcd}$)	73,179	8.6	2.9	6.5	8.8	10.8
Number of products (NProducts$_{fc}$)	73,179	22.1	82.5	3.0	6.0	15.0
Number of destinations (NDestinations$_{fc}$)	73,179	7.3	10.3	1.0	3.0	9.0
Number of suppliers (NSuppliers$_{kcd}$)	73,179	19.7	43.4	2.0	5.0	16.0
Contiguity (contiguity$_{cd}$)	73,179	0.2	0.4	0.0	0.0	0.0
Common language (com_language$_{cd}$)	73,179	0.5	0.5	0.0	0.0	1.0
Colonial link dummy (colony$_{cd}$)	73,179	0.2	0.4	0.0	0.0	0.0
Distance in logs (distance$_{cd}$)	73,179	7.9	0.9	7.3	8.1	8.6
Total Export (total_export$_{kfc}$)	73,179	9.1	3.1	6.8	9.2	11.3
Multiple spell dummy (multiple$_{kfcd}$)	73,179	0.1	0.3	0.0	0.0	0.0
Interaction terms						
Private credit to GDP×Sanitary risk	73,179	1.0	1.9	0.0	0.2	1.3
Ease of getting credit×Sanitary risk	65,791	397.8	542.4	0.0	185.8	604.6
Private credit to GDP×Perishability	73,179	0.2	0.2	0.0	0.1	0.5
Logistics Performance Index× Sanitary risk	73,179	10.3	13.6	0.0	6.7	14.7
GDPpc×Sanitary risk	73,179	4808.7	25472.0	0.0	623.0	4087.6
Alternative measures						
Alternative sanitary risk	73,179	4.2	5.4	0.0	3.6	6.2
Private credit to GDP measured at spell initiation	73,179	0.3	0.2	0.1	0.1	0.5
GDPpc measured at spell initiation	73,179	1672.9	4184.7	486.3	562.6	1931.8
Private credit to GDP×Alternative sanitary risk	73,179	1.2	2.4	0.0	0.3	1.7
Private credit to GDP at spell initiation×Sanitary risk	73,179	1.2	2.3	0.0	0.2	1.5
Private credit to GDP at spell initiation×Alternative sanitary risk	73,179	1.5	2.8	0.0	0.3	2.0
Private credit to GDP at spell initiation×Perishability	73,179	0.2	0.3	0.0	0.1	0.5
GDPpc at spell initiation×Sanitary risk	73,179	6756.4	32575.3	0.0	1048.0	6330.8

Note: The summary statistics for all variables in our sample include number of observations, mean, standard deviation, first quartile, median, and third quartile.

Table 9.3
Prima facie evidence.

Product sanitary risk	Country financial development	Number of spells	Spell duration		Mean difference	Test of mean equality	
			Mean	Std. Dev.		T-statistic	Significance
Low (sanitary risk$_k$ < Q1)	Low (FD$_c$ < Q1)	10,957	1.41	0.96	−0.06	−3.93	***
	High (FD$_c$ > Q3)	7,069	1.47	1.02			
High (sanitary risk$_k$ > Q3)	Low (FD$_c$ < Q1)	5,322	1.33	0.79	−0.31	−16.35	***
	High (FD$_c$ > Q3)	5,797	1.64	1.18			

Note: The table shows preliminary evidence of the differential impact of financial development on export survival, depending on the Sanitary Risk Index of products. In particular, it reports magnitude and statistical significance of the difference in average export spell duration between countries with high (top quartile) versus low (bottom quartile) levels of financial development, both for products with low (bottom quartile) and high (top quartile) values of the Sanitary Risk Index.
*** significant at 1%

such as bilateral distance between exporting country c and destination country d (distance$_{cd}$)[3] and a dummy variable that equals 1 if the exporting and destination countries share a border (contiguity$_{cd}$). Bilateral trade can also be fostered by countries' cultural proximity. We control for this possibility by using two dummies: one equal to 1 if a language is spoken by at least 9 percent of the population in both countries (com_language$_{cd}$) and the other equal to 1 if both partners have had a colonial relationship (colony$_{cd}$).

Table 9.2 reports the summary statistics for our sample. Table 9.3 provides some preliminary evidence for the importance of finance for trade survival of exported products. While financial development seems to increase the average spell duration for all products, the effect seems to be both economically and statistically stronger for products with high export-related financing needs as measured by the Sanitary Risk Index.

9.4 Main Results

Table 9.4 reports the results of various baseline estimations corresponding to equation (9.1). The dependent variable is hazard rate—the risk of exiting the foreign destination market d for a product k exported by firm f from country c. The lower the hazard rate, the better the prospect of long-term survival for a given export. All regressions are estimated by a Cox PH model stratified across firms. As all exporting firms are

Table 9.4
Financial development and export survival.

	(1)	(2)	(3)	(4)
$FD_c \times$ sanitary risk$_k$	−0.0098*	−0.0096*	−0.0133**	−0.0114**
	(0.0055)	(0.0053)	(0.0052)	(0.0052)
sanitary_risk$_k$	0.0008	0.0010		
	(0.0025)	(0.0024)		
initial_export$_{kfcd}$	−0.0854***	−0.0831***	−0.0858***	−0.0870***
	(0.0057)	(0.0059)	(0.0059)	(0.0059)
NProducts$_{fc}$	0.0007***	0.0006***	0.0005***	0.0005***
	(0.0002)	(0.0002)	(0.0002)	(0.0002)
NDestinations$_{fc}$	−0.0187***	−0.0138***	−0.0136***	−0.0136***
	(0.0035)	(0.0032)	(0.0031)	(0.0031)
NSuppliers$_{kcd}$	−0.0059***	−0.0053***	−0.0056***	−0.0056***
	(0.0009)	(0.0009)	(0.0007)	(0.0007)
contiguity$_{cd}$	−0.0349	−0.0454	−0.0670	−0.0726
	(0.0242)	(0.0471)	(0.0480)	(0.0478)
com_language$_{cd}$	−0.0132	−0.0340	−0.0382	−0.0380
	(0.0131)	(0.0242)	(0.0243)	(0.0245)
colony$_{cd}$	−0.0751***	−0.0015	−0.0037	−0.0031
	(0.0235)	(0.0331)	(0.0334)	(0.0336)
distance$_{cd}$	0.0359***	0.0641***	0.0631***	0.0601***
	(0.0116)	(0.0183)	(0.0181)	(0.0181)
GDPpc$_c$	0.0023***	0.0027***	0.0028***	0.0027***
	(0.0003)	(0.0004)	(0.0004)	(0.0004)
multiple$_{kfcd}$	0.2307***	0.2388***	0.2582***	0.2613***
	(0.0208)	(0.0212)	(0.0207)	(0.0207)
total export$_{kfc}$	−0.0150***	−0.0178***	−0.0150***	−0.0150***
	(0.0044)	(0.0044)	(0.0043)	(0.0043)
Observations	73,179	73,179	73,179	73,179
Firm strata	Yes	Yes	Yes	Yes
Industry (HS-4) fixed effects	Yes	Yes	No	No
Spell initiation year fixed effects	Yes	No	No	No
Destination × spell initiation year fixed effects	No	Yes	Yes	Yes
Product (HS-8) fixed effects	No	No	Yes	Yes
Exporting country × HS-2 fixed effects	No	No	No	Yes

Note: The dependent variable is the hazard rate of trade relationships for product k of firm f exporting from country c to destination country d. All regressions are estimated using the Cox proportional hazards model stratified by firm. The main variable of interest is the interaction of sanitary risk of product k (sanitary_risk$_k$) with financial development in country c ($FD_c \times$ sanitary_risk$_k$). Financial development (FD_c) is measured as a ratio of private credit (i.e., credit from banks to the private sector) to GDP. The direct effect of sanitary risk (sanitary_risk$_k$) in columns 3 and 4 and the direct effect of financial development of country c (FD_c) in all columns are captured by fixed and strata effects. The control variables include initial export value (initial_export$_{kfcd}$), number of products exported by firm f from country c to the world market (NProducts$_{fc}$), number of destinations serviced by firm f (NDestinations$_{fc}$), number of firms from the same exporting country c exporting a given product k to a given destination market d (NSuppliers$_{kcd}$), gravity variables (contiguity$_{cd}$, com_language$_{cd}$, colony$_{cd}$, distance$_{cd}$), real GDP per capita of the exporting country c expressed in constant US dollars (GDPpc$_c$), a dummy variable equal to 1 if a given export spell is part of a multiple spell when a given firm exits a given destination market with a given product and later reenters the same destination with the same product (multiple$_{kfcd}$), and value of total exports of product k by firm f from country c to the world market (total_export$_{kfc}$). All columns include firm strata effects. The estimations also include additional fixed effects at the level of HS-4 industry (columns 1 and 2), spell initiation year (column 1), destination x spell initiation year (columns 2, 3, and 4), HS-8 product level (columns 3 and 4), and exporting country x HS-2 broad industry (column 4). Robust standard errors clustered at the (exporting country)*HS-4 sector level are in parentheses.
* Significant at 10%; ** significant at 5%; *** significant at 1%.

based in a specific exporting country, there is no need to include additional exporting country fixed effects, as those would be fully absorbed by the firm strata effects. The firm strata effects thus control for a possible omitted variable bias at both the firm level and the exporting country level. In addition to the stratification, we also include fixed effects to control for heterogeneity alongside other dimensions.

In column 1 of table 9.4, we control for year of the spell initiation fixed effects and industry fixed effects at the HS-4 level. Our main variable of interest ($FD_c \times sanitary\_risk_k$) is negative and significant, suggesting that financial development decreases the hazard rate, especially for those agricultural products that face high costs of SPS compliance. The direct effect of these export-related costs ($sanitary\_risk_k$) is not significant. The size of the initial shipment ($initial\_export_{kfcd}$) and number of destinations to which a given firm exports ($NDestinations_{fc}$) also decrease the hazard rate significantly. The former variable controls for trust of a foreign business partner vis-à-vis the exporting firm at the beginning of their trade relationship, and the latter is a proxy for the experience a given firm has in exporting. The variable controlling for the experience of a given firm in exporting a specific product k ($total\_export_{kfc}$) also decreases the hazard rate of exports. A higher number of exporters of a given product from the same country to the same destination ($NSuppliers_{kcd}$) significantly decreases the hazard rate of exports. This suggests the potential importance of positive externalities and network effects among the exporters in the developing countries from the MENA and SSA regions. The number of products exported by a given firm ($NProducts_{fc}$) should control for the export diversification achieved by this firm and could thus be expected to decrease the overall hazard rate. However, in our sample, this variable has a positive sign. Repeated exits and reentries into a given destination market increase the hazard rate, as can be seen in the positive and significant sign for the multiple spells dummy variable ($multiple_{kfcd}$). The gravity variables capturing physical (common border: $contiguity_{cd}$), cultural (common language: $com\_language_{cd}$), and historical (colonial links: $colony_{cd}$) affinities all have the expected negative sign. Also intuitively, the distance between exporting and destination country ($distance_{cd}$) increases the hazard rate for exports, as can be seen in the positive and significant estimated coefficient for this variable. The GDP per capita of the exporting country ($GDPpc_c$) has a positive and significant effect on the hazard rate. Jaud, Kukenova, and Strieborny (2018) provide an explanation for this seemingly counterintuitive result. When controlling for exporting-country fixed effects (implemented via firm strata effects in this chapter), the impact of GDPpc$_c$ is identified solely from variations within countries over time that often emerge from business cycle fluctuations. At the same time, we measure GDP per capita in the first year of an export spell. Economically, the positive estimated coefficient for GDPpc$_c$ would then imply that exports initiated at the peak of a business cycle in the country of origin face a higher risk of failure. This could be explained by the overconfidence of exporters during a boom and/or difficulties maintaining the costly presence in foreign markets once the business climate at home deteriorates.

In columns 2 to 4 of table 9.4, we are successively increasing the stringency of the included fixed effects (in addition to stratification at the firm level). In column 2, we add the fixed effects for the (destination country)*(year of the export spell initiation). In column 3, we replace the industry fixed effect at the HS-4 level by a product fixed effect at the HS-8 level. This means that in column 3 and all subsequent estimations, the direct effect of export-related financial vulnerability (sanitary_risk$_k$) is captured by these product fixed effects. In column 4, we add an interactive fixed effect of broad industry (measured at the HS-2 level) with exporting country. These fixed effects control for unobservable patterns of country-industry specialization whether they are driven by Ricardian forces of technology or Heckscher-Ohlin forces of factor endowments. In column 4 of table 9.4, we thus control for stratification at the firm level as well as for fixed effects at the level of (destination country)*(year of the export spell initiation), HS-8 product, and (exporting country)*(HS-2 industry). This most stringent specification is our preferred one, and we use it in the subsequent estimations.

Our main variable of interest (FD$_c$ × sanitary risk$_k$) remains negative and significant in all specifications of table 9.4. The firm- and product-related control variables also keep their sign from the first column and remain significant. Among the gravity control variables, the physical distance between exporting and destination country (distance$_{cd}$) seems to be the most robust force, significantly increasing the hazard rate of exports.

Please note that independent of the applied sets of fixed effects, we are able to estimate the direct impact of the exporting country's GDP per capita but not the direct effect of its financial development. This is because in our sample the GDP per capita is measured at the beginning of a given export spell and is thus time-varying, while financial development is measured at the beginning of the sample and consequently varies only across countries and not across time. The direct effect of the time-invariant variable FD_c is therefore captured by exporting firm strata effects, while the direct effect of time-varying $GDPpc_c$ is not.[4]

Before moving on to further estimations, let us briefly discuss the economic significance of our results. A natural way to interpret the economic magnitude of the coefficient on our main variable of interest is to ask how an improved financial development in a given country would affect the export survival of the products with high costs of SPS compliance versus the export survival of the "nonrisky" products (i.e., products with Sanitary Risk Index equal to 0). The following example can shed some light on the issue. In 2003, Jordan's ratio of private credit to GDP (FD_c) was 69 percent. In the case of Senegal, the value of this variable was 18 percent. Let us consider the case of poultry meat that is exported by both countries and has a Sanitary Risk Index ($sanitary\_risk_k$) equal to 17.724. We consider the estimated coefficient α for the main interaction term ($FD_c \times sanitary\_risk_k$) from the most stringent specification reported in column 4 of table 9.4, which is –0.0114. This estimate would imply that if Senegal reached the same level of financial development as Jordan, the hazard rate of its exports of poultry meat would decrease relative to the hazard rate of its "nonrisky" exports by approximately 10 percent ($\alpha^*sanitary\_risk_k^*\Delta FD_c = -0.0114 * 17.724 * (0.69 - 0.18) = -0.103$).

In table 9.5, we first examine the robustness of our results to alternative measures of export-related financial needs and financial development and then control for an alternative channel at the product level that could bias our results. In column 1 of table 9.5, we recompute our measure of export-related needs at the product level by using a Poisson model rather than a negative binomial empirical model (the appendix provides technical details about computing the measure). In column 2 of table 9.5, we measure financial development by the Ease of Getting Credit Index of the World Bank (EGC_c) rather than by the ratio of private bank credit to GDP (FD_c). In both columns, our main variable of interest remains negative and significant. In columns 3 and 4 of table 9.5, we control for the interaction between perishability index at the product level and financial development at the country level ($FD_c \times perishability_k$). This controls for the possibility that our measure of high costs related to SPS compliance does not capture the need for external financing but rather the problems fulfilling the SPS requirements in the case of products that cannot be stored without refrigerator facilities. The sign and significance of our main measure ($FD_c \times sanitary\_risk_k$) are not affected by inclusion of this additional control. The control itself ($FD_c \times perishability_k$) is

Table 9.5
Alternative measures of the main variable and perishability index.

	Alternative measures		Perishability index	
	(1)	(2)	(3)	(4)
$FD_c \times$ (alternative) sanitary_risk$_k$	−0.0081*			
	(0.0042)			
$EGC_c \times$ sanitary_risk$_k$		−0.0002***		
		(0.0001)		
$FD_c \times$ perishability$_k$			0.0100	0.0403
			(0.1016)	(0.1020)
$FD_c \times$ sanitary_risk$_k$				−0.0116**
				(0.0052)
initial_export$_{kfcd}$	−0.0870***	−0.0922***	−0.0870***	−0.0870***
	(0.0059)	(0.0063)	(0.0059)	(0.0059)
NProducts$_{fc}$	0.0005***	0.0002	0.0005***	0.0005***
	(0.0002)	(0.0002)	(0.0002)	(0.0002)
NDestinations$_{fc}$	−0.0136***	−0.0092***	−0.0136***	−0.0136***
	(0.0031)	(0.0034)	(0.0031)	(0.0031)
NSuppliers$_{kcd}$	−0.0056***	−0.0054***	−0.0056***	−0.0056***
	(0.0007)	(0.0007)	(0.0007)	(0.0007)
contiguity$_{cd}$	−0.0724	−0.0988	−0.0724	−0.0725
	(0.0478)	(0.0601)	(0.0478)	(0.0478)
com_language$_{cd}$	−0.0379	−0.0384	−0.0378	−0.0380
	(0.0245)	(0.0249)	(0.0245)	(0.0245)
colony$_{cd}$	−0.0031	0.0016	−0.0030	−0.0031
	(0.0336)	(0.0376)	(0.0336)	(0.0336)
distance$_{cd}$	0.0602***	0.0577***	0.0601***	0.0601***
	(0.0181)	(0.0217)	(0.0181)	(0.0181)
GDPpc$_c$	0.0027***	0.0026***	0.0027***	0.0027***
	(0.0004)	(0.0004)	(0.0004)	(0.0004)
multiple$_{kfcd}$	0.2613***	0.2656***	0.2613***	0.2612***
	(0.0207)	(0.0213)	(0.0207)	(0.0207)
total_export$_{kfc}$	−0.0150***	−0.0178***	−0.0150***	−0.0150***
	(0.0043)	(0.0048)	(0.0043)	(0.0043)
Observations	73,179	73,179	73,179	73,179

Note: The dependent variable is the hazard rate of trade relationships for product k of firm f exporting from country c to destination country d. All regressions are estimated using the Cox proportional hazards model. We control for (destination country)*(spell initiation year), product (HS-8), and (exporting country)*HS-2 fixed effects, and allow the baseline hazard to vary across firms. The variables of interest are defined in table 9.4. In column 1, sanitary risk is computed using a Poisson model rather than a negative binomial model. Additional variables are World Bank ranking of Ease of Getting Credit (EGC_c) and perishability index (perishability$_k$). Robust standard errors clustered at the (exporting country)*HS-4 sector level are in parentheses.
* Significant at 10%; ** significant at 5%; *** significant at 1%.

not significant whether it enters the regression alone in column 3 or together with the main interaction term in column 4.

In table 9.6, we control for alternative channels at the country level that could bias our results. In particular, the level of financial development is usually highly correlated with other aspects of economic development in exporting countries that could shape the survival of agricultural exports in foreign markets. In column 1, we include the interaction term between the export-related financial needs and logistic performance index ($LPI_c \times sanitary\_risk_k$). In column 2, we interact the product measure with the GDP per capita in a given exporting country ($GDPpc_c \times sanitary\_risk_k$). Finally, column 3 includes an interaction of SPS-related costs with the Ease of Doing Business Index of the World Bank ($EDB_c \times sanitary\_risk_k$). In all three columns, our main interaction term remains negative and significant. Among the three controls capturing the alternative channels, only the logistic performance index seems to disproportionately help products with high export-related financial needs.

Table 9.7 looks more closely into the issue of various destination markets. One could expect that SPS requirements would be particularly high when it comes to exports to developed countries. Therefore, the exports to those countries should face particularly high financial costs of compliance with SPS. Firms exporting products with high SPS-related costs to developed countries should thus particularly benefit from a high level of financial development in their home country. This is indeed what table 9.7 shows. In column 1 of table 9.7, we reestimate our preferred specification on the subsample of high-income destination countries. The main variable of interest ($FD_c \times sanitary\_risk_k$) remains negative and significant. On the contrary, when we look at the subsample of low-income destination markets in column 2, the significance disappears. As our sample of exporting countries includes solely MENA and SSA countries, in the last three columns we look at those regions also as destination markets. Columns 3 and 4 of table 9.7 look separately at exports into the MENA and SSA regions, respectively. Column 5 includes exports from our ten countries (Jordan, Kuwait, Morocco, Yemen, Ghana, Mali, Malawi, Senegal, Tanzania, and Uganda) into the destination of the combined region of MENA and SSA. As both MENA and SSA are developing regions, we would expect the coefficient for our main variable of interest ($FD_c \times sanitary\_risk_k$) to be insignificant, similar to the subsample of low-income destination countries from column 2 of table 9.7. This is indeed what we find.

Table 9.6
Alternative channels at the country level.

	Logistic performance	Economic development	Ease of doing business
$FD_c \times$ sanitary $risk_k$	−0.0114**	−0.0115**	−0.0131**
	(0.0052)	(0.0055)	(0.0063)
$LPI_c \times$ sanitary_$risk_k$	−0.0428***		
	(0.0094)		
$GDPpc_c \times$ sanitary_$risk_k$		0.0000	
		(0.0000)	
$EDB_c \times$ sanitary_$risk_k$			−0.0000
			(0.0001)
initial_export$_{kfcd}$	−0.0870***	−0.0870***	−0.0922***
	(0.0059)	(0.0059)	(0.0063)
NProducts$_{fc}$	0.0005***	0.0005***	0.0002
	(0.0002)	(0.0002)	(0.0002)
NDestinations$_{fc}$	−0.0136***	−0.0136***	−0.0092***
	(0.0031)	(0.0031)	(0.0034)
NSuppliers$_{kcd}$	−0.0056***	−0.0056***	−0.0054***
	(0.0007)	(0.0007)	(0.0007)
contiguity$_{cd}$	−0.0726	−0.0726	−0.0978
	(0.0478)	(0.0477)	(0.0601)
com_language$_{cd}$	−0.0380	−0.0380	−0.0385
	(0.0245)	(0.0245)	(0.0249)
colony$_{cd}$	−0.0031	−0.0031	0.0020
	(0.0336)	(0.0336)	(0.0376)
distance$_{cd}$	0.0601***	0.0601***	0.0575***
	(0.0181)	(0.0181)	(0.0217)
GDPpc$_c$	0.0027***	0.0027***	0.0026***
	(0.0004)	(0.0004)	(0.0004)
multiple$_{kfcd}$	0.2613***	0.2613***	0.2655***
	(0.0207)	(0.0207)	(0.0207)
total_export$_{kfc}$	−0.0150***	−0.0150***	−0.0178***
	(0.0043)	(0.0043)	(0.0048)
Observations	73,179	73,179	73,179

Note: The dependent variable is the hazard rate of trade relationships for product k of firm f exporting from country c to destination country d. All regressions are estimated using the Cox proportional hazards model. We control for (destination country)*(spell initiation year), product (HS-8), and (exporting country)*HS-2 fixed effects, and allow the baseline hazard to vary across firms. The variables of interest are defined in table 9.4. Additional controls include logistic performance index (LPI_c), GDP per capita ($GDPpc_c$), and Ease of Doing Business Index (EDB_c). Robust standard errors clustered at the (exporting country)*HS-4 sector level are in parentheses.
* Significant at 10%; ** significant at 5%; *** significant at 1%.

Table 9.7
Destination markets.

	(1)	(2)	(3)	(4)	(5)
					MENA
	High-income	Low-income	MENA	SSA	and SSA
$FD_c \times sanitary\_risk_k$	−0.0198***	0.0458	−0.0032	0.0181	−0.0059
	(0.0068)	(0.0285)	(0.0102)	(0.0123)	(0.0063)
$initial\_export_{kfcd}$	−0.0914***	−0.0769***	−0.0754***	−0.0833***	−0.0698***
	(0.0072)	(0.0258)	(0.0206)	(0.0133)	(0.0116)
$NProducts_{fc}$	0.0004**	0.0048**	0.0015***	0.0015***	0.0013***
	(0.0002)	(0.0020)	(0.0003)	(0.0004)	(0.0002)
$NDestinations_{fc}$	−0.0124***	−0.0296*	−0.0287***	−0.0211***	−0.0240***
	(0.0033)	(0.0178)	(0.0047)	(0.0049)	(0.0035)
$NSuppliers_{kcd}$	−0.0052***	−0.0213	−0.0160***	−0.0090***	−0.0149***
	(0.0007)	(0.0147)	(0.0027)	(0.0030)	(0.0022)
$contiguity_{cd}$	−0.1271*	−0.0139	−0.0558	0.0043	−0.0062
	(0.0730)	(0.1330)	(0.0540)	(0.0782)	(0.0441)
$com\_language_{cd}$	−0.0232	−0.0619	−0.1559	0.0319	−0.0995**
	(0.0245)	(0.1566)	(0.1730)	(0.0735)	(0.0488)
$colony_{cd}$	−0.0280				
	(0.0392)				
$distance_{cd}$	0.0418	0.2179**	−0.0317	0.2161***	0.0909***
	(0.0285)	(0.0928)	(0.0322)	(0.0577)	(0.0317)
$GDPpc_c$	0.0029***	0.0077***	0.0020***	0.0061***	0.0024***
	(0.0005)	(0.0009)	(0.0004)	(0.0008)	(0.0003)
$multiple_{kfcd}$	0.2890***	0.2758***	0.2901***	0.1918***	0.2201***
	(0.0246)	(0.0492)	(0.0466)	(0.0313)	(0.0262)
$total\_export_{kfc}$	−0.0158***	−0.0322	−0.0069	−0.0079	−0.0129
	(0.0055)	(0.0248)	(0.0116)	(0.0113)	(0.0079)
Observations	55,031	3,870	11,492	12,092	23,584

Note: The dependent variable is the hazard rate of trade relationships for product k of firm f exporting from country c to destination country d. All regressions are estimated using the Cox proportional hazards model. We control for (destination country)*(spell initiation year), product (HS-8), and (exporting country)*HS-2 fixed effects and allow the baseline hazard to vary across firms. The variables of interest are defined in table 9.4. Sample description: exports to high-income countries (column 1), exports to low-income countries (column 2), exports to MENA countries (column 3), exports to SSA countries (column 4), and exports to both MENA and SSA countries (column 5). Robust standard errors clustered at (exporting country)*HS-4 sector level are in parentheses.
* Significant at 10%; ** significant at 5%; *** significant at 1%.

9.5   Robustness Tests

In this section, we report the results of several robustness checks testing various econometric issues that arise in the context of the survival analysis. These include the proportionality assumption in the Cox model, measurement of financial development, and the issue of left censoring. For a more detailed discussion of these econometric issues, see Jaud, Kukenova, and Strieborny (2018).

In table 9.8, we reestimate our main specification from column 4 of table 9.4, replacing the hazard rate as our dependent variable with the probability of survival S_{ck,t_0}. S_{ck,t_0} is a dummy variable that equals 1 if firm f from country c, which started to export the product k to the destination market d in the year t_0, is still serving this destination market after L years. We run a linear probability model (an OLS estimation) for spell lengths $L = 1, 3, 6, 9$. This econometric framework imposes fewer restrictions on the time profile of survival than a hazard function does, as the effects of explanatory variables are allowed to vary across survival periods. In other words, it relaxes the hazard proportionality assumption of the Cox model (see also Araujo, Mion, and Ornelas 2014; Jaud, Kukenova, and Strieborny 2018).

As the dependent variable is now the probability of export survival rather than the hazard rate of exit from the export market, all variables in table 9.8 have the opposite signs compared to the rest of the chapter. In particular, our main variable of interest ($FD_c \times sanitary\_risk_k$) has an expected positive sign, which would confirm that financial development disproportionately increases the probability of export survival for those products that have high financing needs for exporting because of the costly compliance with the SPS regulations. We see that this is indeed the case in all columns of table 9.8.

In all previous estimations, we measured financial development (FD_c) at the beginning of the sample so that its direct effect was captured by the exporting firm's strata effects. In table 9.9, we instead measure financial development at the beginning of each particular spell, similar to our treatment of GDP per capita of the exporting country. In column 1, we reestimate our preferred specification from the fourth column of table 9.4. In column 2 of table 9.9, we control for the possible alternative channel working through the different degree of perishability of the exported products, reestimating the specification from the fourth column of table 9.5. In column 3 of table 9.9, we control for the possible bias emerging as a result of the high correlation between financial and

Table 9.8
Linear probability model.

	$L=1$	$L=3$	$L=6$	$L=9$
$FD_c \times$ sanitary risk$_k$	0.0124***	0.0037**	0.0009*	0.0006**
	(0.0026)	(0.0017)	(0.0005)	(0.0003)
initial_export$_{kfcd}$	0.0383***	0.0182***	0.0059***	0.0029***
	(0.0029)	(0.0020)	(0.0010)	(0.0006)
NProducts$_{fc}$	0.0003***	−0.0001	−0.0002***	−0.0001***
	(0.0001)	(0.0000)	(0.0000)	(0.0000)
NDestinations$_{fc}$	−0.0045***	−0.0019***	−0.0002	0.0001
	(0.0010)	(0.0006)	(0.0003)	(0.0002)
NSuppliers$_{kcd}$	−0.0001	0.0001	0.0001**	0.0001*
	(0.0001)	(0.0001)	(0.0001)	(0.0000)
contiguity$_{cd}$	0.0443**	0.0223*	0.0004	−0.0049*
	(0.0205)	(0.0117)	(0.0073)	(0.0026)
com_language$_{cd}$	0.0300***	0.0157**	0.0081**	0.0038**
	(0.0100)	(0.0066)	(0.0033)	(0.0017)
colony$_{cd}$	0.0110	0.0293***	0.0084	0.0046**
	(0.0172)	(0.0108)	(0.0055)	(0.0021)
distance$_{cd}$	−0.0067	−0.0068	−0.0105***	−0.0069***
	(0.0081)	(0.0058)	(0.0039)	(0.0019)
GDPpc$_c$	0.0000***	−0.0000***	−0.0000***	−0.0000***
	(0.0000)	(0.0000)	(0.0000)	(0.0000)
multiple$_{kfcd}$	−0.0543***	−0.1028***	−0.0643***	−0.0312***
	(0.0074)	(0.0090)	(0.0098)	(0.0067)
total_export$_{kfc}$	0.0102***	0.0032***	0.0014**	0.0003
	(0.0022)	(0.0012)	(0.0006)	(0.0005)
Observations	73,179	73,179	73,179	73,179
R^2	0.421	0.361	0.335	0.295

Note: The dependent variable is the probability of survival $S_{ck,t0}$, which is a dummy variable that equals 1 if firm f from country c, which started to export the product k to the destination market d in the year t_0, is still serving this destination market after L years. Note that all variables have the opposite expected sign compared to the other tables, where the dependent variable was the hazard rate. We run a linear probability model (an OLS estimation) for spell lengths $L = 1, 3, 6, 9$. The specifications otherwise correspond to the fourth column of table 9.4. Robust standard errors clustered at the (exporting country)*HS-4 sector level are in parentheses.
* Significant at 10%; ** significant at 5%; *** significant at 1%.

Table 9.9
Measuring financial development at the initiation of export spells.

	(1)	(2)	(3)	(4)
	Main specification	Alternative channels		HIC
$FD_c \times$ sanitary risk$_k$	−0.0084*	−0.0090*	−0.0085*	−0.0125**
	(0.0048)	(0.0048)	(0.0051)	(0.0062)
$FD_c \times$ perishability$_k$		0.0911		
		(0.1012)		
GDPpc$_c \times$ sanitary risk$_k$			0.0000	
			(0.0000)	
FD_c	3.8341***	3.7778***	3.8344***	4.0118***
	(0.5847)	(0.5770)	(0.5845)	(0.6917)
initial_export$_{kfcd}$	−0.0866***	−0.0866***	−0.0866***	−0.0911***
	(0.0059)	(0.0059)	(0.0059)	(0.0072)
NProducts$_{fc}$	0.0004**	0.0004**	0.0004**	0.0003*
	(0.0002)	(0.0002)	(0.0002)	(0.0002)
NDestinations$_{fc}$	−0.0110***	−0.0109***	−0.0110***	−0.0098***
	(0.0031)	(0.0031)	(0.0031)	(0.0033)
NSuppliers$_{kcd}$	−0.0055***	−0.0055***	−0.0055***	−0.0051***
	(0.0007)	(0.0007)	(0.0007)	(0.0007)
contiguity$_{cd}$	−0.0953**	−0.0951**	−0.0953**	−0.1305*
	(0.0464)	(0.0465)	(0.0464)	(0.0740)
com_language$_{cd}$	−0.0446*	−0.0448*	−0.0446*	−0.0340
	(0.0245)	(0.0245)	(0.0245)	(0.0246)
colony$_{cd}$	0.0023	0.0023	0.0023	−0.0198
	(0.0332)	(0.0332)	(0.0332)	(0.0391)
distance$_{cd}$	0.0532***	0.0531***	0.0532***	0.0323
	(0.0172)	(0.0172)	(0.0172)	(0.0279)
GDPpc$_c$	0.0014***	0.0014***	0.0014***	0.0014***
	(0.0003)	(0.0003)	(0.0003)	(0.0003)
multiple$_{kfcd}$	0.2624***	0.2623***	0.2624***	0.2922***
	(0.0206)	(0.0206)	(0.0206)	(0.0245)
total_export$_{kfc}$	−0.0163***	−0.0163***	−0.0163***	−0.0169***
	(0.0043)	(0.0043)	(0.0043)	(0.0055)
Observations	73,179	73,179	73,179	55,031

Note: The dependent variable is the hazard rate of trade relationships for product k of firm f exporting from country c to destination country d. All regressions are estimated using the Cox proportional hazards model. We measure financial development (FD$_c$) at the beginning of each spell rather than at the beginning of the sample. Otherwise, the specifications in columns 1, 2, 3, and 4 correspond to the fourth column of table 9.4, the fourth column of table 9.5, the second column of table 9.6, and the first column of table 9.7, respectively. Robust standard errors clustered at the (exporting country)*HS-4 sector level are in parentheses.
* Significant at 10%; ** significant at 5%; *** significant at 1%.

overall economic development across countries. In particular, we control for the interaction term between our measure of financial needs at the product level and the GDP per capita at the exporting country level, thus reestimating the specification from the second column of table 9.6. Finally, in column 4 of table 9.9, we check the robustness of our result regarding the particular importance of our channel for the exports to the developed countries. We reestimate the specification from the first column of table 9.7, restricting the destination markets to the high-income countries only. In all four columns, our main variable of interest ($FD_c \times sanitary\_risk_k$) has the expected negative sign and is statistically significant. The seemingly counterintuitive positive coefficient for the financial development itself (FD_c) can be explained by business cycle considerations similar to those for the positive coefficient of GDP per capita discussed in table 9.4.

In table 9.10, we address three features of trade survival data that could affect our previous estimation results: censoring, the existence of multiple spells, and the possibility of tied-spells terminations. All columns reestimate our preferred specification from column 4 of table 9.4. In column 1 of table 9.10, we drop all left-censored observations. These are the spells that we observe in the first year of our sample and that could thus have already been active for many years before. The related issue of right censoring (the existence of spells that are observed in the last year of the sample and that thus could continue to exist) is directly accounted for in the estimation of the Cox model, with Stata including a dummy variable that is equal to 1 if a spell exists in the last year of the sample and equal to 0 otherwise. Columns 2 and 3 of table 9.10 provide two robustness checks for our treatment of multiple spells. Multiple spells occur when a given firm enters a destination market with a given product, then exits the export market and reenters with the same product later. In previous estimations, we used a dummy variable equal to 1 for multiple spells and 0 otherwise. In column 2, we instead restrict the sample to single spells and first spells of the multiple spells, thus dropping later reentries after the original exits from the export market. In column 3, we restrict our sample further, including only single spells, thus also dropping the first spells of multiple-spell events. Column 4 of table 9.10 addresses the fact that sometimes two spells terminate at exactly the same time. Such events violate the assumption of a continuous hazard function in the Cox proportional hazards model. In the previous estimations, we applied the usual

Table 9.10
Left censoring, multiple spells, tied-spells terminations.

	(1)	(2)	(3)	(4)
	Left censoring	First and single spells	Single spells	Efron method
$FD_c \times sanitary\_risk_k$	−0.0084*	−0.0106**	−0.0090*	−0.0177**
	(0.0048)	(0.0051)	(0.0054)	(0.0073)
$initial\_export_{kfcd}$	−0.0741***	−0.0847***	−0.0825***	−0.1132***
	(0.0062)	(0.0057)	(0.0063)	(0.0079)
$NProducts_{fc}$	0.0003	0.0006***	0.0009***	0.0002
	(0.0002)	(0.0002)	(0.0002)	(0.0002)
$NDestinations_{fc}$	−0.0126***	−0.0172***	−0.0179***	−0.0119***
	(0.0037)	(0.0033)	(0.0035)	(0.0038)
$NSuppliers_{kcd}$	−0.0150***	−0.0059***	−0.0059***	−0.0066***
	(0.0016)	(0.0007)	(0.0008)	(0.0008)
$contiguity_{cd}$	−0.0753	−0.0552	−0.0279	−0.0762
	(0.0515)	(0.0484)	(0.0487)	(0.0605)
$com\_language_{cd}$	−0.0250	−0.0410	−0.0277	−0.0441
	(0.0281)	(0.0272)	(0.0280)	(0.0320)
$colony_{cd}$	0.0268	0.0045	−0.0085	−0.0081
	(0.0402)	(0.0325)	(0.0340)	(0.0434)
$distance_{cd}$	0.0509***	0.0509***	0.0644***	0.0660***
	(0.0196)	(0.0184)	(0.0195)	(0.0228)
$GDPpc_c$	0.0038***	0.0027***	0.0030***	0.0034***
	(0.0005)	(0.0004)	(0.0004)	(0.0005)
$multiple_{kfcd}$	0.1687***	0.4847***		0.2955***
	(0.0166)	(0.0260)		(0.0252)
$total\_export_{kfc}$	−0.0115**	−0.0137***	−0.0159***	−0.0229***
	(0.0048)	(0.0043)	(0.0050)	(0.0062)
Observations	59,777	67,902	63,317	73,179

Note: The dependent variable is the hazard rate of trade relationships for product k of firm f exporting from country c to destination country d. All regressions are estimated using the Cox proportional hazards model. The specifications correspond to the fourth column of table 9.4. In column 1, we drop all left-censored spells, in column 2 we restrict the sample to the single spells and first spells of multiple spells, in column 3 we further restrict the sample to single spells only, and in column 4 we use the Efron method (Efron 1988) instead of the usual Breslow method (Breslow 1974) to address the issue of possible tied-spells terminations. Robust standard errors clustered at the (exporting country)*HS-4 sector level are in parentheses.
* Significant at 10%; ** significant at 5%; *** significant at 1%.

Breslow method (Breslow 1974) to address this issue. In column 4, we apply instead the alternative Efron method (Efron 1988).

Also, this last set of robustness checks confirms our main result. Our variable of interest ($FD_c \times sanitary\_risk_k$) remains negative and significant in all four columns of table 9.10, in accordance with our hypothesis that financial development disproportionately decreases the hazard of exiting an exporting market for those products that have high financing needs associated with exporting because of the cost of compliance with the SPS regulations.

9.6   Concluding Remarks

This chapter explores the effects of financial development in the developing countries on the long-term success of their exports. It uses unique firm, product, and destination data collected by customs authorities in four Middle Eastern and North African (MENA) countries (Jordan, Kuwait, Morocco, and Yemen) as well as in six countries of sub-Saharan Africa (SSA) (Ghana, Mali, Malawi, Senegal, Tanzania, and Uganda). Using a measure of export-related financial needs arising from compliance with Sanitary and Phytosanitary Standards (SPS), we show that finance plays an important role in promoting agricultural exports from the selected countries in the MENA and SSA regions. In particular, the long-term export survival of products with high export-related financial needs particularly benefits from financial development. The result is robust to controlling for stratification and various sets of fixed effects capturing the heterogeneity across firms, products, and countries. The positive impact of financial development on export survival also remains significant when controlling for various alternative channels that could be correlated with our mechanism.

Similarly to Jaud, Kukenova, and Strieborny (2015), our results seem to be driven by exports to the developed countries. This is not surprising, given that those countries have particularly strict SPS in general and for imports from developing countries in particular. From the policy perspective, this adds another reason why governments of developing countries, such as those in the MENA and SSA regions, should consider promoting domestic financial development. A well-developed financial system implies better access to credit for exporting firms, helping them establish a long-term presence in the attractive markets of developed countries. Those developing countries that consider agricultural exports an important part of their exporting strategy might be especially interested in the results presented in this chapter.

Appendix

This appendix describes the construction of the Sanitary Risk Index and briefly motivates its use as a measure of financing needs at the product level. Subsection 2a from Jaud, Kukenova, and Strieborny (2015) provides a more detailed discussion.

The risk index is computed using data from the EU Rapid Alert System for Food and Feed (RASFF). The RASFF database reports all agrifood shipments to the European Union between 2001 and 2008 that have suffered rejection because of food safety reasons. The database provides rejections by product, exporting country, importing country (EU member state), and year. The index is the coefficient on the product dummy (δ_k) in the regression

$$\text{Alert}_{ck} = f\ (\beta \text{Imp\_Share}_{ck}^{EU} + \gamma \text{Controls}_k + \delta_c + \delta_k + \varepsilon_{ck}), \tag{9.2}$$

where ε_{ck} is an error term. For a product k exported from country c, the dependent variable is the combined count of notifications from all EU member states between 2001 and 2008.[5] The unit of observation is the exporting country × product pair, and the regression is cross-sectional. To avoid picking up on any particularities generated by exporting countries' export volume, protectionist agenda, or limited competition, a set of control variables is included: share of exporting country c in EU imports of product k in the year 2000 (one year before the sample start) ($\text{Imp\_share}_{ck}^{EU}$), the ad valorem equivalent of the MFN (most favored nation) tariff imposed by the European Union on product k,[6] a dummy variable indicating whether product k is affected by a quota during the sample period, and a dummy variable indicating whether product k has been the object of a dispute at the WTO between the European Union and any other country. Including a dummy variable indicating whether exporting country c is affected by a ban on product k during the sample period controls for decreases in the incidence of notifications resulting from reduced imports rather than reduced risk. The initial value of EU imports of product k in the year 2000 is also included, as products imported in large volumes are likely to be inspected—and thus likely to fail inspections—more often than others. Finally, the inclusion of exporting country fixed effect (δ_c) controls for all suppliers' characteristics that may affect the quality of the product, including overall economic development.[7] Because the number of notifications is a count, negative binomial or Poisson estimation is used.[8]

In this econometric framework, the product dummy captures the share of alerts resulting from product characteristics, after controlling for exporters' characteristics and other variables that may affect the probability of being rejected. A high risk index reflects a high sensitivity to food safety regulations. Since rejection occurs when a product does not comply with food safety requirements as set forth in the regulation, the index can be interpreted as the gap between standard and actual product quality. "Risky" products are products far away from the standard. The gap deepens if the regulation is changing and/or if current production technologies do not allow adequate quality to be reached. As a consequence, being far away from the standard leaves firms with two options: conform or exit the market. However, compliance is a costly process. For complying firms, the risk index thus captures the need for capital to conform with EU markets' food safety requirements and acts as a proxy for financing needs related both to exporting a product in general and exporting it into countries with strict food safety regulations (similar to the ones in the European Union) in particular.

Notes

This chapter is part of a World Bank program. Martin Strieborny highly appreciates the ongoing financial support from the Handelsbanken Research Foundation. Melise Jaud appreciates the financial support from the Swiss National Science Foundation. We would like to thank Tibor Besedeš and the participants at the CESifo workshop "Disrupted Economic Relationships: Disasters, Sanctions, Dissolutions" in Venice for very helpful comments and suggestions.

1. We thank Denisse Pierola and Paul Brenton.

2. Bricongne et al. (2010) compute an external finance dependence measure—motivated by Rajan and Zingales (1998)—at the HS-2 industry level.

3. Distances are calculated as the sum of the distances between the biggest cities of both countries, weighted by the share of the population living in each city.

4. We measure the financial development (FD_c) at the beginning of the sample because of possible endogeneity concerns. The rising importance of exports that require external funding for the costly compliance with the SPS regulations might accelerate the process of financial development in the exporting country. In a series of robustness tests reported in table 9.9, we also measure financial development in the first year of a given export spell. The variable FD_c thus becomes time-varying and is not captured by exporting firm strata effects in these estimations, so table 9.9 reports direct effects of both FD_c and $GDPpc_c$.

5. Indeed, there are consistent differences in the number of notifications among notifying EU states. In an average year, Germany, with 20 percent of notifications, is among the

top notifying countries, while Ireland only accounts for 0.21 percent of notifications. Aggregating the number of notifications across all importing (notifying) countries and all years smooths temporal fluctuations and reduces the effects of outliers.

6. We take tariff data for the year 2005.

7. The limited time span of our data on alerts does not allow us to include country-sector fixed effects.

8. Most of the estimations presented use a negative binomial model, with a Poisson model serving as a robustness check. The Poisson and negative binomial estimates should give similar results, as the consistency of second-stage estimates does not depend on the correct specification of the first-stage equation. In addition, we have overdispersion and little excess of zeros in the sample. The negative binomial model is to a reasonable extent adequate in tackling both problems. However, estimation using a zero-inflated negative binomial model could be a good alternative.

References

Albornoz, F., H. Calvo Pardo, G. Corcos, and E. Ornelas. 2010. "Sequential Exporting." London School of Economics. Mimeo.

Amiti, M., and D. E. Weinstein. 2011. "Exports and Financial Shocks." *Quarterly Journal of Economics* 126 (4): 1841–1877.

Araujo, L., G. Mion, and E. Ornelas. 2014. "Institutions and Export Dynamics." London School of Economics. Mimeo.

Beck, T. 2002. "Financial Development and International Trade: Is There a Link?" *Journal of International Economics* 57:107–131.

Beck, T. 2003. "Financial Dependence and International Trade." *Review of International Economics* 11 (2): 296–316.

Beck, T., A. Demirguc-Kunt, and R. Levine. 2006. "A New Database on Financial Development and Structure." *World Bank Economic Review* 14:597–605.

Berman, N., and J. Héricourt. 2010. "Financial Factors and the Margins of Trade: Evidence from Cross-Country Firm-Level Data." *Journal of Development Economics* 93 (2): 206–217.

Besedeš, T. 2013. "The Role of NAFTA and Returns to Scale in Export Duration." *CESifo Economic Studies* 59 (2): 306–336.

Besedeš, T., B.-C. Kim, and V. Lugovskyy. 2014. "Export Growth and Credit Constraints." *European Economic Review* 70: 350–370.

Besedeš, T., and T. Prusa. 2006a. "Ins, Outs and the Duration of Trade." *Canadian Journal of Economics* 39 (1): 266–295.

Besedeš, T., and T. Prusa. 2006b. "Production Differentiation and Duration of U.S. Import Trade." *Journal of International Economics* 70 (2): 339–358.

Besedeš, T., and T. Prusa. 2011. "The Role of Extensive and Intensive Margins and Export Growth." *Journal of Development Economics* 96: 371–379.

Brenton, P., C. Saborowski, and E. von Uexkull. 2010. "What Explains the Low Survival Rate of Developing Country Export Flows?" *World Bank Economic Review* 24 (3): 474–499.

Breslow, N. 1974. "Covariance Analysis of Censored Survival Data." *Biometrics* 30 (1): 89–99.

Bricongne, J-C., F. Fontagné, G. Gaulier, D. Taglioni, and V. Vicard. 2010. "Firms and the Global Crisis: French Exports in the Turmoil." ECB Working Paper 1245. Frankfurt: European Central Bank.

Bugamelli, M., F. Schivardi, and R. Zizza. 2010. "The Euro and Firm Restructuring." In *Europe and the Euro*, edited by A. Alesina and F. Giavazzi, 99–138. Chicago: University of Chicago Press.

Cadot, O., L. Iacovone, M. D. Pierola, and F. Rauch. 2013. "Success and Failure of African Exporters." *Journal of Development Economics* 101: 284–296.

Chaney, T. 2016. "Liquidity Constrained Exporters." *Journal of Economic Dynamics and Control* 72: 141–154.

Chor, D., and K. Manova. 2012. "Off the Cliff and Back? Credit Conditions and International Trade during the Global Financial Crisis." *Journal of International Economics* 87: 117–133.

Crinò, R., and L. Ogliari. 2017. "Financial Imperfections, Product Quality, and International Trade." *Journal of International Economics* 104: 63–84.

Efron, B. 1988. "Logistic Regression, Survival Analysis, and the Kaplan-Meier Curve." *Journal of the American Statistical Association* 83 (402): 414–425.

Fan, H., E. L.-C. Lai, and Y. A. Li. 2015. "Credit Constraints, Quality, and Export Prices: Theory and Evidence from China." *Journal of Comparative Economics* 43: 390–416.

Görg, H., and M. A. Spaliara. 2014. "Financial Health, Exports and Firm Survival: Evidence from UK and French Firms." *Economica* 81: 419–444.

Greenaway, D., A. Guariglia, and R. Kneller. 2007. "Financial Actors and Exporting Decisions." *Journal of International Economics* 73: 377–395.

Jaud, M., O. Cadot, and A. Suwa-Eisenmann. 2009. "Do Food Scares Explain Supplier Concentration? An Analysis of EU Agri-food Imports." Paris School of Economics Working Paper 2009–28. Paris: Paris School of Economics.

Jaud, M., M. Kukenova, and M. Strieborny. 2015. "Financial Development and Sustainable Exports: Evidence from Firm-Product Data." *World Economy* 38 (7): 1090–1114.

Jaud, M., M. Kukenova, and M. Strieborny. 2018. "Finance, Comparative Advantage, and Resource Allocation." *Review of Finance* 22 (3): 1011–1061.

Levchenko, A. A., L. T. Lewis, and L. L. Tesar. 2011. "The Role of Trade Finance in the U.S. Trade Collapse: A Skeptic's View." In *Trade Finance during the Great Trade Collapse*, edited by J.-P. Chauffour and M. Malouche, 133–147. Washington, DC: World Bank.

Manova, K. 2008. "Credit Constraints, Equity Market Liberalizations and International Trade." *Journal of International Economics* 76: 33–47.

Manova, K. 2013. "Credit Constraints, Heterogeneous Firms and International Trade." *Review of Economic Studies* 80: 711–744.

Manova, K., S.-J. Wei, and Z. Zhang. 2015. "Firm Exports and Multinational Activity under Credit Constraints." *Review of Economics and Statistics* 97 (3): 574–588.

Minetti, R., and S. C. Zhu. 2011. "Credit Constraints and Firm Export: Microeconomic Evidence from Italy." *Journal of International Economics* 83: 109–125.

Muûls, M. 2015. "Exporters, Importers and Credit Constraints." *Journal of International Economics* 95: 333–343.

Nitsch, V. 2009. "Die Another Day: Duration in German Import Trade." *Review of World Economics* 145 (1): 133–154.

Paravisini, D., V. Rappoport, P. Schnabl, and D. Wolfenzon. 2015. "Dissecting the Effect of Credit Supply on Trade: Evidence from Matched Credit-Export Data." *Review of Economic Studies* 82: 333–359.

Rajan, R., and L. Zingales. 1998. "Financial Dependence and Growth." *American Economic Review* 88 (3): 559–586.

Rauch, J., and J. Watson. 2003. "Starting Small in an Unfamiliar Environment." *International Journal of Industrial Organization* 21 (7): 1021–1042.

Svaleryd, H., and J. Vlachos. 2005. "Financial Markets, the Pattern of Industrial Specialization and Comparative Advantage: Evidence from OECD Countries." *European Economic Review* 49 (1): 113–144.

Wei-Chih, C. 2012. "Innovation and Duration of Exports." *Economics Letters* 115 (2): 305–308.

10 Did an Oil Shock Cause the Collapse of the Soviet Economy?

Marvin Suesse

10.1 Introduction

Seminal events in economic history have both structural and situational causes. This holds for the final collapse of the economy of the Soviet Union (USSR) between 1985 and 1992. Much has been written about the structural inefficiencies of the centrally planned economy, indeed from its very inception (von Mises 1920). After 70 years of Soviet economic growth and 25 years of postmortem analysis, scholars have arrived at an impressive diagnosis of chronic Soviet ailments (Ofer 1987; Nove 1986; Gregory and Harrison 2005). The same cannot be said for the immediate cause of the patient's demise. Why did an economy that had been growing slowly for decades go into freefall in the late 1980s?

As is often the case with sudden deaths, theories have ranged from the plausible to the conspiratorial. One theory that has become increasingly influential, especially within Russia itself, ascribes the Soviet Union's final demise to the vagaries of global oil markets (Gaidar 2007a; Mau and Starodubrovskaya 2001). Given the purported influence of oil on a wide range of economic outcomes, this theory cannot be dismissed out of hand.[1] Yet the oil theory has undergone little academic scrutiny.[2] This chapter presents an attempt to examine the role of oil in the Soviet collapse conceptually and empirically. Conceptually, it argues that substantial links between the world economy and the domestic Soviet economy are difficult to establish. Empirically, it finds that the oil hypothesis cannot explain the behavior of key macroeconomic aggregates from 1965 to 1992. Moreover, evidence shows that the purchasing power of Soviet oil exports did not change radically between 1980 and 1991. The oil hypothesis is subsequently contrasted with two other explanations of the Soviet collapse: policy and territorial disintegration. It is suggested that these explanations carry substantially greater explanatory power than oil for understanding the Soviet collapse.

10.2   Postwar Soviet Growth, Decline, and Collapse

Figure 10.1 shows the trajectory of gross domestic product (GDP) per capita for the Soviet Union and the post-Soviet countries. The vertical line marks the date of the Soviet Union's formal dissolution. Three stylized facts stand out. First, growth was fast until the mid-1960s. This was the era of extensive growth in factor inputs. Second, growth rates slowed down markedly but remained broadly positive in the 1970s and early 1980s. This period is the focus of the bulk of the literature on the structural causes of the Soviet decline.[3] Finally, recorded output dropped markedly in the final years of the Soviet Union. This output fall continued after the end of the Soviet Union until 1996, when macroeconomic stabilization was achieved in all former Soviet countries (Roland 2000). At that point, output was at 55 percent of its 1989 peak.

The accuracy and veracity of the GDP figures presented here has been questioned, and some have even hypothesized that the Soviet output collapse is mainly an accounting fiction (Aslund 2001), that real

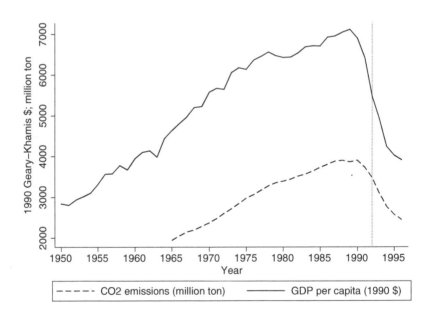

Figure 10.1
GDP per capita in the (former) Soviet Union and carbon dioxide emissions. GDP data from Bolt and van Zanden (2014); CO_2 data from BP (2015).

output did not fall, just the distribution of output changed. It is true that the data should be regarded with some suspicion. Although the figures used here are based on Western reevaluations of the (probably inflated) Soviet output figures (Maddison 1998), difficulties remain regarding the aggregation of output without meaningful prices. However, volume indicators of output show a remarkably similar story. The data for total carbon dioxide emission graphed in figure 10.1 is able to trace the hump-shaped trajectory of growth quite well.

In any case, the abruptness of the output collapse in the Soviet Union's final years justifies the search for a different set of mechanisms than those leading to the growth slowdown. After all, Soviet planners had always allocated a lot of resources to the military, Soviet enterprises had always produced goods that were not needed, and Soviet managers had always been cautious when it came to introducing new technologies. These things did not change suddenly.

This does not mean that structural factors are irrelevant to understanding the Soviet Union's end. A theory of collapse that goes beyond outlining pure chance or coincidence must outline how some "trigger" interacted with existing structural features and weaknesses of the Soviet economy. Oil may have constituted one such trigger.

10.3   A Soviet Oil Curse?

10.3.1   Oil Prices and GDP

The idea that an oil shock was the final blow to the Soviet economy has been most forcefully argued by Yegor Gaidar in *Collapse of an Empire: Lessons for Modern Russia* (Gaidar 2007a). The book quickly became a best seller in Russia. Gaidar had been one of the leading architects of market reform in early 1990s Russia. After his exit from active politics, he became worried about the increasing dependence of the modern Russian economy on hydrocarbon exports. He argued that, historically, resource dependence had always led to collapse. The Soviet Union was no exception in this regard. Its inept leaders had been able to sustain the economy only as long as high oil prices brought in hard currency earnings from oil exports. As oil prices collapsed during the 1980s oil glut, hard currency earnings diminished, sending the inefficient economy into a steep decline. Like modern Russia, the USSR is portrayed as a petrostate at the mercy of world oil markets.

As seen in figure 10.2(a), the coincident movement of oil prices and GDP indeed seems strong for modern post-Soviet countries (whose

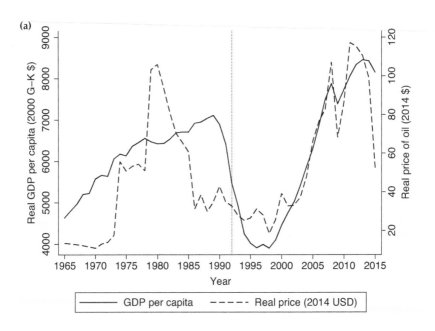

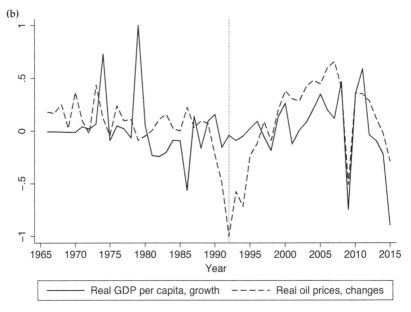

Figure 10.2
(a) GDP per capita in the (former) Soviet Union and the real oil price. (b) Soviet and
post-Soviet GDP and oil prices, year-over-year change. GDP data from Bolt and van
Zanden (2014); oil price data from BP (2015). Changes are standardized by each variable's
maximum annual change over the observed time period.

GDP is mainly accounted for by the Russian Federation). As for the Soviet Union, its economic collapse did indeed coincide with a period of historically low oil prices. However, the preceding oil price boom only spanned a short time (from the mid-1970s to the early 1980s), and the Soviet economy was growing well before the 1970s oil peak. Growth rates were even comparatively low during the peak of the oil boom. Figure 10.2(b) takes first differences from the previous series and reinforces the picture. GDP growth and oil prices move in unison after 1992, but the correspondence is tenuous for Soviet times. Growth actually spiked before the 1973 oil peak and fell during the 1979–1980 oil boom. Soviet output then recovered as oil prices continued to fall. Accordingly, a simple Granger causality test on the first differences of GDP and the real oil price does not indicate a causality running from oil to GDP from 1965 to 1992 ($p=0.424$). If anything, causality is more likely to run the other way ($p=0.108$), which may be the result of the increasing penetration of global markets by Soviet oil during the period.[4]

However, it may be that a simple regression of oil prices on GDP is not able to detect the underlying mechanisms linking both aggregates. A closer look at the oil hypothesis may guide the empirical strategy in a more fruitful direction. There are, in fact, two oil hypotheses. The first, which I call the "domestic hypothesis," concentrates on Soviet oil production, while the second, the "international hypothesis," focuses on Soviet trade with the rest of the world.

10.3.2 The Domestic Oil Hypothesis

The domestic oil hypothesis points out that oil production in the Soviet Union had reached its peak in 1980. The subsequent decline in production starved energy-inefficient industries of their main input, thus leading to a decline in total output (Reynolds and Kolodziej 2008; Gaddy and Ickes 2005). To some extent, as oil production itself is a component of GDP, this effect is mechanical. However, Gaddy and Ickes (2005) go further than this by pointing out that the forms of resource dependence were more extreme in the Soviet Union than is common in other contexts. Because of the underpricing of energy in the internal Soviet trading system, enterprises and whole regions became accustomed to high levels of cheap energy input, determining their factor input ratios. These subsidies or rents shaped the country's political economy by creating powerful lobbies. The withdrawal of oil rents destabilized that system, both politically and economically.

The domestic view is right in pointing to the inefficiency of the Soviet oil industry. Its equipment was outdated. It also absorbed an increasing share of the country's resources. By 1985, the energy sector was sucking in 35 percent of industrial investment (Stern 1987). Moreover, the Soviet oil industry had to import expensive Western technology to exploit increasingly inaccessible locations (Office of Technology Assessment 1981).[5] The productivity of new oil wells was declining, and eventually oil output declined (figure 10.3).

A key weakness of the argument, however, is apparent from the two other lines of the figure. Throughout the late Soviet period, domestic oil consumption was broadly constant, reacting only marginally to changes in production. Instead, the production shortfall was passed on to exports.[6] There was thus no negative energy supply shock to domestic production. This is also borne out econometrically. Figure 10.4 displays the possible channels of causation between Soviet oil production, Soviet GDP, and oil prices. Dark arrows represent relationships that are Granger causal at the 5 percent level. The relevant p-values are indicated

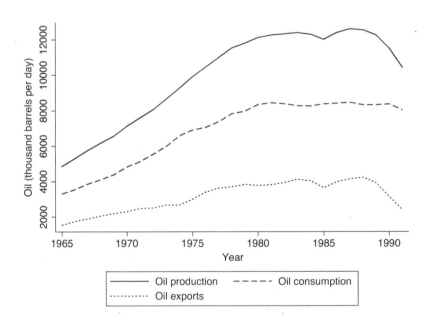

Figure 10.3
Soviet oil production, consumption, and exports. *Source:* BP (2015). Exports are calculated as the difference between production and domestic consumption and include exports to non–hard currency markets.

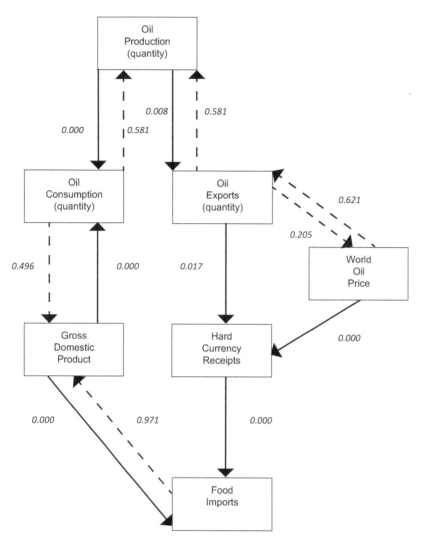

Figure 10.4
Soviet oil production, GDP, and world oil prices. For data, see the appendix. Sample
covers 1965–1992, except for hard currency receipts (1971–1989) and food imports (1965–
1990). Dark arrows indicate a statistically significant Granger causal relationship at the
5 percent level based on a VAR with two lags on the variables shown on either side of
the drawn arrow. An exception is the relationship between oil price and currency receipts,
which is the contemporaneous regression between both variables with Newey-West standard errors. All series are in first differences.

next to each arrow.[7] The left-hand side of figure 10.4 represents the mechanism emphasized by domestic oil theory: a decline in production should lead to a decline in GDP through a decline in oil consumption. Although we can reject the null hypothesis of non-Granger causality between production and consumption at the 0.000 level, we cannot reject it for the link between consumption and GDP. Instead, GDP seems to predict oil consumption rather than the other way around. Domestic energy consumption does not seem to have affected GDP, casting doubt on the domestic oil hypothesis.[8] We therefore turn to the examination of the external energy trade.

10.3.3   The International Oil Hypothesis

This hypothesis focuses on the hard currency revenue from selling oil on foreign markets, which is mainly influenced by the prevailing world market price. Although production shortfalls play some role in this version, Soviet hard currency earnings are ultimately depressed by the 1980s fall in oil prices (Gaidar 2007a). The main consequence of lost hard currency earnings is that it would have necessitated a cut in imports. This is mainly supposed to have restricted the import of agricultural products and, to a lesser extent, advanced machinery. Food imports, especially grain and animal feeds, are particularly important in this hypothesis, as the productivity of Soviet agriculture was lagging far behind that of Western countries (Gaidar 2007a). The story is therefore essentially one of a balance-of-payments crisis.

The right-hand side of figure 10.4 shows the extent to which the time series data support this version of the oil hypothesis. There is indeed a statistically significant link running from oil production to the quantity of oil exports. Furthermore, oil prices and oil exports determine hard currency receipts, which in turn affect food imports. The relationship between food imports and GDP growth, however, is not in accordance with the oil hypothesis. Food imports do not seem to predict GDP growth. Instead, and maybe quite intuitively, incomes are a good predictor of food imports.[9]

The missing causation from hard currency or food imports to GDP growth is not surprising if one pays closer attention to the underlying mechanism linking the external and internal sectors of the late Soviet economy. It is important to note at this point that the only mechanism linking foreign exchange and domestic output is imports. The Soviet government did not need foreign currency to pay its civil servants or to buy domestic production, as the ruble was not convertible, and domestic prices were set by the government (Nove 1986). An increase in the Soviet government's external purchasing power therefore would not directly have increased its domestic purchasing power. What then could the effects of a balance-of-payments crisis have been for the Soviet economy?

One possibility is that the Soviet government was trying to maintain a constant quantity of imports with declining oil receipts. It would then have needed to deplete its gold reserves or borrow from abroad to balance its external accounts. This did in fact happen (Gaidar 2007a). As loans could mainly be raised from foreign governments rather than from private banks, loans were political in nature and tied to political concessions to Western governments. These concessions made it more difficult for the Soviet leadership to use force, especially in controlling its client states in Central Europe. This may have been a factor in the abrupt end of the Soviet-controlled Council for Mutual Economic Assistance (CMEA) after 1989 (Gaidar 2007a). The welfare consequences to the Soviet economy of the "loss" of the CMEA are far from clear, however. It certainly led to reduced barter imports from CMEA countries, mainly machinery.[10] This may have had negative effects on growth in the longer term. On the other hand, the political changes in Central Europe absolved the Soviet government from the need to continue subsidizing their former client states. Energy exports to these states could now be charged in hard currency.

Another possible mechanism is that, in an effort to hold essential food imports constant in the face of a worsening balance-of-payments situation, Soviet policymakers cut back on the import of advanced Western technology, as well as durable consumer goods. This, too, did happen to some degree, if only rather late (Gaidar 2007a). A cutback on advanced technology imports certainly would have had negative consequences for long-run growth and would have depressed potential output in the import-dependent oil and gas sectors even further. These are, however, more likely to have been long-run effects depressing the trend rate of Soviet growth rather than leading to an immediate fall in output. Finally, the reduced import of durable consumer goods would not affect output directly, although it may have increased discontent in the population and put pressure on the Soviet government's internal state budget.[11]

The main focus of the international oil hypothesis, however, is on food imports, especially grain (Gaidar 2007b). Clearly, the immediate consequence of a radical cut in food imports would be a strain on the already fragile retail trade in foods, and at fixed domestic prices this would exacerbate shortages. Unspent purchasing power would also lead to a monetary overhang and repressed inflation. Eventually, consumers would have had to cut back food consumption, an unpalatable prospect for the Soviet leadership. In fact, all these processes are well recorded for the late Soviet Union. Food shortages increased, rationing was intensified, pressure on the artificially low retail prices mounted, and discontent with the system became palpable (Gaidar 2007a; Nove 1992). What is not clear, however, is the extent to which these processes can be attributed to an external supply shock in foods. The first basic goods to which rationing was applied were sugar and products containing alcohol. This was connected to President Mikhail Gorbachev's antialcohol campaign, which resulted from "policy" rather than from import problems (Ellman and Kontorovich 1998). The fact that food shortages increased locally may also be attributed to the increasing dislocation of the economy as the command system was demolished (Harrison 2003), or the disintegration of the trading system as regions became more independent (Nove 1992). After all, shortages increased for all goods, not only for foods. As was usually the case in Soviet economic history, shortages in consumption were primarily caused not by a physical unavailability of goods but rather by misallocation.[12]

The preceding discussion takes for granted that both hard currency receipts and food imports did actually decrease substantially during the Soviet Union's final years. Do the data support this? Figure 10.5(a) shows net imports of all agricultural goods into the USSR, evaluated at constant US dollars, and hard currency receipts from oil exports. Hard currency receipts are calculated as the difference between domestic production and consumption, evaluated at the world market price of oil in real US dollars. The graph suggests a dramatic collapse in foreign currency earnings. At the same time, food imports are broadly constant. This does suggest a worsening balance-of-payments situation for the USSR, even though it does not suggest that the country suffered a dramatic negative supply shock in foods.

Figure 10.5(b) refines the picture further and makes two crucial changes to the calculation of Soviet export proceeds from oil. First, it adjusts for the fact that not all the Soviet Union's oil exports went to hard currency markets. This offered Soviet policymakers an additional margin of substitution by shifting exports away from barter trade with the CMEA. They did so extensively: whereas the CMEA accounted for

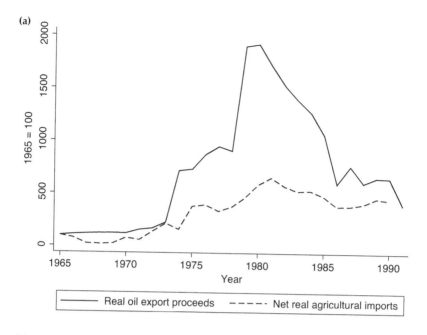

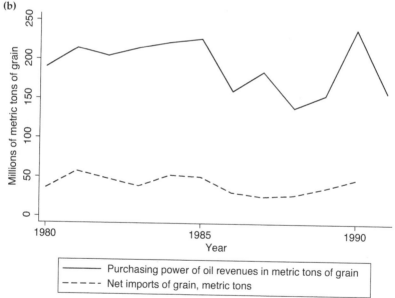

Figure 10.5
(a) Value of oil exports and food imports at constant US$ prices. (b) Value of oil exports in metric tons of grain and net grain imports in metric tons. For data, see the appendix. In (a), export proceeds are calculated oil exports (production–domestic consumption) multiplied by the real price of oil. Net agricultural imports is the agricultural trade balance at 2000 US$ prices. In (b), export proceeds are calculated oil exports (production–domestic consumption) adjusted by non–hard currency (CMEA) trade multiplied by the current oil price and evaluated at current grain prices. Net grain imports are calculated from the grain trade balance adjusted by current grain prices.

46 percent of Soviet oil exports in 1980, this share had dropped to barely 16 percent in 1990.[13] This increased hard currency earnings. Second, export earnings are no longer calculated at constant US dollars in figure 10.5(b). The US price index is hardly appropriate to deflate Soviet imports (as the consumption baskets are likely to differ). If the main concern of the Soviet leadership was to use export proceeds to buy grain internationally, export proceeds should be deflated by the international price of grain. Similarly, food imports in value terms are now replaced with grain imports in volume. This yields a different picture in figure 10.5(b): the USSR was actually importing more tons of grain in 1990 than in 1980. Despite some fluctuations, there was thus no sustained supply shock to the domestic economy. In fact, there was no need to radically cut back grain imports. As the graph shows, the purchasing power of Soviet oil exports measured in units of grain did fall, but did not collapse. This suggests that an external oil shock is unlikely to have had a major impact on the Soviet economy, thus calling into question oil-based explanations for the Soviet collapse.

10.4   Policy, Reform, and the Loss of Control

If the disruptions in the retail and distribution sectors of the Soviet economy mentioned in the last section were not caused by a negative external shock, then what was their cause? Gorbachev's drive to limit the sale of alcohol between 1985 and 1987 led to a burgeoning demand for sugar, which was used to distill alcohol at home. It also led to panic buying as consumers feared further shortages. Apart from disrupting retail markets, this policy was also one of the main factors causing a disequilibrium in the Soviet government's finances, as alcohol taxes were a major source of revenue for the domestic budget. The anti-alcohol policy has since become a prime example of the unintended consequences of well- intentioned policies by the Gorbachev administration. Hanson (2003, 177) puts the point strongly: "Mikhail Gorbachev was the first Soviet leader who ... did not understand the Soviet system. He was therefore the last Soviet leader." Similarly, observers have derided Gorbachev's failure to institute a price reform early enough, his outdated emphasis on heavy investment at a time when funds were stretched thin, his underestimation of separatist tendencies, his radicalism, his "turn to the right," or his indecisiveness (Ellman and Kontorovich 1992). However, the "Gorbachev factor" (Brown 1997) may not be satisfying as an all-encompassing explanation for the final collapse, as it does not explain why such misguided policies were carried out in the first place.

Another version of the policy view holds that any policy that transforms a command economy into a market economy will inevitably lead to temporary disruptions and an output fall. This has been termed the "transformational recession" (Kornai 1994). For example, an influential strand of theory pioneered by Blanchard and Kremer (1997) and Roland and Verdier (1999) posits that price liberalization breaks off existing supplier contracts that were determined under the planned economy. Firms can now look for partners that are more profitable. However, imperfect institutions in transition economies, such as weak legal systems, or search frictions, will lead to delays in finding new suppliers. This leads to an output fall in the meantime.

Although these explanations are well accepted as factors in explaining the recessions in Central Europe, it is undetermined to what degree they can shed light on the late Soviet and early post-Soviet experience. Price reform did not get under way in earnest until after the Soviet Union's dissolution (Roland 2000). Some have even claimed there was no transformational recession in the former Soviet Union, as the pace of reform was too slow (Harrison 2003).

Still, even though many of the perestroika-era reform efforts can hardly be described as "market oriented," some policies did entail liberalization, even if that word was not used. A classic case was the 1988 Law on Cooperatives, which in effect legalized small private businesses. These new firms could employ workers, sell output at unregulated prices, and were not bound to state production orders or to the state banking system. Although they never employed a large share of the workforce, their operations had far-reaching ramifications. Most importantly, private cooperatives were able to bid inputs away from the state-run sector, as they were able to pay prices above the fixed state sector prices. In a well-known paper, Murphy, Shleifer, and Vishny (1992) argued that this setup of de facto partial price liberalization can decrease aggregate output in the economy if the state sector values these inputs more.

Yet even when we accept that liberalizing reforms may have had some impact on the economy of the late USSR, it still leaves unexplained why leaders instituted policies with detrimental short-term effects. Even a dictator's lot is tied to public acceptance, and unless we are willing to accept a very low discount rate for the future, most political leaders would shy away from demanding heavy sacrifices in peacetime. One possible answer is that Soviet leaders gave up running the command economy because it had become too expensive to continue to do so (Harrison 2002). In this line of thought, the dictator has to pay costs to monitor, reward, and punish agents who carry out production plans. However, structural trends can increase these costs. Increasing the complexity of the economy increases monitoring costs, while punishments are more costly if perpetrators possess higher human capital. A decreasing rate of growth in turn restricts the dictator's ability to reward. For some time, the economy may continue operating if agents are not aware of the true costs the dictator faces in punishing shirkers. Once mass unrest breaks out, however, the dictator is forced to renege on his promise of punishing, and the command economy breaks down.

This model has the merit of explaining why Soviet leaders may have voluntarily dismantled the command economy. It is also in accordance with basic facts about the long-term evolution of the Soviet economy. Monitoring did indeed place a heavy burden on the Soviet economy (Harrison 2013), human capital was rising, and growth was slowing down. The Soviet breakup was also concurrent with large-scale demonstrations and other forms of mass unrest. By the end of 1989, authorities had effectively lost control and protests were left unchecked. If these trends carried over to the degree of control Soviet authorities had over plan execution, the "command and control" framework could indeed explain the production shortfalls in the Soviet economy after 1989. However, research has also suggested that the vast majority of protesters were concerned not about issues of economic reform or political liberalization but exclusively with ethnic or nationalist issues (Beissinger 2002). It is to these that we now turn.

10.5   Political and Economic Disintegration: A Missing Link?

The wave of ethnonationalist protests that engulfed the Soviet Union from 1989 onward was concurrent with an increase in separatist activity by local leaders (Walker 2003).[14] Separatism took various forms, including the refusal of local authorities to supply goods to nonlocals in state stores, the refusal to supply conscripts to the Soviet army, or simply the refusal to carry out the production and supply plan devised by central Gosplan authorities (Nove 1992; Fowkes 1997). The most visible of the increasing centrifugal tendencies pulling the Soviet Union apart was the issuance of so-called sovereignty declarations by local leaders. These unilateral declarations showed the degree to which a territory was moving toward independence from the Soviet Union, although not all territories that issued sovereignty declarations did eventually attempt to secede (Hale 2000). Even as separatism was most visible at the upper federal level (the 15 Soviet republics), it extended to the oblast, district, and even municipal levels (Herrera 2004).

Observers have long suspected that this political disintegration had economic effects. Alec Nove wrote in 1992: "Now, however, there was real freedom. Nationalism was strengthened by, and contributed to, economic disintegration. The economic links between republics and regions were close. ... Separation led to a disruption of supplies and led to collapse and conflict" (Nove 1992, 415). Soviet economists, not without self-interest, were quick to point out how closely integrated Soviet regions were and how costly a separation would be (Granberg 1993). Soviet enterprises were indeed often large, integrated monopolies, whose production relied on inputs from single plants from other regions (Snyder 1993). What is, however, crucial to understanding the role of disintegration in explaining the collapse of the Soviet economy (rather than the postseparation recession) is the realization that separatism started several years before the formal end of the Soviet Union.

The declarations of sovereignty (1988–1990) referred to above shed light on this disintegration before the collapse. Suesse (2018) shows how the issuance of these declarations reduced bilateral trade between pairs of republics (figure 10.6a). The reason is that loyal local authorities refused to trade with more separatist regions, as separatist regions were less likely to reciprocate received goods with reverse trade flows. The expectation of dissolution was enough to depress trade volumes and subsequently output (figure 10.6b).[15]

Although trade disintegration explains up to 30 percent of the output fall according to these estimates, other forms of disintegration may also have contributed to the late Soviet and early postindependence decline in incomes. For example, the rising tide of nationalism made the position of minorities increasingly untenable. Although this affected many peoples, the most quantifiable effect was on the millions of Russians who lived in the non-Russian parts of the Soviet Union. This led to large migration flows from the Caucasus, the Baltics, and Central Asia to Russia as 1.7 million Russians migrated between 1989 and 1995 (van Selm 1997). As Russians had constituted the most skilled section of the

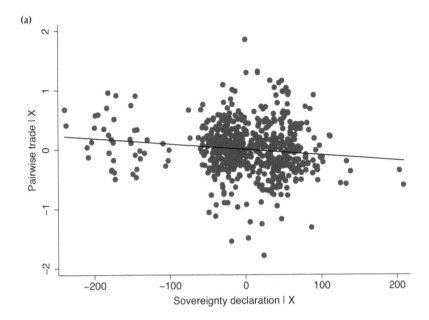

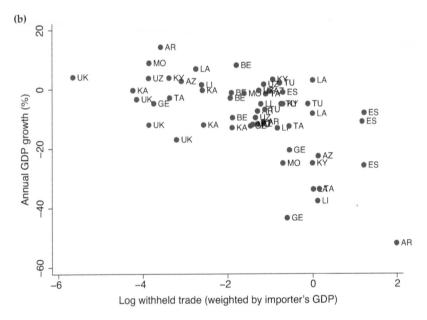

Figure 10.6
(a) Pairwise trade between Soviet republics and sovereignty declarations 1987–1991.
(b) Withheld trade and growth, Soviet republics 1988–1992. *Source:* Suesse (2014, 2017). (a)
Partial plot of a regression of pairwise trade (in rubles) between Soviet republics on the
date of sovereignty declaration, conditional on pairwise controls and republic-year specific fixed effects. (b) Withheld trade is the component of trade withheld by each republic
that can be attributed to the sovereignty declaration from (a), lagged one year and excluding Russia.

workforce in many industries, this exodus may have led to disruptions in the production process. In the Caucasus and Central Asia, violent ethnic conflict created additional economic costs.

One crucial dimension of disintegration was fiscal disintegration, which stemmed from the fact that, as central authorities lost control over the regions, these regions became less and less willing to forward tax receipts to central state coffers. For example, the Russian authorities only submitted 5 percent of the allotted receipts to the central Soviet authorities in 1991 (Hanson 2003). As most enterprise operations were still dependent on central government subsidies, the central government deficit may have had ramifications for the wider economy.

Haphazard fiscal disintegration also had other severe consequences. Each republic had taken full control of its budget and therefore could set its own fiscal policies. Given that all republics were still part of a ruble zone and did not control monetary policies, they had an incentive to engage in extremely expansionary policy. The cost of expansion would be borne by all, in the form of inflation (Havrylyshyn and Williamson 1991). As a result, budget deficits became rampant at both the Soviet Union and republic levels, as did inflation.

Policy coordination between central and local authorities became a real stumbling block. The Russian part of the Soviet Union, governed by Boris Yeltsin, was prepared to move toward radical market reform by 1990, while the Soviet government under Gorbachev was still committed to fixed prices (Ellman and Kontorovich 1998). This effectively made further market reforms impossible. The different pace of economic reforms further fueled the power struggles between local and central authorities, the clearest manifestation of which was the "War of Laws," in which different levels of the federal hierarchy issued competing, and often contradictory, laws and economic decrees.

As local autonomy developed, it became increasingly unclear who controlled the production of local enterprises. This was all the more serious given the egregiously slow development of market institutions discussed earlier. Command economies have been able to survive despite decades of inimical growth and poverty, but a command economy where it was not clear who was in command simply could not produce. Output fell further, and the Soviet state was finally dissolved by Gorbachev on December 25, 1991.

10.6   Conclusion

One attractive feature of the disintegration approach is that it forges a link from the fall in Soviet output to the post-Soviet recessions. Disintegration may well have continued after the end of the Soviet Union, as its successor states erected new barriers to trade and migration. These included export controls, tariff barriers, or discrimination against foreign enterprises in still largely state-run economies. Moreover, political conflict has often inhibited trade in this region (Djankov and Freund 2002). Other barriers were less voluntary but nonetheless nefarious for trade: the difficulties in establishing a clearing mechanism for trade balances between former Soviet countries in the early 1990s (Eichengreen 1993) or the difficulty of reconciling trade regulations with institutions in a state of constant flux. If disintegration led to large output declines in the Soviet Union, there is reason to suppose similar results might be visible in the immediate postindependence period.

Yet it is also clear that disintegration cannot account for the entirety of the Soviet economic collapse. The approach takes secessionist tendencies as given and analyzes their results. It does not explain why Soviet authorities were no longer able to repress dissent. This implies that an explanation along the lines of Harrison (2002), focusing on the payoffs and costs of command and control, may be needed to complement the picture of the Soviet output collapse.

The oil shock, on the other hand, may not have been of first-order importance. The data analyzed in this chapter suggest that neither domestic oil consumption nor oil exports had much effect on GDP growth. The balance-of-payments crisis did decrease the available options for the Soviet leadership in a time when options were few, but it is hard to spell out how this could have had immediate consequences for output. In fact, this chapter has shown that oil revenues did not decrease radically in terms of their grain purchasing power, and that there was little shortfall in imported foods. Oil may be what keeps the wheels of industrial economies turning, but they stopped turning in the Soviet Union for a different reason.

Appendix: Data for Energy Statistics

Variable	Time period	Source	Definition
Oil production	1965–1992	BP (2015)	Annual oil production in thousands of barrels per day, includes crude oil, tight oil, oil sands, and natural gas liquids
Oil consumption	1965–1992	BP (2015)	Annual oil consumption in thousands of barrels per day, includes inland demand plus international aviation and marine bunkers and refinery fuel and loss
Oil exports	1965–1992	Calculated from BP (2015)	Difference between oil production and consumption, in thousands of barrels per day
World oil price	1965–2014	BP (2015)	Annual mean price of oil, in constant 2014 US$ per barrel
Hard currency receipts	1971–1989	Stern (1987), Gaidar (2007a)	Annual Soviet hard currency earnings from all energy exports (without reallowance for reexports) in US$
Food imports	1965–1990	Gaidar (2007a)	Annual agricultural products' net imports (imports–exports) in millions of 2000 dollars
Value of oil exports	1965–1992	Calculated from BP (2015)	Oil exports in thousands of barrels per day (annualized) * price of oil in 2014 US$
Value of oil exports (grain units)	1980–1991	Calculated from BP (2015) and USDA (2016)	Oil exports adjusted by non–hard currency (CMEA) trade, multiplied by current oil price in US$ and evaluated at current grain prices in US$
Grain imports (quantity)	1980–1990	Calculated from Gaidar (2007a) and USDA (2016)	Annual grain net imports (imports–exports) in millions of current US$ divided by grain price in current US$
GDP	1965–2015	Bolt and van Zanden (2014), World Bank (2016)	Real GDP per capita, in 1990 international Geary-Khamis $
CO_2	1965–2015	BP (2015)	Carbon dioxide emissions from the energy sector, in millions of tons per year

Notes

I wish to thank the editors and two anonymous referees for their helpful comments. A previous version of this chapter was presented as a 2014 public lecture at the Institute of Slavic, Eastern European and Eurasian Studies at the University of California, Berkeley.

1. See Barsky and Kilian (2004) on the relationship between oil and macroeconomic dynamics, and van der Ploeg (2011) for a survey of the resource curse literature.

2. Gaddy and Ickes (2005) refer to the importance of resource rents for the functioning of the Soviet economy. Reynolds and Kolodziej (2008) stress the importance of oil output for Soviet GDP, and Mau and Starodubrovskaya (2001) blame the fall in oil prices for the Soviet collapse. Neither offers a mechanism. Finally, general histories of Soviet economic history sometimes refer to oil in passing (Hanson 2003).

3. Factors ranging from the end of extensive growth and overinvestment in the military (Allen 2001) to increasing complexity (Bergson and Levine 1983) have been emphasized as the causes of the growth slowdown. Others have pointed to the Soviet inability to develop new technologies (Ofer 1987) or to the low rate of substitution between capital and labor (Easterly and Fischer 1995).

4. Even the coincidence of GDP growth and oil price changes for the modern post-Soviet countries should not necessarily be taken as causal. As opposed to its Soviet predecessor, the modern Russian economy is susceptible to global shocks, such as the 2007–2008 financial crisis, that affect both GDP and oil prices (see Ahn and Ludema, chapter 5, this volume).

5. Similar difficulties were observed in the natural gas industry, which could only unfold its huge potential slowly because of bottlenecks in the infrastructure supplying Western markets. Equipment for the construction of gas export pipelines needed to be imported at great expense, as Soviet industry was unable to manufacture these goods itself (Stern 1987).

6. This may not be surprising, since lower oil prices in the 1980s decreased the opportunity cost of domestic oil consumption, thus making exports less attractive.

7. See the appendix for details on the variables used and their sources.

8. The same relationship is observed between natural gas consumption and GDP, and persists if GDP growth is proxied by growth in CO_2 emissions.

9. Similarly, the data show no evidence linking hard currency receipts directly to GDP growth at the 10 percent significance level (not shown).

10. Nearly 47 percent of imports from socialist countries were machinery and equipment in the mid-1980s (Chadwick, Long, and Nissanke 1987).

11. High-quality durable consumption goods were unavailable in the USSR and could therefore be resold at high domestic ruble prices by the Soviet government, which as a (near) monopolist on foreign trade transactions recorded a book profit in its domestic budget from these imports (Hanson 2003).

12. "Food supplies to the cities were deteriorating. This was nothing to do with shortfalls in production. ... Urban workplaces became less obedient to instructions from above. ... Also, local trade wars developed" (Hanson 2003, 228–229).

13. Oil exports from the Soviet Union to the rest of the CMEA are calculated as the difference between total Soviet oil exports and oil exports from the whole of the CMEA bloc

(BP 2015). This rests on the assumption that all oil exported by the CMEA was Soviet oil, which is likely to have been the case, as the other CMEA economies were not major oil producers. Finally, I adjust for the fact that CMEA trade started to use hard currency in 1991 (Slay 2014). The results for the substitution away from the CMEA bloc are not qualitatively different if I use the estimates by Chadwick, Long, and Nissanke (1987) for socialist oil trade, available up to 1984.

14. See Suesse (2016) on the causality of the correlation between mass protests and separatist policies by local leaders.

15. This link between separatism, trade disintegration, and the Soviet output collapse can be interpreted as causal, based on exogenous variation stemming from foreign trade potential or state history (Suesse 2018).

References

Allen, R. C. 2001. "The Rise and Decline of the Soviet Economy." *Canadian Journal of Economics / Revue canadienne d'économique* 34 (4): 859–881.

Aslund, A. 2001. "The Myth of Output Collapse after Communism." Carnegie Endowment Working Papers 18. Washington, DC: Carnegie Endowment for International Peace.

Barsky, R. B., and L. Kilian. 2004. "Oil and the Macroeconomy since the 1970s." *Journal of Economic Perspectives* 18 (4): 115–134.

Beissinger, M. 2002. *Nationalist Mobilization and the Collapse of the Soviet State*. Cambridge: Cambridge University Press.

Bergson, A., and H. S. Levine, eds. 1983. *The Soviet Economy: Toward the Year 2000*. London: Allen and Unwin.

Blanchard, O., and M. Kremer. 1997. "Disorganization." *Quarterly Journal of Economics* 112 (4): 1091–1126.

Bolt, J., and J. L. van Zanden. 2014. "The Maddison Project: Collaborative Research on Historical National Accounts." *Economic History Review* 67 (3): 627–651.

BP. 2015. *Statistical Review of World Energy*. bp.com/statisticalreview.

Brown, A. 1997. *The Gorbachev Factor*. Oxford: Oxford University Press.

Chadwick, M., D. Long, and M. Nissanke. 1987. *Soviet Oil Exports: Trade Adjustments, Refining Constraints and Market Behaviour*. Oxford: Oxford University Press.

Djankov, S., and C. Freund. 2002. "Trade Flows in the Former Soviet Union, 1987–1996." *Journal of Comparative Economics* 30 (1): 76–90.

Easterly, W., and S. Fischer. 1995. "The Soviet Economic Decline: Historical and Republican Data." *World Bank Economic Review* 9 (3): 341–371.

Eichengreen, B. J. 1993. "A Payments Mechanism for the Former Soviet Union: Is the EPU a Relevant Precedent?" *Economic Policy* 8 (17): 309–353.

Ellman, M., and V. Kontorovich. 1992. *The Disintegration of the Soviet Economic System*. New York: Routledge.

Ellman, M., and V. Kontorovich. 1998. *The Destruction of the Soviet Economic System: An Insider's History*. New York: M. E. Sharpe.

Fowkes, B. 1997. *The Disintegration of the Soviet Union: A Study in the Rise and Triumph of Nationalism*. London: Macmillan.

Gaddy, C., and B. Ickes. 2005. "Resource Rents and the Russian Economy." *Eurasian Geography and Economics* 46 (8): 559–583.

Gaidar, Y. 2007a. *Collapse of an Empire: Lessons for Modern Russia*. Washington, DC: Brookings Institution Press.

Gaidar, Y. 2007b. *The Soviet Collapse: Grain and Oil*. Washington, DC: American Enterprise Institute for Public Policy Research.

Granberg, A. 1993. "The Economic Interdependence of the Former Soviet Republics." In *Economic Consequences of Soviet Disintegration*, edited by J. Williamson, 47–77. Washington, DC: Institute for International Economics.

Gregory, P., and M. Harrison. 2005. "Allocation under Dictatorship: Research in Stalin's Archives." *Journal of Economic Literature* 43 (3): 721–761.

Hale, H. E. 2000. "The Parade of Sovereignties: Testing Theories of Secession in the Soviet Setting." *British Journal of Political Science* 30 (2): 31–56.

Hanson, P. 2003. *The Rise and Fall of the Soviet Economy: An Economic History of the USSR from 1945*. New York: Pearson.

Harrison, M. 2002. "Coercion, Compliance and the Collapse of the Soviet Economy." *Economic History Review* 55 (3): 397–433.

Harrison, M. 2003. "Are Command Economies Unstable? Why Did the Soviet Economy Collapse?" Warwick Economics Research Papers 604. Warwick, UK: Department of Economics, University of Warwick.

Harrison, M. 2013. "Accounting for Secrets." *Journal of Economic History* 73 (4): 1017–1049.

Havrylyshyn, O., and J. Williamson. 1991. *From Soviet disUnion to Eastern Economic Community?* Washington, DC: Institute for International Economics.

Herrera, Y. M. 2004. *Imagined Economies: The Sources of Russian Regionalism*. Cambridge: Cambridge University Press.

Kornai, J. 1994. "Transformational Recession: The Main Causes." *Journal of Comparative Economics* 19 (1): 39–63.

Maddison, A. 1998. "Measuring the Performance of a Communist Command Economy: An Assessment of the CIA Estimates of the USSR." *Review of Income and Wealth* 44 (3): 307–323.

Mau, V., and I. Starodubrovskaya. 2001. *The Challenge of Revolution: Contemporary Russia in Historical Perspective*. Oxford: Oxford University Press.

Mises, L. von 1920. "Die Wirtschaftsrechnung im sozialistischen Gemeinwesen" [Economic Calculation in the Socialist Commonwealth]. *Archiv fuer Sozialwissenschaften und Sozialpolitik* 47 (1): 86–121.

Murphy, K., A. Shleifer, and R. Vishny. 1992. "The Transition to a Market Economy: Pitfalls of Partial Reform." *Quarterly Journal of Economics* 107 (3): 889–906.

Nove, A. 1986. *The Soviet Economic System*. London: Allen and Unwin.

Nove, A. 1992. *An Economic History of the USSR 1917–1991*. London: Penguin.

Ofer, G. 1987. "Soviet Economic Growth: 1928–1985." *Journal of Economic Literature* 25 (4): 1767–1833.

Office of Technology Assessment (OTA). 1981. *Technology and Soviet Energy Availability*. Washington, DC: Office of Technology Assessment.

Reynolds, D. B., and M. Kolodziej. 2008. "Former Soviet Union Oil Production and GDP Decline: Granger Causality and the Multi-cycle Hubbert Curve." *Energy Economics* 30:271–289.

Roland, G. 2000. *Transition and Economics: Politics, Markets, and Firms*. Cambridge, MA: MIT Press.

Roland, G., and T. Verdier. 1999. "Transition and the Output Fall." *Economics of Transition* 7 (1): 1–28.

Slay, B. 2014. *The Polish Economy: Crisis, Reform and Transformation*. Princeton, NJ: Princeton University Press.

Snyder, T. 1993. "Soviet Monopoly." In *Economic Consequences of Soviet Disintegration*, edited by J. Williamson, 175–243. Washington, DC: Institute for International Economics.

Stern, J. P. 1987. *Soviet Oil and Gas Exports to the West: Commercial Transaction or Security Threat*. Aldershot: Gower.

Suesse, M. 2014. "Breaking the Unbreakable Union: Nationalism, Trade Disintegration and the Soviet Economic Collapse." Working Paper 2/14. Berkeley, CA: Berkeley Economic History Lab.

Suesse, M. 2016. "Shaping the Size of Nations: Empirical Determinants of Secessions and the Soviet Breakup." VIVES Discussion Papers 54. Leuven, Belgium: VIVES.

Suesse, M. 2018. "Breaking the Unbreakable Union: Nationalism, Disintegration and the Soviet Economic Collapse." *Economic Journal* 128 (615): 2933–2967.

US Department of Agriculture (USDA). 2016. "U.S. and Foreign Wheat Prices." In *Wheat Yearbook*. Washington, DC: US Department of Agriculture.

Van der Ploeg, F. 2011. "Natural Resources: Curse or Blessing?" *Journal of Economic Literature* 49 (2): 366–420.

Van Selm, B. 1997. *The Economics of Soviet Breakup*. London: Routledge.

Walker, E. W. 2003. *Dissolution: Sovereignty and the Breakup of the Soviet Union*. Lanham, MD: Rowman and Littlefield.

World Bank. 2016. "GDP Per Capita: World Bank National Accounts Data." data.worldbank.org/indicator/NY.GDP.PCAP.PP.KD.

Contributors

Tibor Besedeš
Georgia Institute of Technology

Volker Nitsch
Technische Universität
Darmstadt

Enrico Spolaore
Tufts University

Romain Wacziarg
University of California, Los
Angeles

Arthur Silve
Université Laval

Thierry Verdier
Paris School of Economics

Julian Hinz
European University Institute

Tristan Kohl
University of Groningen

Chiel Klein Reesink
University of Groningen

Daniel P. Ahn
Johns Hopkins University

Rodney D. Ludema
Georgetown University

Kilian Heilmann
University of Southern California

Chenmei Li
Peking University

Peter A. G. van Bergeijk
Erasmus University Rotterdam

Wolfgang Hess
Lund University

Maria Persson
Lund University

Melise Jaud
University of Lausanne

Madina Kukenova
Business School Lausanne

Martin Strieborny
Lund University

Marvin Suesse
Trinity College Dublin

Index